MW01627161

# Family Friendly
## Mediterranean-style Cooking

with a Groundbreaking Guide to Weight Loss, Weight Control and Cardiovascular Health

**Dr. Arnold Slyper**

# Family Friendly

## Mediterranean-style Cooking

with a Groundbreaking Guide to Weight Loss,
Weight Control and Cardiovascular Health

**Dr. Arnold Slyper**

First published 2017

ISBN: 978-1-56871-624-4



Published by

**Targum Publishers**
Shlomo ben Yosef 131a/1
Jerusalem 9380581
editor@targumpublishers.com

**Distributed by:**
**Feldheim Publishers**
208 Airport Executive Park
Nanuet, NY 10954

www.feldheim.com

*Printed in Israel*

This book is dedicated to my dear wife Judy.

***"She watches over the ways of her household,***
***and never eats the bread of idleness.***
***Her children rise and call her happy; her husband also praises her:***
***Many women have excelled, but you surpass them all."***
(Proverbs 31)

# Contents

# List of Recipes

CHAPTER 1

# Mediterranean-style Eating

Typically in Western countries the starch for the main meal of the day, such as potato or rice, is placed separately on the plate from the meat, and there may be a vegetable or salad dish on the side. Mediterranean-style cooking, on the other hand, not only uses more vegetables, fruits, grains, beans and spices, but different foods are often mixed together in combinations. Vegetables may be cooked together with grains, and meat added to vegetables and grains. This provides the potential for delicious dishes. It also means that less meat is eaten in a dish than if it were served alone, which is helpful when trying to limit one's intake of red meat.

This type of mixing is not easy to do with potato, but is very easy to do with popular Mediterranean starches such as pasta, couscous and rice.

Not all the Mediterranean-style recipes in this book are from Mediterranean countries, but most have this feature of mixing of ingredients. In fact, part of the fun of preparing Mediterranean-style dishes is looking for ethnic recipes. There are lots of treasures out there!

The Mediterranean-style diet described in this book is not low in dairy, fowl and eggs, since in moderation these foods are not harmful. This diet is not, therefore, low in fat. This provides the potential for extremely tasty recipes that your family are guaranteed to enjoy.

# Chicken Stir Fry with Peanuts

**MARINATING** *30 minutes* ▪ **COOKING TIME** *14 minutes* ▪ **SERVES** *5*

*For a quick and appealing meal, this dish definitely makes the grade. The peanuts provide a pleasant crunchy taste, and the different vegetables provide plenty of healthful ingredients.*

- 4 boneless skinless chicken breast halves (1 pound)
- 3 tablespoons of cornstarch
- 2½ tablespoons of soy sauce
- ½ teaspoon of ground ginger
- ¼ teaspoon of garlic powder
- 3 tablespoons of olive oil, divided
- 1⅓ cups of uncooked rice, preferably brown rice
- 2 cups of broccoli florets
- 3 stalks of celery, sliced into ½ inch pieces
- 2 large carrots, thinly sliced
- 1 small onion, cut into wedges
- 1 cup of chicken broth
- 2 oz of roasted, unsalted peanuts

## DIRECTIONS:

1. Cut the chicken into ½-inch strips and place in a re-sealable plastic bag. Add cornstarch and toss to coat.
2. Add the soy sauce, ginger and garlic powder to the bag and shake well.
3. Refrigerate the chicken mixture for 30 minutes.
4. Cook the brown rice in twice its volume of water for 45 minutes.
5. In a large non-stick skillet or wok, heat 2 tablespoons of oil. Stir-fry the chicken until it is no longer pink, about 3-5 minutes. Remove and keep warm.
6. Add the remaining 1-tablespoon of oil to the skillet. Stir-fry the broccoli, celery, carrots and onion for 4-5 minutes or until crisp tender.
7. Add the chicken broth.
8. Return the chicken to the skillet and add the peanuts. Cook and stir until the mixture is thickened.
9. Serve the chicken dish over the rice.

### NUTRITIONAL INFORMATION

Per serving: 52 g total carbohydrate, 466 cals, 16 g fat, 3 g saturated fat, 4 g fiber, 585 mg sodium.

# Chicken Couscous

**COOKING TIME** *30 minutes* ▪ **SERVES** *4*

*With its mixture of vegetables, grain, and chicken, this tasty dish is Mediterranean-style to the core. Couscous is a form of pasta. Like pasta, it is often made from semolina and durum wheat and therefore has a low-glycemic index.*

- 1 onion, chopped
- 1 clove garlic, minced
- 1 tablespoon of olive oil
- 12 oz of boneless, skinless chicken (breasts or thighs), cut into 1-inch cubes
- 3 medium carrots, cut into ¼-inch pieces
- 2 stalks of celery, sliced
- 1 ¼ cups of chicken stock
- ¼ teaspoon of salt or to taste
- ¼ teaspoon of cumin
- ¼ teaspoon of turmeric
- ⅛ teaspoon of cayenne pepper
- 1 medium zucchini, cut into ½ × ½ × 1-inch strips
- 2 medium tomatoes, seeded and chopped (or one 8-oz can of chopped tomatoes with juice)
- 15-oz can of garbanzo beans, rinsed and drained
- 1 cup of uncooked couscous, preferably wholewheat

## DIRECTIONS:

1. In a large frying pan, sauté the onion and garlic in hot oil until tender but not brown.
2. Add the chicken, carrots, celery, chicken stock, salt, cumin, turmeric, and cayenne pepper. Bring the mixture to a boil, and then reduce the heat, cover, and simmer for 20 minutes.
3. Add the zucchini, tomatoes and garbanzo beans. Cover and cook for 10 minutes more or until the vegetables and chicken are tender.
4. In the meantime, prepare the couscous according to the packet instructions. (Once the pot of water is boiled, this takes just over 10 minutes to cook).
5. Serve the chicken dish over the couscous.

**NUTRITIONAL INFORMATION**

Per serving: 87 g total carbohydrate, 558 cals, 9 g fat, 2 g saturated fat, 12 g fiber, 546 mg sodium.

# Chicken Kabobs

**MARINATING** *6 to 12 hours* ▪ **COOKING TIME** *6 to 12 minutes* ▪ **SERVES** *4*

*Kids find "doing things" with food a lot of fun and are usually keen on eating their creations. It shouldn't be difficult to find helpers to make these kabobs. The kids can even plan what vegetables they want to use. Other veggies besides those listed here, and even fruit, can be put on the skewers.*

1 lb of boneless, skinless chicken breasts, cut into 1½-inch cubes

1 cup of button mushrooms

½ of a red pepper, cut into 2 inch chunks

½ of a yellow pepper, cut into 2 inch chunks

Cherry tomatoes

Small onions

Marinade:

2 tablespoons of olive oil

2 tablespoons of soy sauce

2 tablespoons of lemon juice

2 tablespoons of fresh parsley, chopped

½ teaspoon of salt or to taste

⅛ teaspoon of pepper

**DIRECTIONS:**

1. Mix the marinade mixture in a bowl and marinate the chicken and mushrooms for 6 to 12 hours.
2. If you are using wooden skewers, soak them in water for 30 minutes to prevent them from igniting.
3. Alternate the chicken and vegetables on the skewers.
4. Grill the kabobs close to the heat for about 6 minutes or broil for about 12 minutes, turning every so often.

# Chicken Dijon with Vegetables and Noodles

**COOKING TIME 80 minutes ▪ SERVES 5**

*This recipe is an entire dinner in one dish! And it's easily reheated.*

1 chicken, cut up, skinned
1 medium zucchini, cut into chunks
1 medium yellow squash, cut into chunks
1 medium onion, sliced
1 medium tomato, cut into wedges
2 cups of uncooked whole-wheat rotini.

**Sauce:**

¼ cup of Dijon mustard
¼ cup of olive oil
1 tablespoon of red wine vinegar
½ tablespoon of oregano
¼ teaspoon of salt
¼ teaspoon of pepper

**DIRECTIONS:**

1. Preheat the oven to 375°F.
2. Cook the noodles according to the packet instructions and set aside.
3. Combine the sauce ingredients.
4. Coat the chicken with half the sauce and arrange the chicken in a 9 × 13-inch pan. Bake uncovered for 30 minutes.
5. Stir together the pan drippings, the rest of the sauce, squash, cooked noodles and half the onion.
6. Spoon this mixture under and around the chicken in the baking dish.
7. Bake uncovered for 15 minutes longer.
8. Top with tomato wedges and the rest of the onion and bake for an additional 10 minutes.

**NUTRITIONAL INFORMATION**

Per serving: 21 g total carbohydrate, 600 cals, 30 g fat, 6 g saturated fat, 4 g fiber, 399 mg sodium.

# CHICKEN CANTONESE

**MARINATING** *30 minutes* ▪ **COOKING** *12 minutes* ▪ **SERVES** *5*

*OK, so Canton is nowhere near the Mediterranean. Nevertheless, this recipe illustrates well the concept of "Mediterranean-style cooking," with the vegetables enhancing the chicken and vice versa. The result is less chicken, more vegetables and a very tasty dish. Make sure the egg noodles are made from semolina and durum wheat and are not Chinese noodles, as Chinese noodles are made from regular flour and not semolina.*

1 stalk of celery, thinly cut diagonally
1 small green and/or red bell pepper, thinly sliced
5 medium mushrooms, sliced
1 small carrot, sliced
1 medium onion, chopped
2 cloves of garlic, minced
⅓ cup of coarsely chopped almonds
6 oz of egg noodles, uncooked
5 teaspoons of cornstarch, divided
2 tablespoons of soy sauce
1 cup of chicken stock, divided
1 teaspoon of sesame oil
1 tablespoon of olive oil
2 teaspoons of grated ginger root
12 oz of boneless, skinless chicken breast halves, cut into thin bite-sized strips

## DIRECTIONS:

1. In a medium-size bowl, stir together the soy sauce, 3 teaspoons of chicken stock and 2 teaspoons of cornstarch. Stir in the chicken and let stand at room temperature for 30 minutes for the chicken to marinate.
2. Cook the egg noodles according to the packet instructions. Drain and add the sesame oil.
3. In a small bowl, stir together 1 cup of chicken stock and 3 teaspoons (1 tablespoon) of cornstarch. Set aside.
4. In a large skillet, preheat the oil over medium-high heat. Stir-fry all the vegetables with the grated ginger root until soft. Remove all the vegetables from the frying pan and put aside.
5. Add the almonds to the skillet and stir-fry for 2 minutes. Remove and put aside.
6. Add the un-drained chicken to the skillet, and stir-fry for 4 minutes or until the chicken is tender and no pink remains.
7. Stir in the mixture of chicken stock and cornstarch. Cook and stir until the mixture is thickened and bubbly.
8. Return the vegetables and almonds to the skillet and stir all the ingredients together for about 1 minute until heated through.
9. Serve over the cooked egg noodles.

### NUTRITIONAL INFORMATION

Per serving: 30 g total carbohydrate, 7 g sugars, 282 cals, 15 g fat, 2 g saturated fat, 6 g fiber, 589 mg sodium.

# GRILLED MOROCCAN CHICKEN

**COOKING TIME** *10-12 minutes* ▪ **SERVES** *4*

*This chicken recipe is a delight eaten on its own and also goes extremely well cut up in salads, as in the next recipe.*

4 boneless skinless chicken breasts
¼ cup of chopped scallions (white part only)
¼ cup of chopped parsley
½ of olive oil
1 tablespoon of minced garlic
¼ cup of chopped fresh cilantro
2 teaspoons of paprika
2 teaspoons of ground cumin
1 teaspoon of salt
¼ teaspoon of turmeric
¼ teaspoon of cayenne pepper

## DIRECTIONS:

1. Combine all the contents of this recipe other than the chicken in the container of a food processor and process until smooth.
2. Rub the mixture on both sides of the chicken breasts and let stand for 30 minutes.
3. Preheat the grill to medium hot.
4. Grill the chicken breasts for 5 to 7 minutes on each side.

# Chicken Salad

**SERVES** *6*

*Use the previous Grilled Moroccan Chicken recipe in this salad and you are in for a treat.*

2 whole boneless, skinless chicken breasts
3 heads of Romaine lettuce, torn into bite-sized bits
1 red onion, thinly sliced
1 container (1 pint) of grape or cherry tomatoes, halved
1 10-oz packet of shredded carrots

### Dressing:

3 tablespoons of mayonnaise
1 tablespoon of Dijon mustard
2 teaspoons of lemon juice
3 tablespoons of minced garlic
1 tablespoon of sugar
Salt to taste
Pepper to taste

### Homemade croutons:

6 slices of whole wheat bread, cut into small cubes
2 tablespoons of olive oil
½ teaspoon of salt
½ teaspoon of garlic powder
¼ teaspoon of pepper

## DIRECTIONS:

1. Grill the two chicken breasts sprinkled with salt, pepper and olive oil, 3-4 minutes per side, and cut into cubes once they have cooled. Alternatively, use the Grilled Moroccan Chicken recipe from the previous page.
2. To make the croutons, preheat the oven to 350°F.
3. Put the bread cubes in a plastic bag, and add oil, salt, pepper and garlic. Mix well.
4. Transfer the coated bread cubes to a baking sheet and cook in the oven for 15-20 minutes.
5. Allow the croutons to cool before serving. They can also be stored in a container or frozen.
6. Combine the dressing ingredients.
7. Toss the chicken, lettuce, red onions, tomatoes and carrots with the dressing.
8. Top with the croutons.

**NUTRITIONAL INFORMATION (WITH CROUTONS)**

Per serving: 31 g total carbohydrate, 308 cals, 12 g fat, 2 g saturated fat, 10 g fiber, 560 mg sodium.

# Chicken Salad with Fruit

**SERVES** *4*

*This is another great chicken salad recipe your family is sure to appreciate.*

¼ cup of dried apricots, quartered

¼ cup of chopped onion, chopped

½ cup of seedless red or green grapes, halved

1 11-oz can of mandarin oranges, drained

1 2.25 oz package of sliced almonds

¼ cup of fresh parsley, chopped

2 cups of cut up, cooked chicken or turkey

⅓ cup of orange juice

½ teaspoon of salt or to taste

½ teaspoon of pepper

## DIRECTIONS:

1. Toast the almonds in a small dry frying pan for 2 to 3 minutes until lightly brown.
2. Combine all the ingredients and chill for a while.
3. For class, the salad can be served on lettuce.

**NUTRITIONAL INFORMATION**

Per serving: 23g total carbohydrate, 308 cals, 14 g fat, 2 g saturated fat, 5 g fiber, 349 mg sodium.

# CHICKEN SALAD WITH STRAWBERRIES

**COOKING TIME** *14 minutes* ▪ **SERVES** *4*

*This highly recommended salad is a blend of delicious tastes.*

4 1″-inch thick boneless skinless chicken breasts (about 4 oz each)

3 tablespoons plus 2 teaspoons of olive oil, divided

1 6-oz package of fresh spinach

2 cups of sugar snap peas (about ¼ lb)

1 cup of strawberries, quartered

1 ripe avocado, cut into ½″ cubes

¼ red onion, finely chopped (about ½ cup)

2 tablespoons of vinegar

Salt and pepper to taste

## DIRECTIONS:

1. Season the chicken with salt and pepper, and cook it in a large skillet over medium heat in 2 teaspoons of olive oil for about 7 minutes each side, until the chicken is no longer pink.
2. Remove the chicken from the skillet and allow it to cool for a few minutes
3. Toss the spinach, snap peas, strawberries and onion in a large salad bowl.
4. Slice the chicken into thin strips and add them to the salad.
5. Whisk the remaining oil and vinegar in a small bowl and season with salt and pepper to taste.
6. Add this dressing to the salad mixture and gently toss.

**NUTRITIONAL INFORMATION**

Per serving: 13 g total carbohydrate, 402 cals, 22 g fat, 4 g saturated fat, 6 g fiber, 125 mg sodium.

# Turkey Meatballs, Lentils and Mint

**COOKING TIME** *65 minutes* ▪ **SERVES** *6*

*The spices give this recipe a very pleasant Middle-Eastern flavor. Serve it as a thick soup or pour over couscous or other starch.*

1 lb of ground turkey

1 cup of bread crumbs, preferably whole-wheat

4 cloves of garlic, minced, divided

1 cup of dried brown lentils

2 teaspoons of dried mint

2 tablespoons of fresh parsley, chopped

1 teaspoon of paprika

¾ teaspoon of ground cumin

½ teaspoon of ground cloves

¼ teaspoon of pepper

¾ teaspoon of salt or to taste

1 small carrot, peeled and cut into ¼-inch dice

1 small onion, cut into ¼-inch dice

¼ cup of olive oil

1 15-oz can of plum tomatoes, drained with juice reserved

4 cups of chicken broth

**DIRECTIONS:**

1. Preheat the oven to 350°F.
2. In a bowl, combine the turkey, breadcrumbs, half of the garlic, the mint, parsley, paprika, cumin, cloves, the salt and pepper, and mix well.
3. Divide the mixture into 24 balls, place them on a baking sheet and bake for 10 minutes. Remove from the oven and set aside.
4. Warm the olive oil over a medium heat in a large sauté pan. Add the onion, carrot and remaining garlic and sauté, stirring until the onion is soft, for about 10 minutes.
5. Add the lentils, the reserved tomato juice from the canned tomatoes and the chicken stock and simmer gently, uncovered, until the lentils are tender, about 30 minutes longer.
6. Chop up the tomatoes, and add the meatballs and tomatoes to the lentils, and simmer for 15 minutes to blend the flavors and finish cooking the meatballs. Season to taste with extra salt and pepper.

**NUTRITIONAL INFORMATION**

Per serving: 40 g total carbohydrate, 424 cals, 18 g fat, 4 g saturated fat, 12 g fiber, 696 mg sodium.

# Ground Turkey Kubbeh

**SOAKING TIME** *10 minutes* ▪ **REFRIGERATION TIME** *30 minutes*
**COOKING TIME** *21 minutes* ▪ **YIELDS** *13 cakes*

*With this recipe, you can easily imagine yourself in the middle of the Middle East.*

1 lb of ground turkey
⅔ cup of finely ground bulgur wheat
1 ½ onion, chopped
⅓ cup of fresh parsley
⅓ cup of pecans, chopped
4 or more tablespoons of olive oil
1 teaspoon of salt
¼ teaspoon of pepper
1 teaspoon of paprika
½ teaspoon of cinnamon
¼ teaspoon of cayenne
3 tablespoon of cold water

## DIRECTIONS:

1. Heat 2 tablespoons of oil in a small skillet over a medium heat. Add 1 chopped onion and sauté for 5 minutes or until it begins to turn golden.
2. Pour 2 cups of cold water over the bulgur wheat. Let soak for 10 minutes (if using medium bulgur soak for 15 to 20 minutes).
3. In a food processor, place half an onion, parsley and spices, and chop them fine.
4. In a large bowl, mix the ground turkey and the onion/spice mixture from the food processor. Add the sautéed onions and the chopped pecans and mix well.
5. Drain the bulgur well in a strainer and squeeze out the extra water. Add it to the turkey mixture and mix well.
6. Cover and refrigerate for about 30 minutes.
7. Shape the mixture into small round patties, using ¼ cup for each, and flatten them.
8. Heat 4 tablespoons of oil in a large skillet and sauté each cake for 3 to 4 minutes per side or until golden brown and cooked through. Add more oil if necessary.
9. Place on a paper towel to drain. Serve hot or cold.

### NUTRITIONAL INFORMATION

Per serving (1 cake): 7 g total carbohydrate, 139 cals, 9 g fat, 2 g saturated fat, 2 g fiber, 214 mg sodium.

# Broccoli Quiche

**COOKING TIME** *33 minutes* ▪ **SERVES** *8*

*This dish will impress everyone in your family. They may not even realize they are eating vegetables!*

### Crust:

1 cup of whole-wheat flour
1 cup of white flour
1 teaspoon of salt
½ cup of canola oil
5 tablespoons of warm water

### Filling:

½ cup of grated cheddar cheese
1 ½ cups of chopped frozen broccoli, defrosted and drained
1 medium onion, chopped
3 large eggs
½ cup of milk
½ teaspoon of oregano
¼ teaspoon of basil
Salt to taste
Pepper to taste

### DIRECTIONS:

1. Preheat the oven to 375°F.
2. Prepare the pie shell by mixing the flour and salt in a large bowl.
3. In a separate bowl, whisk together the oil and water until the mixture is thick.
4. Stir the mixture into the flour until dough forms.
5. Roll out the dough and place in a 9-inch pie pan.
6. Sauté the onion.
7. In the unbaked pie shell, layer as follows: cheese, broccoli and sautéed onion.
8. In a separate bowl, mix the eggs, milk, spices, and salt and pepper to taste, and pour over the quiche filling.
9. Bake at 375°F for 30 minutes.

**NUTRITIONAL INFORMATION**

**(Using whole milk)**

Per serving: 27 g total carbohydrate, 304 cals, 19 g fat, 4 g saturated fat, 3 g fiber, 374 mg sodium.

# SPINACH QUICHE

**COOKING TIME** *48 minutes* ▪ **SERVES** *8*

### PIE SHELL:

1 cup of whole-wheat flour
1 cup of white flour
1 teaspoon of salt
½ cup of canola oil
5 tablespoons of warm water

### FILLING:

1 10-oz package of frozen chopped spinach, thawed and squeezed dry
1 medium onion, chopped
1 15-oz container of ricotta cheese
8 oz of mozzarella cheese, grated
⅓ cup of Parmesan cheese, grated
3 large eggs, beaten
3 tablespoons of olive oil
Salt to taste
½ teaspoon of pepper
¼ teaspoon of nutmeg

## DIRECTIONS:

1. Preheat the oven to 375°F.
2. To prepare the pie shell, mix the flour and salt in a large bowl.
3. In a separate bowl, whisk together the oil and water until the mixture is thick.
4. Stir the mixture into the flour until dough forms.
5. Roll out the dough and place in a 9-inch pie pan.
6. Sauté the onion in the olive oil in a medium-sized skillet until tender.
7. Mix in the spinach, salt, pepper and nutmeg, and sauté until all the liquid from the spinach evaporates, about 3 minutes.
8. Combine the cheeses in a large bowl.
9. Mix in the eggs.
10. Add the spinach mixture to the large bowl and blend well.
11. Fill the pie shell with the spinach-cheese mixture
12. Bake for about 40 minutes until the filling is set in the center and brown on top.

**NUTRITIONAL INFORMATION**

**(Using whole milk ricotta cheese)**

Per serving: 35 g total carbohydrate, 503 cals, 33 g fat, 9 g saturated fat, 4 g fiber, 647 mg sodium.

# Mushroom Quiche

**COOKING TIME** *48 minutes* ▪ **SERVES** *8*

*This is another winning quiche recipe.*

### Pie shell:

1 cup of whole-wheat flour
1 cup of white flour
1 teaspoon of salt
½ cup of canola oil
5 tablespoons of warm water

### Filling

1 large onion, chopped
8 oz of mushrooms, sliced
2 tablespoons of olive oil
4 eggs
½ cup of milk
1 cup of shredded cheddar cheese, divided
¼ teaspoon of salt
⅛ teaspoon of pepper

## DIRECTIONS:

1. Preheat the oven to 375°F.
2. To prepare the pie crust, mix the flour and salt in a large bowl.
3. In a separate bowl, whisk together the oil and water until the mixture is thick.
4. Stir the mixture into the flour until dough forms.
5. Roll out the dough and place in a 9-inch pie pan.
6. Sauté the onion and mushrooms in the olive oil, and keep separate.
7. In a bowl, whisk the eggs and milk and add the salt and pepper.
8. In the unbaked pie shell, layer: ½ cup of shredded cheddar cheese, then the onion/mushroom sauté mixture, and then the remaining ½ cup of shredded cheddar cheese.
9. Pour the egg mixture over all this.
10. Bake at 375°F for 30 minutes

**NUTRITIONAL INFORMATION**

**(Using whole milk)**

Serving size: Per serving: 27 g total carbohydrate, 399 cals, 23 g fat, 5 g saturated fat, 3 g fiber, 462 mg sodium.

# Middle East Vegetable Tacos

**COOKING TIME** *10 minutes* ▪ **YIELDS** *12 taco shells*

*This is a very tasty dish that can be served with tacos, spaghetti or other pasta.*

1 tablespoon of olive oil

1 medium eggplant, peeled and cut into ½-inch cubes

1 medium red bell pepper, cut into ½-inch cubes

1 medium onion, cut into ½-inch wedges

2 cloves of garlic, minced

1 14.5-oz can of diced tomatoes

¼ teaspoon of salt or to taste

¼ teaspoon of oregano

1 10-oz container of hummus

12 medium tacos shells

## DIRECTIONS:

1. In a 10-inch skillet, heat the oil on a medium-high heat and sauté the eggplant, bell pepper, onion, and garlic in oil for 5-7 minutes, stirring occasionally until the vegetables are crisp-tender.
2. Stir in the tomatoes, salt and oregano and reduce the heat to medium. Cover and cook for about 5 minutes or until the eggplant is tender.
3. Spread about 2 tablespoons of hummus inside each taco shell and spoon the vegetable mixture over the hummus in each shell.

**NUTRITIONAL INFORMATION**

**(Serving size: 1 taco)**

Per serving: 13 g bean and starch carbohydrate, 18 g total carbohydrate, 140 cals, 7 g fat, 1 g sat fat, 4 g fiber, 346 mg sodium.

# RATATOUILLE RICE

**COOKING TIME** *30 minutes* ▪ **SERVES** *8*

*This is an easy to make, colorful and tasty rice dish. It can be made as either a side dish or veggie main dish.*

1 small eggplant, peeled, cut in small dice

6 tablespoons of olive oil

¼ teaspoon of salt or to taste

⅛ teaspoon of pepper

1 medium onion, chopped

1 small green pepper, diced

1 small red pepper, diced

½ lb of zucchini or summer squash, cut into small dice

28-oz can of chopped tomatoes, drained

4 large garlic cloves, minced

1 teaspoon of dried thyme

1 teaspoon of basil

1½ cups of uncooked rice, preferably brown rice

**DIRECTIONS:**

1. Heat 2 tablespoons of oil in a large skillet. Add the eggplant, salt and pepper, and sauté over a medium-high heat for 3 minutes. Transfer to a bowl.
2. Add 2 tablespoons of oil to the pan and heat over medium-high heat. Add onion and peppers and cook for 8 minutes or until the onion is tender, but not brown.
3. Add zucchini and cook, stirring for 2 minutes.
4. Return the eggplant to the large skillet. Add the tomatoes, garlic, thyme, and basil and heat until sizzling. Cover and simmer over a low heat, stirring occasionally, for 15 minutes or until the vegetables are tender and the mixture is thick.
5. Boil the rice as per the directions on the package. Drain and rinse with cold water.
6. Heat 2 tablespoons of oil in a large saucepan. Add the rice and heat over a medium heat, stirring with a fork.
7. Add the hot ratatouille to the rice, and heat, tossing gently, for 2 minutes.

**NUTRITIONAL INFORMATION**

Per serving: 40 g total carbohydrate, 275 cals, 12 g fat, 2 g saturated fat, 6 g fiber, 212 mg sodium.

# Pasta Primavera

**COOKING TIME** *33 minutes* ▪ **SERVES** *14*

*This tasty family recipe is full of healthy vegetables.*

- 12 oz of uncooked fettuccine
- 1 cup of chicken broth
- 5 medium-sized carrots, sliced thin
- ½ lb of thin asparagus, trimmed and cut into 2-inch lengths
- 1 large red pepper, seeded and cut into 2-inch long thin strips
- 1 large yellow pepper, seeded and cut into 2-inch long thin strips
- 2 medium-sized zucchini or yellow squash, thinly sliced
- 1 ½ tablespoon of whole-wheat flour
- 1 ⅓ cups of milk
- ½ cup of grated Parmesan cheese
- 3 tablespoons of olive oil
- ½ teaspoons of pepper

**DIRECTIONS:**

1. Cook the fettuccine according to the package instructions. Set aside.
2. In a large pot, bring the chicken broth to a boil.
3. Add the carrots, cover and cook over medium heat for 10 minutes.
4. Stir in the asparagus, peppers and zucchini, cover and cook 3 minutes longer, or until the vegetables are crisp tender.
5. In a small bowl, whisk the flour into the milk.
6. Add the milk and flour mixture to the pot. Bring to a boil, and then simmer, stirring constantly for 1 to 2 minutes until slightly thickened.
7. Pour this mixture over the warm pasta in a serving dish. Add the cheese, oil and pepper and mix well to coat.

**NUTRITIONAL INFORMATION**

Per serving: 23 g total carbohydrate, 160 cals, 5 g fat, 1 g saturated fat, 2 g fiber, 136 mg sodium.

# Creamy Spaghetti

**COOKING TIME** *15 minutes* ▪ **YIELDS** *4*

*This spaghetti dish is a meal in itself. Leftovers (if there are any) can also be served as a cold spaghetti salad.*

½ pound fresh broccoli, broken into florets

1½ cups of zucchini, sliced

1½ cups of fresh mushrooms, sliced

1 large carrot, sliced

3 tablespoons of olive oil, divided

8 oz of uncooked spaghetti, preferably whole-wheat

¼ cup of onion, chopped

3 cloves of garlic, minced

2 tablespoons of whole wheat flour

2 teaspoons of chicken bouillon granules

1 teaspoon of dried thyme

2 cups of whole milk

¾ cup of shredded mozzarella cheese

**DIRECTIONS:**

1. In a large skillet, sauté the broccoli, zucchini, mushrooms and carrots in 1 tablespoon of oil until crisp-tender, about 3 minutes. Remove from the heat and set aside.
2. Cook the spaghetti according to the package directions. Drain and set aside.
3. In another saucepan, sauté the onion and garlic in the remainder of the olive oil until tender.
4. Stir in the flour, chicken bouillon and thyme until blended.
5. Add the milk gradually. Bring to a boil and cook for 2 minutes or until thickened, stirring constantly.
6. Reduce the heat to low and stir in the cheese until melted.
7. Add the vegetables and heat through.
8. Toss the spaghetti into the vegetable mixture.

**NUTRITIONAL INFORMATION**

Per serving: 18 g grain carbohydrate, 33 g total carbohydrate, 354 cals, 20 g fat, 7 g saturated fat, 1 g fiber, 230 mg sodium.

# Pasta Ratatouille Bake

**COOKING TIME** *45 minutes* ▪ **SERVES** *8*

8 oz of dry macaroni, preferably whole-wheat

2 tablespoons of olive oil

2 medium onions, chopped

1 clove of garlic, chopped

1 teaspoon of dried oregano

1 teaspoon of dried basil

4 medium tomatoes, chopped

4 small zucchinis, sliced

15-oz (1¼ cups) of cooked white beans (fresh, frozen or canned)

½ cup of vegetable stock

½ cup of grated parmesan cheese

2 teaspoons of salt or to taste

## DIRECTIONS:

1. Cook the macaroni according to the package instructions and drain.
2. Preheat oven to 350°F.
3. In a large skillet, heat the oil, and cook the onion and garlic until golden.
4. Stir in the herbs, tomato, zucchini, beans, stock and seasoning and simmer for 5 minutes.
5. Combine the pasta and vegetables in a baking dish and sprinkle the cheese on top.
6. Bake for 35 minutes at 350°F.

**NUTRITIONAL INFORMATION**

Per serving: 36 g total carbohydrate, 223 cals, 6 g fat, 1 g saturated fat, 7 g fiber, 752 mg sodium.

# Spinach Lasagna

**COOKING TIME** *75 minutes* ▪ **SERVES** *6*

*Your family will love this dish. The kids may not even notice they are eating spinach.*

1 lb of small curd cottage cheese

1½ cup of shredded mozzarella cheese, divided

1 egg

¾ teaspoon of oregano

⅛ teaspoon of pepper

1 10-oz package of frozen chopped spinach, thawed and drained

1 24-oz jar of spaghetti sauce

8 oz of dry lasagna noodles

1 cup of water

**DIRECTIONS:**

1. Preheat the oven to 350°F.
2. In a large bowl, mix the cottage cheese, 1 cup of mozzarella cheese, egg, spinach and spices.
3. Layer ½ cup of spaghetti sauce, ⅓ of the raw noodles, and half of the cheese mixture in a 9 × 13-inch pan.
4. Repeat this one more time.
5. Top with the remaining noodles and remaining sauce.
6. Sprinkle with the remaining ½ cup of mozzarella cheese.
7. Pour 1 cup of water around the edges.
8. Cover tightly with foil and bake at 350°F for 1 hour 15 minutes.
9. Let sit for 15 minutes before serving so it becomes a bit more solid.

**NUTRITIONAL INFORMATION**

Per serving: 45 g total carbohydrate, 377 cals, 12 g fat, 7 g saturated fat, 5 g fiber, 916 mg sodium.

# BAKED PASTA SHELLS WITH SPINACH AND CHEESE

**COOKING TIME** *55 minutes* ▪ **SERVES** *8*

*This recipe makes a filling, inexpensive and guaranteed popular supper.*

12 oz of dry jumbo pasta shells, preferably whole-wheat

½ lb of fresh or 1 cup of frozen spinach leaves

2 cloves of garlic, minced

½ lb of ricotta cheese

½ lb of mozzarella cheese, grated

1 egg

1 tablespoon of fresh basil leaves, minced, or 1 teaspoon of dried basil leaves

1½ cups of pasta sauce

¼ cup of grated Parmesan cheese

Salt to taste

Black pepper to taste

**DIRECTIONS:**

1. Cook the pasta shells until al dente, according to the package instructions.
2. Preheat the oven to 375°F.
3. If using fresh spinach, place the leaves in a pan with a bit of water. Cover and cook over low until the leaves are just wilted. Drain the water from the spinach and chop finely. If using frozen spinach, thaw completely, and squeeze all liquid from the spinach. Chop finely.
4. Beat the egg.
5. In a large mixing bowl, blend the spinach, garlic, ricotta and mozzarella cheese, egg, basil, salt and pepper to make the filling.
6. Spread a few tablespoons of pasta sauce on the bottom of a shallow baking dish that is large enough to hold the shells in one layer.
7. Fill each shell with about one tablespoon of filling.
8. Arrange the shells in the dish. Pour the remaining sauce over and around the shells.
9. Top the dish with Parmesan cheese.
10. Cover the dish with aluminum foil and bake for about 40 minutes.

**NUTRITIONAL INFORMATION**

Per serving: 41 g total carbohydrate, 329 cals, 11 g fat, 6 g saturated fat, 2 g fiber, 459 mg sodium.

# Veggie Macaroni and Cheese

*COOKING TIME 27 minutes ▪ SERVES 8*

*Who doesn't love macaroni and cheese? The added vegetables very much enhance this recipe.*

12 oz of dry macaroni, preferably whole-wheat
1½ cups of broccoli florets
1 cup of fresh caulifloweret s
1½ cups of carrots, thinly sliced
1 celery stalk, sliced
½ cup of zucchini, sliced
½ medium onion, chopped
½ tablespoon of olive oil
⅛ cup of whole-wheat flour
½ cup of milk
½ cup of soup broth
6 oz (about 1¾ cups) of shredded cheddar cheese
½ teaspoon of dry mustard
⅛ teaspoon of salt
Dash of pepper
⅛ teaspoon of paprika

## DIRECTIONS:

1. Preheat the oven to 350°F.
2. Cook the macaroni in a medium-sized pot according to the package instructions.
3. In the same pot, for the last 6 minutes of cooking, add the vegetables.
4. Transfer the macaroni and vegetables to a 13 × 9 × 2-inch baking dish.
5. In a large frying pan, sauté the onion in the olive oil until tender.
6. Stir in the flour until blended.
7. Stir in the milk and soup broth.
8. Bring the mixture to a boil, cook, and stir for 2 minutes until thickened.
9. Stir in the cheese, mustard, salt and pepper.
10. Pour the cheese mixture over the macaroni and vegetable mixture in the baking dish and stir to coat the macaroni.
11. Sprinkle with paprika.
12. Bake uncovered at 350°F for 15-20 minutes or until heated through.

**NUTRITIONAL INFORMATION**

Per serving: 39 g total carbohydrate, 278 cals, 9 g fat, 5 g saturated fat, 5 g fiber, 278 mg sodium.

# THIN CRUST WHOLE WHEAT PIZZA

**COOKING TIME** *20 minutes* ▪ **SERVES** *8*

*A family recipe book would be incomplete without a pizza recipe. Pizza is a tasty way to eat vegetables. This recipe uses a mixture of whole-wheat and white flour.*

### PIZZA DOUGH:

- 2 cups of white flour, with additional flour as needed, about ¼ cup
- 1 cup of whole-wheat flour
- 2 teaspoons of yeast
- ½ teaspoon of salt
- ½ teaspoon of dried basil
- 1 tablespoon of sugar
- 1 cup of water
- 1 tablespoon of olive oil
- ⅛ teaspoon of garlic powder

### TOPPING:

- 1 cup of pasta sauce
- 8 oz of grated Mozzarella cheese
- ½ cup of zucchini, thinly sliced
- ¾ cup mushroom, sliced
- ⅓ cup of scallion, chopped
- ½ of a medium green pepper, cut into small pieces

### GARNISH:

- ¼ teaspoon of dried basil or dried oregano
- ¼ teaspoon of dried rosemary

## DIRECTIONS:

1. Preheat the oven to 400°F.
2. In a large bowl, mix the ingredients for the pizza dough and knead for about 2 minutes to form the dough.
3. Stretch and roll out the dough to fit a 16-inch pizza pan that has been lightly sprayed with oil.
4. Spread the pizza sauce onto the dough, up to 1 inch from the end of the dough.
5. Top with cheese.
6. Spread the vegetables onto the sauce.
7. Sprinkle the garnish onto the vegetables.
8. Bake in the oven for 20 minutes at 400°F.

**NUTRITIONAL INFORMATION**

Per serving: 52 g total carbohydrate, 350 cals, 10 g fat, 4 g saturated fat, 6 g fiber, 330 mg sodium.

# BURRITO GRANDE

**COOKING TIME** *45 minutes (for the rice)* ▪ **SERVES** *6*

*This delicious burrito dish with its mixture of beans and vegetables is very much in a Mediterranean mode.*

1 cup of uncooked brown rice
1 15-oz can of black beans, rinsed and well-drained
1 15-oz can of pinto beans, rinsed and well-drained
4 oz of frozen whole kernel corn, defrosted
½ of a 15-oz can of diced tomatoes and green chilies
½ of a medium green pepper, chopped
4 scallions, chopped
1 garlic clove, minced
¼ cup of fresh cilantro, chopped
2 tablespoons of lime juice
⅔ tablespoon of olive oil
1 teaspoon ground cumin
½ teaspoon of salt or to taste
4 oz of shredded cheddar cheese
6 burrito-size whole-wheat tortillas

## DIRECTIONS:

1. Cook the brown rice according to the package instructions.
2. Combine all the ingredients together and mix well.
3. Serve cold or at room temperature inside a whole-wheat tortilla.

**NUTRITIONAL INFORMATION**
**(without the tortilla)**

Per serving: 35 g total carbohydrate, 262 cals, 8 g fat, 4 g saturated fat, 9 g fiber, 864 mg sodium.

# ROASTED VEGETABLE CHILI

**COOKING TIME** *30 minutes* ▪ **SERVES** *8*

1 medium butternut squash, peeled and cut into 1-inch pieces
2 large carrots, sliced
2 medium zucchini, cut into 1-inch pieces
2 medium green peppers, diced
1 large onion, chopped
2 14½-oz cans of diced tomatoes
2 15-oz cans of cannelloni or white kidney beans, rinsed and drained
3 14½-oz cans of chicken broth
2 tablespoons of olive oil, divided
1½ teaspoons of ground cumin
1 cup of salsa
1 cup of water
3 teaspoons of chili powder
6 garlic cloves, minced

## DIRECTIONS:

1. Preheat the oven to 450°F.
2. Place the squash, carrots, and zucchini in a baking pan.
3. Combine 1 tablespoon of olive oil with the cumin, drizzle over the vegetables, and toss to coat.
4. Bake uncovered at 450°F for 25-30 minutes, stirring once.
5. In a large soup pot, sauté the green peppers and onion in the remaining 1 tablespoon of oil for 3-4 minutes until tender.
6. Stir in the broth, tomatoes, beans, water, salsa, chili powder and garlic.
7. Bring to a boil. Reduce heat and simmer uncovered for 10 minutes.
8. Stir in the roasted vegetables.
9. Return to a boil. Reduce heat and simmer uncovered for 5-10 minutes or until heated through.

**NUTRITIONAL INFORMATION**

Per serving: 44 g total carbohydrate, 287 cals, 6 g fat, 1 g saturated fat, 10 g fiber, 287 mg sodium

# Chopped Meat in Artichoke Bottoms

**COOKING TIME** *45 minutes* ▪ **SERVES** *6*

*This is a delicious and classy recipe. If artichokes are not to your taste, use squares of raw green pepper.*

½ cup onion, finely grated
¼ cup of fresh parsley, chopped
½ teaspoon of salt
1 clove garlic, crushed
¾ lb of chopped meat
Dash of turmeric
2 large eggs
¼ cup of tomato paste
¼ teaspoon of pepper
¾ teaspoon of cumin
¼ teaspoon of cinnamon
12 large artichoke bottoms, frozen
½ cup of whole-wheat flour
¼ cup of olive
1 14-oz can of crushed tomatoes

**DIRECTIONS:**

1. In a bowl, mix the grated onion, garlic, parsley, salt, turmeric and meat.
2. Stir in one of the eggs, tomato paste, black pepper, cumin and cinnamon into the meat mixture.
3. Shape about 2 tablespoons of meat into the artichoke bottom.
4. Beat the second egg in a small bowl with 1 tablespoon of tomato paste.
5. Sprinkle the flour into another bowl. Dip the meatballs/artichoke bottoms into the egg mixture and then into the flour.
6. Heat the oil in a large skillet. Fry the meatballs/artichoke bottoms until brown on all sides.
7. Place the cooked meatballs/artichoke bottoms into a large wide pot.
8. Dilute the crushed tomatoes with 1 cup of water and add this to the pot with the meatballs/artichoke bottoms, plus enough water to almost cover them. Cover and bring to a boil.
9. Reduce the heat and simmer slowly for 20 minutes.

**NUTRITIONAL INFORMATION**

Per serving: 25 g total carbohydrate, 311 cals, 20 g fat, 5 g saturated fat, 7 g fiber, 201 mg sodium

# CHOPPED MEAT SERVED ON HUMMUS

**SERVES** *4*

*This is a popular Israeli dish. Hummus is a Mediterranean dish made from garbanzo beans and tahini and is available in tubs in most big supermarkets in America. It is a healthy and filling food containing fiber, protein and fat.*

½ lb of chopped meat
½ of a medium onion, chopped
1 clove of garlic, minced
2 tablespoon of tomato paste
1 teaspoon of onion soup mix
Salt and pepper to taste
12 oz container of hummus

## DIRECTIONS:

1. Sauté the onion and garlic for about 4 minutes in a small skillet.
2. Add in the chopped meat and cook until the meat is no longer pink.
3. Mix in the tomato paste and seasoning.
4. Serve over hummus.

**NUTRITIONAL INFORMATION**

Per serving: 5 g total carbohydrate, 258 cals, 16 g fat, 6 g saturated fat, 1 g fiber, 197 mg sodium

# Beef Stew with Green Beans

**COOKING TIME** *2 hours 17 minutes* ▪ **SERVES** *5*

*The combination of meat and vegetables in this recipe is very Mediterranean-style. Because the meat and vegetables are combined, less red meat is needed than if it was eaten separately.*

2 large onions, sliced thin

2 tablespoons of olive oil

1 lb of stew meat cubes

2 garlic cloves, minced

1 14½-oz can of stewed tomatoes

1 sweet red, green or yellow pepper, cut in thin strips

Salt to taste

⅛ teaspoon of pepper

2 beef bouillon cubes

1 cup of water

1½ lb of green beans, with ends removed

1 teaspoon of sugar

1 teaspoon of sweet paprika

## DIRECTIONS:

1. Sauté the onions in the oil for about 7 minutes on medium-low heat.
2. Add the beef and sauté for another 7 minutes, stirring often.
3. Stir in the garlic and bouillon cubes, and then add the tomatoes, pepper strips, paprika, salt, pepper and 1 cup of water.
4. Bring to boil, and cover and cook over low heat for 1½ hours.
5. Add the green beans and cook for 30 minutes or until the beef and beans are tender, adding a few tablespoons of water from time to time if needed.
6. Add the sugar and mix well.
7. Cook for another 3 minutes.

**NUTRITIONAL INFORMATION**

Per serving: 16 g total carbohydrate, 120 cals, 5 g fat, 1 g saturated fat, 5 g fiber, 285 mg sodium.

# Beef Moussaka

**COOKING TIME** *45 minutes* ▪ **SERVES** *6*

*Meat together with vegetables can make wonderful combinations. This recipe is a great example.*

1 large eggplant, cut into ½-inch slices
1 large onion, sliced
1 lb of ground beef
2 cloves of garlic, minced
2 large tomatoes, sliced
1 teaspoon of salt
½ teaspoon of pepper
½ teaspoon of cinnamon
Dash of paprika

## DIRECTIONS:

1. Preheat the oven to 350°F.
2. Wash and liberally salt the eggplant slices and leave for 20 minutes.
3. Rinse off the salt well.
4. Bake the eggplant on a cookie sheet for 10 minutes or until soft.
5. In a medium-sized skillet, sauté the onions and set aside.
6. Sauté the ground beef.
7. Add the seasonings, except for the garlic.
8. In a greased 8 × 10-inch casserole dish, layer the ingredients as follows: half the eggplant with garlic, ground beef, tomatoes, half the eggplant with garlic and onions. Top with a dash of paprika.
9. Bake covered at 350°F for 30 minutes.

**NUTRITIONAL INFORMATION**

Per serving: 11 g total carbohydrate, 267 cals, 19 g fat, 7 g saturated fat, 4 g fiber, 444 mg sodium.

# A Really Delicious Cholent

**PREPARATION AND COOKING TIME** *Marinating of the beef overnight, and cooking of the cholent overnight* ▪ **SERVES** *4*

*Cholent is a traditional dish made by Orthodox Jews especially for the Sabbath. Jewish law does not permit cooking a raw dish on the Jewish Sabbath, but it is permitted to keep food warm on a slow burner overnight. A crockpot plugged in on Friday is also permitted. Many cholents contain barley and potato. This one contains wheat berries, potato and chickpeas. This combination congeals less than barley and the leftovers taste as delicious during the rest of the week as they do on the Sabbath!*

1 lb of beef stew
3 potatoes, cut in quarters
½ cup of raw chickpeas
½ cup of wheat berries
2 tablespoon of onion soup mix
1 16-oz can of beer
1½ cups of water or more

**DIRECTIONS:**

1. Marinate the beef stew overnight in the can of beer.
2. Place the meat and the beer in the crockpot together with the other ingredients.
3. Cover with water to fill the crockpot and cook on low overnight.

**NUTRITIONAL INFORMATION**

Per serving: 53 g total carbohydrate, 643 cals, 25 g fat, 6 g saturated fat, 8 g fiber, 429 mg sodium.

# CAULIFLOWER CHEESE PIE

**COOKING TIME** *55 minutes* ▪ **SERVES** *8*

### CRUST:

1 cup of whole-wheat flour
1 cup of white flour
1 teaspoon of salt
½ cup of canola oil
5 tablespoons of warm water

### FILLING:

1 garlic clove, minced
1 cup of chopped onions
3 tablespoons of olive oil
1 small cauliflower, broken into small flowerets
Dash of thyme
½ teaspoon of basil
½ teaspoon of salt
Dash of black pepper
1 cup of grated cheddar cheese
2 eggs
¼ cup of milk
⅛ teaspoon of paprika

## DIRECTIONS:

1. Preheat the oven to 375°F.
2. To prepare the pie crust, mix the flour and salt in a large bowl.
3. In a separate bowl, whisk together the oil and water.
4. Stir the mixture into the flour until dough forms.
5. Roll out the dough and place in a 9-inch pan.
6. In a medium-sized skillet, sauté the onions and garlic in oil until tender.
7. Add the herbs and cauliflower and cook for 10 minutes, stirring occasionally.
8. Spread half the cheese onto the crust, then the sautéed vegetables, followed by the rest of the cheese.
9. Beat the eggs and milk together and pour over the rest of the mixture.
10. Dust with paprika.
11. Bake at 375°F for 35 to 40 minutes until set.

**NUTRITIONAL INFORMATION**

Per serving: 29 g total carbohydrate, 380 cals, 25 g fat, 5 g sat fat, 4 g fiber, 568 mg sodium.

# BUTTERNUT SQUASH WITH GINGER CASSEROLE

**COOKING TIME** *30 minutes* ▪ **SERVES** *6*

1 medium butternut squash
2 tablespoons of olive oil
1 medium onion, minced
1 15½-oz can of white beans
1 cup of canned or frozen corn kernels
4 oz of canned diced tomatoes
1 tablespoon of peeled ginger root, minced
¼ cup of chicken broth or water
½ teaspoon of ground ginger
¼ teaspoon of sugar (optional)
Salt to taste
Pepper to taste

## DIRECTIONS:

1. Halve the squash and remove the seeds and strings.
2. Put the squash halves cut-side down in a microwave-safe baking dish. Add 2 tablespoons of water and cover with wax paper.
3. Microwave on high power for about 15 minutes or until tender.
4. Remove the squash pulp from the peel and roughly dice the pulp.
5. Heat the oil in a large skillet. Add the onion and sauté over a medium heat for about 7 minutes.
6. Add the minced ginger and sauté over a low heat for 30 seconds.
7. Add the squash pieces, the broth, ground ginger, beans, corn, diced tomatoes, salt and pepper. Cover and cook, stirring often, for about 5 minutes.

### NUTRITIONAL INFORMATION

Per serving: 40 g total carbohydrate, 288 cals, 5 g fat, 1 g sat fat, 10 g fiber, 274 mg sodium.

## CHAPTER 2

# Experimenting with Grains

Using whole grains is important in Mediterranean-style meal planning. They are tasty, filling and an excellent source of fiber and anti-oxidants. A variety of grains are presented in this chapter to demonstrate how they can be used. Some are whole grain – while others are not. However, even in recipes that do not use whole grains, the grains used provide a useful base for the addition of veggies, beans and fruits in a Mediterranean mode.

Some of the grains used in this chapter may be unfamiliar to you, but don't be daunted by this. Rather, approach this chapter as an adventure in the discovery of new foods!

Many of the grain recipes included here are *pilafs*. A pilaf is a Middle Eastern or Central Asian dish in which the grain is first browned in oil and then cooked in seasoned broth or other liquid. Pilaf recipes can contain a variety of meats and vegetables and are therefore ideal for Mediterranean-style cooking.

# RICE AND LENTIL PILAF (MAJEDRA)

**COOKING TIME** *95 minutes* ▪ **SERVES** *8*

*This pilaf is loaded with fiber. It also keeps well in the fridge – as do many of the dishes in this chapter.*

- 1 cup of uncooked brown rice
- 1 cup of uncooked brown lentils
- 1 teaspoon of mixed dry herbs
- 5½ cups of hot vegetable stock or water, divided
- 3 medium onions, thinly sliced, divided
- 2 tablespoons of olive oil, divided
- ½ cup of almonds, chopped
- 2½ tablespoons of raisins
- 1 teaspoon of salt or to taste
- ⅛ teaspoon of pepper or to taste

**DIRECTIONS:**

1. Place the rice in a large saucepan with 1 teaspoon of salt, half the dried herbs, and 2½ cups of hot vegetable stock or water. Bring to a boil and simmer gently until all the stock is absorbed (about 45 minutes). Set aside.
2. Sauté two of the onions in the olive oil until they are brown.
3. Add the chopped almonds and fry gently for a few minutes.
4. Add the raisins to the onion and nut mixture and set this mixture aside.
5. In a medium-sized saucepan, gently fry the remaining onion in a little oil.
6. Add the lentils, the rest of the herbs and 3 cups of hot vegetable stock or water to cover them. Bring to the boil and simmer covered until the lentils are soft (about 35 to 40 minutes).
7. Combine the cooked rice that has been set aside and the lentils. Add salt and pepper and warm over a low heat.
8. Serve with the onion, almond and raisin mixture piled on top.

**NUTRITIONAL INFORMATION**

Per serving: 39 g total carbohydrate, 259 cals, 8 g fat, 1 g saturated fat, 9 g fiber, 295 mg sodium.

# Bulgur Pilaf with Pine Nuts

**COOKING TIME** *25 minutes* ▪ **SERVES** *7*

*Bulgur is a whole grain made from different wheat species, but mainly durum wheat. The grain is usually parboiled (partially cooked) and then dried. Bulgur should not to be confused with cracked wheat, which is made from crushed wheat grains that have not been parboiled. The distinction is important since cracked wheat needs a lot more cooking.*

1 ½ cups of dry bulgur
3 cups of chicken broth
¾ cup of celery, chopped
1 cup of onion, chopped
1 tablespoon of olive oil
½ cup of pine nuts
½ teaspoon of salt or to taste

**DIRECTIONS:**

1. In a medium saucepan, heat the chicken stock to boiling.
2. Add the bulgur, cover, and reduce the heat to low. Simmer until the liquid is absorbed, about 10 minutes.
3. Meanwhile, in a large skillet, heat the oil over medium-high heat. Add the onion and celery and cook for about 5 minutes until softened. Remove from the heat and add to the cooked bulgur.
4. Next, place the pine nuts in the skillet used for the onions and celery and sauté over a medium-high heat until the nuts begin to turn golden.
5. Stir the pine nuts into the bulgur mixture and season to taste with salt.

**NUTRITIONAL INFORMATION**

Per serving: 27 g total carbohydrate, 186 cals, 7 g fat, 1g saturated fat, 5.6 g fiber, variable sodium

# ORZO PILAF WITH APRICOTS AND CASHEWS

**COOKING TIME** *22 minutes* ▪ **SERVES** *7*

*Orzo looks like a grain – but it's not. It's a form of pasta. Most orzo is made from semolina, which is coarsely ground durum wheat in which the bran is removed. Because of its hardness, durum wheat has a low glycemic index, but it is not whole grain and its fiber content is not particularly high. However, as for other recipes in this section, this grain can serve as a useful base for veggies and meats. This recipe is simple to make and it looks and tastes very classy. It can also be served cold as a gourmet salad.*

1 medium onion, chopped
3 tablespoons of olive oil
1 ½ cups of uncooked orzo
3 cups of hot chicken broth
½ cup of dried apricots, diced
1 teaspoon of ground ginger
½ cup of roasted cashews
⅓ cup of parsley, chopped
Salt to taste
Pepper to taste

**DIRECTIONS:**

1. Sauté the onion in the oil in a medium-size saucepan for 7 minutes or until it begins to turn brown.
2. Add the uncooked orzo to the onion and cook over a low heat for 3 more minutes, stirring.
3. Add the diced apricots, hot broth and ground ginger to the orzo and bring to a boil.
4. Cover and cook over a low heat for about 12 minutes or until the orzo is tender.
5. Add the cashews, parsley, and seasoning if desired, and stir well. Serve hot or cold.

**NUTRITIONAL INFORMATION**

Per serving: 37 g carbohydrate, 282 cals, 11 g fat, 2 g saturated fat, 2.3 g fiber, variable sodium.

# COUSCOUS WITH DRIED FRUIT

**COOKING TIME** *19 minutes* ▪ **SERVES** *6*

*Couscous is made from semolina, made from coarsely ground durum wheat, which is moistened and tossed with fine wheat flour until it forms into small round balls. It is not whole grain, but also provides a nice base for Mediterranean cooking.*

2 medium onions, chopped
1 red pepper, seeded and chopped
2 cloves of garlic, minced
2 tablespoons of olive oil
1½ cups of uncooked couscous
1 teaspoon of ground cumin
3 cups of hot chicken broth
½ cup of raisins
½ cup of dried dates or apricots
½ cup of fresh parsley or mint, chopped
Salt and pepper to taste

## DIRECTIONS:

1. Heat the oil in a large deep skillet on medium heat. Sauté the onions, red pepper and garlic for 6 to 7 minutes or until golden.
2. Stir in the couscous and cumin and cook for 2 minutes. Add the hot broth and bring to a boil.
3. Reduce the heat to low, and cover and simmer for 10-12 minutes or until the couscous is tender.
4. Stir in the raisins, dried fruit, salt and pepper. Sprinkle with parsley and serve.

**NUTRITIONAL INFORMATION**

Per serving: 58 g carbohydrate, 303 cals, 5 g fat, 1 g saturated fat, 5 g fiber, 498 sodium.

# MUSHROOM KASHA PILAF

**COOKING TIME** *18 minutes* ▪ **SERVES** *6*

*Kasha is usually made from crushed and roasted whole grain buckwheat, although in Russia, the term kasha means a dish made of any kind of grain boiled in water or milk, i.e. a porridge, and it is not necessarily made of buckwheat. Do not overcook the kasha or it can become mushy.*

1 cup of dry kasha

1 egg, beaten

2 cups of boiling chicken broth

1 large onion, chopped

3 cups of mushrooms (about 10 oz), sliced

3 tablespoons of olive oil, divided

½ teaspoon of salt or to taste

⅛ teaspoon of pepper

## DIRECTIONS:

1. In a medium pot, thoroughly mix the kasha and egg.
2. Stirring constantly, cook the mixture on a medium heat until all the kasha is egg-coated, dry and separated.
3. Add 2 cups of boiling chicken broth.
4. Turn the heat to low and cover and simmer until all the liquid is absorbed, about 5 minutes.
5. In a separate pan, sauté the onion and mushrooms in 3 tablespoons of olive oil until soft.
6. Add the vegetables to the kasha, and salt and pepper to taste.

**NUTRITIONAL INFORMATION**

Per serving: 20 g grain carbohydrate, 25.0 g total carbohydrate, 196 cals, 9 g fat, 2 g saturated fat, 4.0 g fiber, 607 sodium.

# Brown Rice and Noodle Pilaf

**COOKING TIME** *45 minutes* ▪ **YIELDS** *4½ cups*

*White rice is made by removing the husk from the rice – and it is the husk that contains the bran and germ layers. White rice therefore has a lot less fiber that white rice; one cup of brown rice contains about 4 g of fiber versus less than 1 g for white rice. Brown rice also has a mild nutty flavor. The bottom line? Try and use brown rice rather than white rice whenever possible.*

1 cup of uncooked brown rice
1 oz of dry angel hair pasta
4 teaspoons of olive oil, divided
½ green pepper, diced
1 medium onion, diced
2 cups of chicken broth
1 cup of water
½ teaspoon of salt or to taste
¼ teaspoon of pepper

## DIRECTIONS:

1. In a medium-sized pot, add the 2 cups of chicken broth and one cup of water to the brown rice and boil gently for 25 minutes.
2. In the meantime, snap the pasta into 1-2-inch pieces and sauté them in a skillet in 2 teaspoons of olive oil until partially brown. Place in a bowl.
3. Sauté the pepper and onion in 2 teaspoons of oil in the same skillet and add to the bowl.
4. Add the pasta and vegetables to the rice, add additional water as needed, and cook for another 20 minutes.

### NUTRITIONAL INFORMATION

Per serving: 45 g total carbohydrate, 260 cals, 6 g fat, 1 g saturated fat, 3 g fiber, 788 mg sodium.

# RICE WITH VEGETABLES AND PECAN

**COOKING TIME** *45 minutes* ▪ **SERVES** *12*

*You can't go wrong with this simple winning rice recipe. From a health perspective, brown rice is preferable to white rice, but if your family doesn't buy into this there are plenty of health benefits from the veggies and nuts.*

2 cups of uncooked brown rice
2 cups of broccoli, chopped
1 large onion, chopped
3 medium carrots, cut into 2-3 inch long strips
2 cups of sliced fresh mushrooms
2 tablespoons of olive oil
3 garlic cloves, minced
¾ teaspoon of dried thyme
¾ teaspoon of dried basil
¾ teaspoon of salt
¼ teaspoon of pepper
½ cup of chopped pecans

## DIRECTIONS:

1. Cook the rice according to the package instructions.
2. Sauté the broccoli, carrots, and onions in olive oil in a large frying pan for 5-7 minutes.
3. Add the rest of the ingredients, except for the rice and pecans, and cook and stir for 2-3 minutes.
4. Add the rice and pecans and cook for an additional 1-2 minutes.

**NUTRITIONAL INFORMATION**

Per serving: 29 g total carbohydrate, 186 cals, 7 g fat, 1 g saturated fat, 3 g fiber, 165 mg sodium

# CHINESE RICE WITH VEGETABLES

**COOKING TIME** *20 minutes* ▪ **SERVES** *8*

*This is another simple recipe that tastes excellent as either a hot dish or cold salad.*

2 cups of uncooked brown rice
1 10-oz package of uncooked frozen peas
1½ cups of celery, chopped
¼ cup of onion, finely chopped
½ cup of olive oil
1 tablespoon of soy sauce
1 teaspoon of celery salt
1 teaspoon of vinegar
1 teaspoon of salt
½ teaspoon of sugar
1 teaspoon of curry powder

## DIRECTIONS:

1. Cook the rice according to the package instructions.
2. Add the peas, celery and onion to the cooked rice.
3. Combine the oil, soy sauce, celery, salt, sugar, and curry powder in a separate jar. Shake well and pour on the rice mixture. Mix well.

**NUTRITIONAL INFORMATION**

Per serving: 40 g total carbohydrate, 313 cals, 15 g fat, 2 g saturated fat, 3 g fiber, 443 mg sodium

# RICE WITH A TOUCH OF GREEN

**COOKING TIME** *44 minutes* ▪ **SERVES** *4*

1 ½ cups of uncooked rice, preferably brown rice

1 cup of scallions, chopped

1 cup of fresh parsley, minced

4 teaspoons of olive oil

4 teaspoons of butter

3 cups of broth

⅛ teaspoon of cayenne pepper

1 bay leaf

## DIRECTIONS:

1. In a medium pot, sauté the scallions and parsley in oil and butter for 1 minute or until tender.
2. Add the rice, and cook over medium-heat for about 3 minutes until the rice is coated with oil and translucent.
3. Stir in the broth, cayenne pepper and bay leaf.
4. Reduce the heat, cover tightly, and simmer the brown rice for about 40 minutes until the water is absorbed (about 18-20 minutes for white rice).
5. Finally, discard the bay leaf.

**NUTRITIONAL INFORMATION**

Per serving: 57 g total carbohydrate, 352 cals, 11 g fat, 4 g saturated fat, 4 g fiber, 751 mg sodium.

# Curried Brown Rice Pilaf with Walnuts

**COOKING TIME** *55 minutes* ▪ **SERVES** *4*

*With its content of nuts, fruit and brown rice this very tasty recipe is full of healthful ingredients.*

½ cup of walnut pieces
2 teaspoon of olive oil
2 cloves garlic, minced
½ medium red pepper, diced
1 large onion, diced
1 teaspoon of curry powder
¼ teaspoon of ground cumin
1 ½ cups of uncooked brown rice
3 cups of boiling chicken broth
Salt and pepper to taste
¼ cup of dried apricots, diced
¼ cup of minced parsley

## DIRECTIONS:

1. In a large skillet, toast the walnuts for about 4-5 minutes on medium heat until lightly browned. Set aside.
2. Heat the oil in the same skillet over medium-high heat, and sauté the garlic, red pepper, and onion for about 3-4 minutes.
3. Add the curry and cumin and sauté, stirring, for 1 minute.
4. Add the brown rice and sauté, stirring for 1 minute.
5. Add the broth, salt and pepper and bring to a boil again. Cover, reduce heat to low and simmer for 40-45 minutes until the rice is done.
6. Add in the reserved walnuts, apricots and parsley.

### NUTRITIONAL INFORMATION

Per serving: 67 g total carbohydrate, 427 cals, 15 g fat, 2.8 g saturated fat, 5 g fiber, 742 mg sodium.

# CHICKPEA AND LENTIL CURRY ON RICE

**COOKING TIME** *75 minutes* ▪ **SERVES** *8*

*You may need to do a bit of shopping for the ingredients for this recipe – but the effort is well worthwhile. Your family will love it.*

1½ tablespoons of olive oil
½ onion, chopped
2 cloves of garlic, minced
½ red pepper, diced
1 carrot, diced
1 small sweet potato, diced
2 tablespoons of fresh ginger, minced
¼ teaspoon of cayenne pepper
½ teaspoon of ground cumin
½ teaspoon of ground coriander
1½ tablespoons of curry powder
½-1 teaspoon of salt
28-oz can of crushed tomatoes
1 13.5-oz can of coconut milk
1 cup of uncooked whole green lentils
1½ tablespoons of honey
1 15-oz can of chickpeas
1 cup of fresh cauliflower florets
½ cup of frozen peas
2 cups of raw brown or white rice

## DIRECTIONS:

1. In a large pot, heat the olive oil on medium heat and sauté the onions until soft.
2. Add the garlic, ginger, red pepper, carrots, sweet potato, curry, spices and salt, and cook for 5 minutes stirring.
3. Add the crushed tomatoes, coconut milk, lentils, and honey. Bring to a boil while stirring well.
4. Cover. Reduce heat to simmer and cook for 45 minutes, stirring occasionally.
5. Add the cauliflower, chickpeas and peas. Cook for another 20 minutes or until the cauliflower is tender.
6. Cook 2 cups of rice according to the packet instructions.
7. Serve the chickpea and lentil curry over the rice.

**NUTRITIONAL INFORMATION**

Per serving: 83 g total carbohydrate, 523 cals, 16 g fat, 16 g saturated fat, 15 g fiber, 563 mg sodium.

# SOPA SECA

**COOKING TIME** *50 minutes* ▪ **SERVES** *6*

- 1 15½-oz can of chickpeas, rinsed and drained (or 1½ cups of dried chickpeas soaked overnight in 2 cups of water)
- 3 tablespoons of olive oil
- 2 onions, chopped
- 2 cloves of garlic, minced
- 1 green pepper, chopped
- 1 cup of uncooked brown rice
- 1½ cups of boiling water
- 1 14½-oz can of chopped tomatoes, with juice
- ¼ teaspoon of oregano
- ½ teaspoon of chili powder
- 1 teaspoon of salt or to taste
- ¼ teaspoon of pepper
- ¼ cup of raisins
- ¼ cup of sliced almonds

## DIRECTIONS:

1. If using dried chickpeas, simmer them in water to cover for 30 minutes, and then drain.
2. Meanwhile, heat the olive oil in a large skillet. Sauté the onions, garlic and green pepper.
3. Add the rice and sauté 1 minute more.
4. Add the boiling water, tomatoes, chickpeas and spices to the skillet. Cover and simmer for 40 minutes.
5. Stir in the raisins and almonds and cook for 5 minutes longer.

### NUTRITIONAL INFORMATION

Per serving: 58 g total carbohydrate, 358 cals, 11 g fat, 1 g saturated fat, 8 g fiber, 728 mg sodium.

# ZUCCHINI PASTA

**COOKING TIME** *30 minutes* ▪ **SERVES** *4*

½ pound of dried pasta, such as ziti or penne

4 medium zucchinis, cut into ribbons or coins

1 large onion, chopped

2 tomatoes, in wedges or chopped, with juice

¼ cup of olive oil

1 teaspoon of dried thyme

Salt to taste

¼ teaspoon pepper

Grated Parmesan cheese or freshly chopped parsley for garnish

## DIRECTIONS:

1. In a large skillet, sauté the zucchini, onion and thyme in the olive oil gently, stirring occasionally. Add the salt and pepper, and adjust the heat so that the onion and zucchini release their liquid without browning, cooking for about 20 minutes.
2. Add the tomatoes and their liquid to the zucchini and heat the mixture until it bubbles.
3. Bring a large pot of water to boil with salt. Cook the pasta until it is almost done.
4. Drain the pasta and finish cooking it in the sauce.
5. Serve garnished with parsley or Parmesan cheese.

**NUTRITIONAL INFORMATION**

Per serving: 47 g total carbohydrate, 357 cals, 15 g fat, 2 g saturated fat, 2 g fiber, 4 mg sodium.

# BASIL, MINT AND VEGETABLE COUSCOUS

**COOKING TIME** *15 minutes* ▪ **SERVES** *10*

*This dish contains a nice selection of vegetables and can be conjured up in a very short time.*

2 tablespoons of olive oil, divided
1 cup of onion, chopped
1 tablespoon of garlic, chopped
1 large yellow squash, coarsely diced
1 large zucchini, coarsely diced
2 cups of tomatoes, coarsely chopped
2 teaspoons of dried basil
2 teaspoons of dried mint
Salt to taste
Pepper to taste
2 cups of uncooked couscous
3 cups of water or vegetable broth

**DIRECTIONS:**

1. Heat 1 tablespoon of olive oil in a large skillet over medium-high heat. Add the onions and cook until they begin to wilt, about 3 minutes.
2. Stir in the garlic and cook for 1 minute.
3. Add the yellow squash and zucchini and cook stirring for 5 to 8 minutes or until the vegetables are tender.
4. Add the tomatoes, basil and mint. Reduce the heat and cook, stirring, 2 to 3 minutes or until the tomatoes are heated through. Season to taste with salt and pepper. Remove from the heat and reserve.
5. Bring the water or stock to boil. Add the couscous, cover and remove from the heat. Set aside until the liquid has been absorbed, about 5 minutes.
6. Stir in the salt to taste and remaining 1 tablespoon of oil.
7. To serve, ladle the vegetable mixture over the couscous.

**NUTRITIONAL INFORMATION**

Per serving: 32 g total carbohydrate, 179 cals, 3.0 g fat, 0.0 g saturated fat, 3.0 g fiber, 23 mg sodium.

# PEPPERS STUFFED WITH CINNAMON BULGUR

**COOKING TIME** *10 minutes* ▪ **SERVES** *4*

2¼ cups of water, divided

½ cup of shredded carrot

¼ cup of chopped onion

1 teaspoon of instant vegetable or chicken bouillon granules

Dash of ground cinnamon

⅛ teaspoon of salt

¾ cup of bulgur

½ cup of dried cranberries or raisins

2 large green peppers

2 tablespoons of sliced almonds

¾ cup of shredded Muenster or mozzarella cheese

## DIRECTIONS:

1. In a large skillet, stir together 1¾ cups of water, carrot, onion, bouillon granules, salt and cinnamon. Bring to boil and then reduce heat and simmer, covered, for 5 minutes.
2. Stir in the bulgur and cranberries. Remove from the heat. Cover and let stand for 5 minutes. Drain off excess liquid.
3. Meanwhile, halve the green peppers lengthwise, removing the seeds and membranes.
4. Stir the shredded cheese into the bulgur mixture. Fill the pepper halves with the mixture.
5. Place the green pepper halves in a skillet. Add ½ cup of water.
6. Bring the peppers and water to boil. Reduce heat and simmer, covered, for 5 to 10 minutes until the green peppers are crisp-tender and the bulgur mixture is heated through.
7. Sprinkle the stuffed peppers with nuts.

**NUTRITIONAL INFORMATION**

Per serving: 37 g total carbohydrate, 257 cals, 9 g fat, 4 g saturated fat, 8 g fiber, 317 mg sodium.

# QUINOA AND BLACK BEANS

**COOKING TIME** *30 minutes* ▪ **SERVES** *6*

*Quinoa? You're in good company if you've never heard of it. Quinoa came originally from the Andean region of South America. It is a grain, although not a member of the grass family. It is modestly high in calcium, is gluten-free and is a good source of fiber. Quinoa is increasing in popularity in this country. This recipe can be served hot as a starch dish or cold as a salad.*

1 teaspoon of olive oil
1 medium onion, chopped
3 cloves of garlic, chopped
1½ cups of vegetable broth
¾ cup of uncooked quinoa
1 teaspoon of ground cumin
¼ teaspoon of cayenne pepper
Salt and pepper to taste
1 cup of frozen corn kernels
1 15-oz can of black beans, rinsed and drained
½ cup of fresh cilantro, chopped

**DIRECTIONS:**

1. In a medium saucepan, heat the oil and sauté the onion and garlic until lightly browned.
2. Add the quinoa and vegetable broth to the saucepan, and season with cumin, cayenne pepper, salt, and pepper.
3. Bring the mixture to the boil, cover, reduce heat and simmer for 20 minutes.
4. Stir the frozen corn into the saucepan and continue to simmer for 5 minutes until heated through.
5. Mix in the black beans and cilantro.

**NUTRITIONAL INFORMATION**

Per serving: 38 g carbohydrate, 240 cals, 6 g fat, 1 g saturated fat, 8 g fiber, variable sodium.

# QUINOA WITH ROASTED BRUSSELS SPROUTS, LEEKS AND SLIVERED ALMONDS

**COOKING TIME** *30 minutes* ▪ **SERVES 6**

*This delicious recipe is another excellent way for introducing quinoa to your family.*

- 1 cup of quinoa
- 2 cups of water
- 1 leek, washed, trimmed and sliced
- 1 lb. of Brussels sprouts, washed, trimmed and halved (or quartered if large)
- ¼ cup of slivered blanched almonds
- ¼ cup of golden raisins, plumped in hot water.
- 1-2 garlic cloves, minced
- 2 tablespoons of golden balsamic vinegar
- 4 tablespoons of olive oil, divided
- 2 teaspoons of dried dill
- 2 tablespoons of fresh Italian parsley, chopped
- Salt to taste
- Pepper to taste

## DIRECTIONS:

1. Preheat the oven to 400°F.
2. Combine the quinoa with 2 cups of water and salt to taste in a medium-sized pot, bring to a boil, and cook the quinoa until all the water is absorbed and the quinoa can be fluffed with a fork.
3. In a roasting pan, toss the prepared leek, Brussels sprouts, almonds and golden raisins in 3 tablespoons of olive oil. Sprinkle with golden balsamic vinegar. Season with salt, minced garlic and dill, and toss to coat.
4. Roast for roughly 20 to 25 minutes, stirring at least once, until the Brussels sprouts are tender and browned a bit.
5. Remove the pan from the oven. Add in the fluffed cooked quinoa and chopped parsley.
6. Drizzle with 1 tablespoon of olive oil to taste. Add salt and ground pepper to taste. Gently toss to combine the roasted Brussels sprouts and hot cooked quinoa.

**NUTRITIONAL INFORMATION**

**Per serving: 36 g total carbohydrate, 286 cals, 14 g fat, 2 g saturated fat, 6 g fiber, 28 mg sodium.**

# Mushroom Barley Casserole

**COOKING TIME** *90 minutes* ▪ **SERVES** *4*

*The mushrooms make a nice addition to this tasty high-fiber starch dish.*

½ cup of onion, diced
4 tablespoons of olive oil
1 cup of uncooked barley
4 cups of chicken broth
2 cups of sliced mushrooms

## DIRECTIONS:

1. In a small skillet, sauté the onion and mushrooms in the olive oil.
2. In a 1½ quart casserole dish, add the barley, chicken broth, salt, and sautéed mushrooms and onions.
3. Bake at 350°F uncovered for 1 hour, stirring several times.
4. Cover tightly and bake for another ½ hour.

**NUTRITIONAL INFORMATION**

Per serving: 42 g total carbohydrate, 321cals, 15 g fat, 2 g saturated fat, 8 g fiber, 485 mg sodium.

# APRICOT BARLEY CASSEROLE

**COOKING TIME** *90 minutes* ▪ **SERVES** *6*

⅔ cup of pine nuts or slivered almonds

¼ cup of olive oil

2 cups of uncooked barley

1 cup of sliced green onions

7 cups of chicken broth

⅔ cup of diced dried apricots

½ cup of golden raisins

## DIRECTIONS:

1. In a medium skillet, sauté the nuts in the olive oil until slightly browned. Remove and set aside.
2. Sauté the barley and onions in the same skillet with the remaining oil until the onions are tender.
3. Add the broth and bring to a boil.
4. Stir in the apricots, raisins and nuts.
5. Put the mixture into a greased 13 × 9 × 2-inch baking dish, and bake uncovered at 325°F for 1¼ hours or until the barley is tender.

### NUTRITIONAL INFORMATION

Per serving: 57 g total carbohydrate, 354cals, 12 g fat, 2 g saturated fat, 10 g fiber, 865 mg sodium.

# CHAPTER 3

# JAZZING UP VEGETABLES

Many American families have given up on vegetables, except as an addition to pizza. When vegetables are absent from meals, starches often take their place, and these are frequently fiber-free and non-satiating. Somehow, veggies have to get back onto your family's plates.

I have two suggestions:

The first is to make vegetables more attractive by cooking them in ways other than boiling. In the past, vegetables that were fried or roasted with oil would rarely have gotten into a recipe book focused on health because of concerns regarding their fat content. But vegetables cooked like this are not at all unhealthy. To the contrary, if one uses healthy oils, such as olive oil, they actually add to health.

My second suggestion is to combine veggies with different starches, grains and protein to make tasty combinations. This is called "Mediterranean-style cooking" in this book.

# Oven Roasted Vegetables

**COOKING TIME** *30 minutes* ▪ **SERVES** *4*

*Oven-roasted vegetables are tastier and more enticing than boiled ones. In this recipe, yellow and red peppers provide a sweeter taste than green peppers and also add bright color. Other vegetables that can be used in this recipe are mushrooms (4 oz) and a baby eggplant cut into ½-inch cubes. A 30-minute cooking time is appropriate for all the vegetables.*

1 zucchini, sliced
1 yellow squash, sliced
1 red bell pepper, cut into broad slices
1 yellow bell pepper, cut into broad slices
1 red onion, cut into medium-sized slices
1 pound of fresh asparagus, cut into medium-sized pieces
3 tablespoons of olive oil
½ teaspoon of salt or to taste
¼ teaspoon of black pepper

**DIRECTIONS:**

1. Preheat the oven to 450°F.
2. Place the zucchini, squash, peppers, asparagus and onion in a large roasting pan. Coat with the olive oil, salt and pepper.
3. Cook in the oven uncovered for 30 minutes at 450°F, stirring occasionally, until the vegetables are lightly browned and tender.

**NUTRITIONAL INFORMATION**

Per serving: 14 g total carbohydrate, 155 cals, 10 g fat, 1.5 g saturated fat, 5 g fiber, 305 mg sodium.

# ROASTED VEGGIE MEDLEY

**COOKING TIME** *53 minutes* ▪ **SERVES** *4*

3 medium carrots, thinly sliced

2 medium yellow summer squash, sliced

2 medium zucchini, sliced

1 small head of cauliflower, broken into florets

2 garlic cloves, minced

4 tablespoons of olive oil, divided

1 cup of chicken broth

1 teaspoon of salt or to taste

½ teaspoon of white pepper

## DIRECTIONS:

1. Preheat the oven to 350°F.
2. In a small saucepan, sauté the garlic in 2 tablespoons of oil for 2-3 minutes. Stir in the broth, 2 more tablespoons of oil, salt and pepper.
3. Place carrots, squash, and cauliflower in a shallow 3-qt baking dish. Pour the oil and broth mixture over the vegetables. Stir to coat.
4. Cover and bake at 350°F for 50 minutes or until the vegetables are tender.

### NUTRITIONAL INFORMATION

Per serving: 11 g total carbohydrate, 136 cals, 10 g fat, 1 g saturated fat, 4 g fiber, 592 mg sodium.

# ROASTED VEGETABLES WITH CHICKPEAS

**COOKING TIME** *45 minutes* ▪ **SERVES** *8*

*This is a colorful and very pleasant tasting recipe that can be used as a starch or vegetable dish.*

1 lb of carrots, cut into chunks

1 lb of sweet potatoes, cut into chunks

1 large red onion, cut into chunks

1 lb of unpeeled red potatoes, cut into cubes

½ lb of parsnip, cut into chunks

6 cloves of garlic, minced

1 16-oz can of chickpeas (garbanzo beans), rinsed and drained

3 tablespoons of olive oil

1 teaspoon of dried rosemary

1 teaspoon of packed brown sugar or granulated sugar

½ teaspoon of salt or to taste

½ teaspoon of black pepper

## DIRECTIONS:

1. Preheat the oven to 425°F.
2. Place all the vegetables, garlic and chickpeas in a large baking pan.
3. In a small bowl, mix the oil, rosemary, sugar, salt and pepper, and drizzle over the vegetables. Stir.
4. Roast for 45 minutes or until the vegetables are lightly browned and tender, stirring occasionally.

### NUTRITIONAL INFORMATION

Per serving: 42 g total carbohydrate, 238 cals, 6 g fat, 1 g saturated fat, 8 g fiber, 397 mg sodium.

# Roasted Brussels Sprouts with Red Peppers

**COOKING TIME** *30 minutes* ▪ **SERVES** *8*

*The combination of Brussels sprouts and red pepper make this a very enticing dish.*

1½ cups of onion, thinly sliced
¾ cups of red pepper, cut into ½ × ½ –inch pieces
3 tablespoons of olive oil
1¼ teaspoons of salt
½ teaspoon of black pepper
½ teaspoon of caraway seeds
3 lb of Brussels sprouts, trimmed and halved
8 garlic cloves, thinly sliced

## DIRECTIONS:

1. Preheat the oven to 400°F.
2. Combine all the ingredients in a large bowl, tossing to coat.
3. Spread on a large roasting pan coated with cooking spray.
4. Bake at 400°F for 30 minutes, stirring occasionally, until the Brussels sprouts are done.

**NUTRITIONAL INFORMATION**

Per serving: 19 g total carbohydrate, 135 cals, 6 g fat, 1 g saturated fat, 7 g fiber, 413 mg sodium.

# WINTER ROASTED CARROTS

**COOKING TIME** *25 minutes* ▪ **SERVES** *6*

*This is a very colorful and tasty way for serving carrots.*

1 lb of baby carrots, cut into halves lengthwise
2 small onions, cut into ⅛'s
6 cloves of garlic, minced
1 large parsnip, cut into 3-inch strips
2 tablespoons of olive oil
½ teaspoon of dried thyme
¼ teaspoon of salt or to taste
⅛ teaspoon of pepper

## DIRECTIONS:

1. Preheat the oven to 450°F.
2. Place the vegetables in a large roasting pan.
3. Drizzle the olive oil over the vegetables. Then sprinkle the thyme, salt and pepper.
4. Bake uncovered for 25 minutes, stirring periodically, until the carrots begin to brown and are tender when pierced with a knife tip.

**NUTRITIONAL INFORMATION**

Per serving: 11g total carbohydrate, 86 cals, 5 g fat, 0.6 g saturated fat, 2 g fiber, 166 mg sodium.

# ROASTED CAULIFLOWER

**COOKING TIME** *15 minutes* ▪ **SERVES** *8 (if you can stop your family coming back for seconds)*

*This dish is guaranteed to turn anyone into a veggie lover. The flowerets taste like a snack food. Try them!*

1 head of cauliflower, cut into small flowerets
4 tablespoons of olive oil
½ teaspoon of salt or to taste
Dash of pepper
½ teaspoon of garlic powder
½ teaspoon of onion powder
½ teaspoon of paprika
½ teaspoon of cumin (optional)

## DIRECTIONS:

1. In a small bowl, mix the oil and spices.
2. Toss the mixture over the flowerets and stir extremely well.
3. Broil for about 15 minutes, stirring after 10 minutes. For the best taste, the florets should be just slightly burnt.

**NUTRITIONAL INFORMATION**

Per serving: 2 g total carbohydrate, 54 cals, 5 g fat, 0.5 g saturated fat, 1 g fiber, 83 mg sodium.

# FRIED CAULIFLOWER WITH A TASTE OF GARLIC

**COOKING TIME** *15 minutes* ▪ **SERVES** *8*

1 head of cauliflower, cut into small flowerets

4 tablespoons of olive oil

2 cloves of garlic, chopped

½ teaspoon of salt or to taste

¼ teaspoon of pepper

¼ cup of black olives (optional)

## DIRECTIONS:

1. In a large frying pan, heat the olive oil and sauté the cauliflower for 3 minutes while sprinkling the salt evenly over the cauliflower.
2. Cover the frying pan, add the garlic, and cook over medium-low heat for about 12 minutes.
3. Add pepper before serving.
4. For an exotic Middle Eastern look, add black olives.

### NUTRITIONAL INFORMATION

Per serving: 3.5 g total carbohydrate, 77 cals, 7 g fat, 1 g saturated fat, 1.5 g fiber, 158 mg sodium.

# Indian Cauliflower

**COOKING TIME** *5 minutes* ▪ **SERVES** *8*

*This wonderful dish has an appealing spicy taste. The timing is important, so use a timer.*

1 head of cauliflower, cut into small flowerets
4 green onions, sliced into 1-inch pieces
1 small red or green pepper, cut into 1-inch squares
1 tablespoon of olive oil
¼ cup of chicken broth
½ teaspoon of dry mustard
¼ teaspoon of turmeric
¼ teaspoon of cumin
⅛ teaspoon of coriander
⅛ teaspoon of red pepper

**DIRECTIONS:**

1. Stir-fry the cauliflower for 3 minutes in large skillet.
2. Add the onions and peppers and stir-fry for another 1½ minutes.
3. In a small bowl, mix all the spices.
4. Add the spices to the vegetables and cook for a further 30 seconds.
5. Stir in the chicken broth and cook for another 1 minute or until heated through.

**NUTRITIONAL INFORMATION**

Per serving: 4 g total carbohydrate, 37 cals, 2 g fat, 0.5 g saturated fat, 2 g fiber, 31 mg sodium.

# Cauliflower Patties

**COOKING TIME** *5 minutes* ▪ **SERVES** *5*

*Getting vegetables onto the plates of your family often needs imagination. This is one way that usually works!*

1 medium cauliflower
1 medium onion, finely chopped
1 egg
1 cup of whole-wheat breadcrumbs or whole-wheat matzo meal, divided
½ teaspoon of oregano
4 tablespoons of olive oil
Salt and pepper to taste

**DIRECTIONS:**

1. Break the cauliflower into flowerets and cook them in water for about 10-15 minutes until soft.
2. Mash the cauliflower and add the onion, egg, ½ cup of breadcrumbs, oregano, salt and pepper.
3. Mix well and shape into patties.
4. Dip both sides of the patty in the remaining ½ cup of breadcrumbs or matzo meal and sauté on both sides until golden brown.

**NUTRITIONAL INFORMATION**

Per serving: 10 g total carbohydrate, 160 cals, 12 g fat, 2 g saturated fat, 3 g fiber, 34 mg sodium.

# Zucchini on the Grill

*Vegetables cooked on the grill are often tastier than those cooked in other ways.*

Zucchini, cut into large slices
Olive oil
Salt to taste
Pepper to taste

**DIRECTIONS:**

1. Lightly coat the vegetables with the olive oil and seasoning.
2. Put on the grill until cooked to satisfaction, flipping once.

# Microwaved Zucchini Parmesan

**COOKING TIME** *5 minutes* ▪ **SERVES** *4*

*Is your garden and kitchen overrun with zucchini? This is a very family-friendly way for eating them.*

3 cups of zucchini, cut into ¼-inch slices (about 1⅓ large zucchini)
1 tablespoon of oil
2 tablespoons of grated Parmesan cheese
1 teaspoon of dried parsley flakes or 1 tablespoon of fresh parsley
Dash of salt
Dash of pepper

## DIRECTIONS:

1. Lightly oil an 8 to 9-inch round baking dish and place the zucchini slices in the dish.
2. Cover the dish with a plastic wrap and microwave at high for 4-6 minutes or until tender crisp. Drain off the fluid.
3. Combine the cheese, parsley, salt and pepper.
4. Sprinkle the cheese mixture over the zucchini before serving.

**NUTRITIONAL INFORMATION**

Per serving: 3 g total carbohydrate, 56 cals, 4 g fat, 1 g saturated fat, 1 g fiber, 50 mg sodium.

# ZUCCHINI WITH TOMATO

**COOKING TIME** *15 minutes* ▪ **SERVES** *6*

*The cumin adds a pleasant Middle Eastern tang to this vegetable dish.*

1 tablespoon of olive oil
½ teaspoon of salt or to taste
⅛ teaspoon of pepper
1 medium onion, diced
2 cloves of garlic, minced
1 15-oz can of baby corn (optional)
1 teaspoon of cumin
3 medium zucchinis, sliced
1 15-oz can of chopped tomatoes

## DIRECTIONS:

1. In a large skillet, sauté the onion and garlic on a moderate heat until they are soft and slightly brown.
2. Add the zucchini and continue cooking until they are cooked but still firm, about 10 minutes.
3. Add the tomato, cumin, salt, pepper and baby corn and continue heating until all the contents are warm.

**NUTRITIONAL INFORMATION**
**(without the corn)**

Per serving: 10 g total carbohydrate, 68 cals, 3 g fat, 3 g fiber, 293 mg sodium.

# ZUCCHINI WITH MUSHROOMS

**COOKING TIME** *20 minutes* ▪ **SERVES** *6*

1 large green pepper, diced
2 cloves of garlic, coarsely chopped
1 medium onion, diced
1 tablespoon of olive oil
½ teaspoon of basil
½ teaspoon of salt
¼ teaspoon of pepper
2 medium zucchini, sliced
4 oz of mushroom, sliced
1 15-oz can of diced tomato
2 tablespoons of tomato ketchup

## DIRECTIONS:

1. In a large skillet, sauté the onion, garlic and pepper on a moderate heat until soft.
2. Add the remainder of the ingredients, cover, and simmer for 10 to 15 minutes until the vegetables are soft, stirring occasionally.

**NUTRITIONAL INFORMATION**

Per serving: 13 g total carbohydrate, 77 cals, 3 g fat, 0 g saturated fat, 3 g fiber, 350 mg sodium.

# SAUTÉED ZUCCHINI

**COOKING TIME** *10 minutes* ▪ **SERVES** *4*

*Zucchini prepared this way are irresistible.*

2 medium zucchini, sliced lengthwise into ¼-inch slices
2 tablespoons of whole-wheat flour
½ cup breadcrumbs, preferably whole-wheat
1 egg
¼ cup of olive oil
¼ teaspoon salt
½ teaspoon of onion powder
Dash of black pepper

## DIRECTIONS:

1. Stir the salt, onion powder and pepper into the egg.
2. Dip each zucchini piece into the flour, then into the egg with the seasoning mixture, and then into breadcrumbs to coat.
3. Gently sauté in oil, turning once, until nicely brown and soft.
4. Drain on a paper towel. Serve warm.

**NUTRITIONAL INFORMATION**

Per serving: 16 g total carbohydrate, 221 cals, 16 g fat, 3 g saturated fat, 2 g fiber, 272 mg sodium.

# Zucchini Patties

**COOKING TIME** *15 minutes* ▪ **SERVES** *4*

*With its eggs and oil, this may not have been regarded in the past as a particularly healthy recipe. However, this is not the case at all. The recipe contains veggies, whole-wheat flour and olive oil – all of which are healthy ingredients. The family will love it. So enjoy!*

2 cups of grated zucchini,

2 eggs

¼ cup of chopped onion

½ cup of whole-wheat flour

½ cup of grated Parmesan cheese

½ cup of shredded mozzarella cheese

¼ teaspoon of salt

3 tablespoons of olive oil

## DIRECTIONS:

1. Heat the olive oil in a large skillet.
2. Mix the rest of the ingredients. Drop by large spoonfuls into the frying pan.
3. Fry until golden on both sides, turning once.

**NUTRITIONAL INFORMATION**

Per serving: 15 g total carbohydrate, 278 cals, 19 g fat, 6 g saturated fat, 2 g fiber, 450 mg sodium.

# STUFFED SQUASH

**COOKING TIME** *63 minutes* ▪ **SERVES** *4*

*This gourmet vegetable dish can be used as either a side dish or main course.*

2 acorn or butternut squash
½ cup of onion, chopped
1 large garlic clove, minced
1 stalk of celery, chopped
3 tablespoons of olive oil
¼ cup of chopped walnuts
¼ cup of sunflower seeds
1 cup of coarsely crumbled whole-wheat bread
½ teaspoon of sage
½ teaspoon of thyme
⅛ teaspoon of salt
⅛ teaspoon of pepper
½ cup of grated cheddar cheese
¼ cup of raisins

## DIRECTIONS:

1. Preheat the oven to 350°F.
2. Split 2 acorn or butternut squash lengthwise down the middle and remove the seeds.
3. Bake the squash face down on an oiled tray for 30 minutes at 350°F.
4. Meanwhile, sauté the onions, garlic, celery, nuts and seeds in the oil in a skillet. Add all the remaining ingredients except for the cheese to the skillet. Cook over a low heat for 5-8 minutes while stirring.
5. Remove from the heat and add in the cheese and raisins.
6. Pack the ingredients into the baked acorn squash halves.
7. Bake the squash an additional 25 minutes at 350°F.

### NUTRITIONAL INFORMATION

Per serving: 40 g total carbohydrate, 375 cals, 22 g fat, 5 g saturated fat, 6 g fiber, 262 mg sodium.

# SPAGHETTI SQUASH PRIMAVERA

**COOKING TIME** *17 minutes* ▪ **SERVES** *8*

*This dish has a very pleasant crunchy taste because of the spaghetti squash.*

1 large spaghetti squash
¼ cup of carrot, sliced
¼ cup of red onion, chopped
¼ cup of red sweet pepper, diced
¼ cup of green pepper, diced
1 garlic clove, minced
2 teaspoons of olive oil
1 cup of yellow summer squash, thinly sliced
1 cup of zucchini, thinly sliced
1 14½-can of stewed tomatoes
½ cup of frozen corn, thawed
½ teaspoon of salt or to taste
½ teaspoon of dried oregano
⅛ teaspoon of dried thyme
4 teaspoons of grated Parmesan cheese
2 tablespoons of minced fresh parsley

**DIRECTIONS:**

1. Cut the spaghetti squash in half and discard the seeds.
2. Place the cut-side up on a microwave-safe plate, cover with waxed paper, and microwave on high for 9 minutes or until tender.
3. In a large skillet, sauté the carrot, onion, peppers and garlic in oil for 3 minutes.
4. Add the yellow squash and zucchini and sauté 2-3 minutes longer or until the squash is tender.
5. Reduce the heat and add the tomatoes, corn, salt, oregano and thyme. Cook for 5 minutes longer or until heated thoroughly, stirring occasionally.
6. Separate the spaghetti squash strands with a fork.
7. Spoon the vegetable mixture into the squash.
8. Sprinkle with Parmesan cheese and parsley.

**NUTRITIONAL INFORMATION**

Per serving: 15 g total carbohydrate, 76 cals, 2 g fat, 0.7 g saturated fat, 3 g fiber, 194 mg sodium.

# ROASTED BUTTERNUT SQUASH WITH RED ONION

**COOKING TIME** *42 minutes* ▪ **SERVES** *6*

*Za'atar is a blend of herbs, sesame and salt that is popular throughout the Middle East. You may be able to buy it at a specialty herb store. Otherwise, use oregano or thyme.*

1 large butternut squash (about 3 lbs), cut into long wedges
2 red onions, cut into long wedges
2 tablespoons of olive oil
3½ tablespoons of tahini
2 tablespoons of water
1½ tablespoons of lemon juice
1 garlic clove, crushed
¼ cup of pine nuts
1 tablespoon of za'atar (or oregano or thyme)
1 tablespoon of parsley
1½ teaspoons of salt, divided
Pepper to taste

## DIRECTIONS:

1. Preheat the oven to 425°F
2. In a large mixing bowl, add the squash, onion, olive oil, 1 teaspoon of salt and pepper.
3. Spread onto a baking sheet with the skin facing down and roast in the oven for 40 minutes.
4. To make the tahini sauce, place the tahini in a small bowl with the water, lemon juice, garlic and ¼ teaspoon of salt. Whisk until smooth. Set aside.
5. In a small frying pan, add the remaining olive oil, pine nuts, and ¼ teaspoon of salt, and cook for 2 minutes on a low-medium heat until the nuts are golden brown.
6. To serve, spread the vegetables onto a large serving platter and drizzle with the tahini sauce. Sprinkle the pine nuts and za'atar on top.

### NUTRITIONAL INFORMATION

Per serving: 31 g total carbohydrate, 236 cals, 13 g fat, 2 g saturated fat, 9 g fiber, 1143 mg sodium.

# SAUTÉED GREEN BEANS

**COOKING TIME** *4 minutes* ▪ **SERVES** *6*

*This and the following three recipes are easy ways for "jazzing up" otherwise ordinary green beans.*

1 lb of fresh green beans, trimmed
5 teaspoons of olive oil
½ teaspoon of garlic powder
¼ teaspoon of salt

**DIRECTIONS:**

1. Heat the oil in a frying pan or wok on high.
2. Add the green beans and stir-fry them over a high heat for 2 to 4 minutes. While frying, add the garlic powder and salt. The beans should be tender-crisp and lightly browned when done.

**NUTRITIONAL INFORMATION**

Per serving: 6 g total carbohydrate, 57 cals, 8 g fat, 0.5 g saturated fat, 3 g fiber, 102 mg sodium.

# SPICED STRING BEANS

**COOKING TIME** *10 minutes* ▪ **SERVES** *6*

2 lbs of fresh string beans, washed and trimmed
2 tablespoons of olive oil
¼ teaspoon of turmeric
½ teaspoon of cumin
¼ cup water

**DIRECTIONS:**

1. Place all the ingredients in a 3-quart saucepan and mix well.
2. Cook, covered, over a small flame for 10 minutes. Serve warm or cold.

**NUTRITIONAL INFORMATION**

Per serving: 11 g total carbohydrate, 88 cals, 5 g fat, 1 g saturated fat, 4 g fiber, 9 mg sodium.

# STRING BEANS AND MUSHROOMS

**COOKING TIME** *10 minutes* ▪ **SERVES** *4*

1 lb of fresh string beans, washed and trimmed

4 oz of mushroom

1 small onion, diced

Salt to taste

Pepper to taste

## DIRECTIONS:

1. Sauté the onions and mushrooms together until brown, about 5 minutes.
2. In a separate pot, boil the beans for about 5 minutes until tender.
3. Drain the string beans and add the sautéed onion and mushrooms.
4. Season with salt and pepper to taste.

**NUTRITIONAL INFORMATION**

Per serving: 10 g total carbohydrate, 68 cals, 3 g fat, 0 g saturated fat, 4 g fiber, 9 mg sodium.

# SESAME STRING BEANS

**COOKING TIME** *20 minutes* ▪ **SERVES** *4*

1 tablespoon of olive oil

1 tablespoon of sesame seeds

1 lb of fresh string beans, washed, trimmed and cut into 2-inch pieces, or frozen cut green beans

¼ cup of chicken broth

¼ teaspoon of salt

Pepper to taste

## DIRECTIONS:

1. Heat the oil in a large skillet and add the sesame seeds. When they start to darken, stir in the green beans. Continue cooking until the beans are bright green, about 2 minutes.
2. Pour in the chicken broth, salt and pepper. Cover and cook until the beans are tender crisp, about 10 minutes.

**NUTRITIONAL INFORMATION**

Per serving: 8 g total carbohydrate, 81 cals, 5 g fat, 1 g saturated fat, 3 g fiber, 216 mg sodium.

# SAUTÉED SNOWPEAS WITH LEEK

**COOKING TIME** *4 minutes* ▪ **SERVES** *4*

8-oz package of snow peas, frozen

1 leek, sliced (use only the white and pale green parts)

1 tablespoon of olive oil

Salt to taste

**DIRECTIONS:**

1. Sauté the vegetables together in the oil until they are tender, about 4 minutes. Serve either warm or cold.

**NUTRITIONAL INFORMATION**

Per serving: 6 g total carbohydrate, 59 cals, 4 g fat, 0 g saturated fat, 2 g fiber, 6 mg sodium.

# BROILED ASPARAGUS

**COOKING TIME** *10 minutes* ▪ **SERVES** *4*

*Broiled asparagus has a much different taste than boiled asparagus.*

1 lb bunch of asparagus, with tough ends removed

1 tablespoons of olive oil

½ teaspoon of salt or to taste

**DIRECTIONS:**

1. Place the asparagus in a pan and sprinkle with the oil and salt.
2. Broil for 10 minutes, stirring once.

**NUTRITIONAL INFORMATION**

Per serving: 4.4 g total carbohydrate, 53 cals, 3.5 g fat, 0.5 g saturated fat, 2.4 g fiber, 293 mg sodium.

# Moussaka

**COOKING TIME** *80 minutes* ▪ **SERVES** *8*

*With its heavy fat content, this dish may fill you more with a guilty conscience than eggplant. But there is no reason for this, since olive oil is full of antioxidants. So enjoy this delicious dish!*

1 15-oz can of chickpeas (equivalent to 1½ cups of dried chickpeas)

Approximately 2 cups of olive oil

2 medium eggplants

3 onions, cut into ¼-inch thick slices

1½ teaspoons of salt or to taste, divided

½ teaspoon of pepper

2 15-oz cans of chopped or crushed tomato

1 cup of water

**DIRECTIONS:**

1. In a heavy skillet, heat about 1 inch of oil until the oil is almost smoking. Drop in the eggplant and stir until all sides are brown, about 2 minutes each side (this can splatter, so you may wish to use gloves and cover nearby surfaces). Transfer the eggplant to a baking pan. Add more oil as needed.
2. Fry the onions in the oil and cook over a moderate heat until soft and lightly browned.
3. Spread the onions and all the cooking oil over the eggplant in the baking pan. Sprinkle with ¾ teaspoon of salt and pepper.
4. Scatter the chickpeas on top and cover this with the tomatoes. Sprinkle with ¾ teaspoon of salt and more pepper. Add the water.
5. Cover and bake in the lower third of the oven at 400°F for 1 hour.

**NUTRITIONAL INFORMATION**

**(Assuming all the oil is eaten – which is usually not the case)**

Per serving: 33 g total carbohydrate, 632 cals, 55 g fat, 8 g saturated fat, 10 g fiber, 767 mg sodium.

# EGGPLANT PARMESAN

**COOKING TIME** *45 minutes* ▪ **SERVES** *6*

2 medium or 1 large eggplant, cut into ½-inch circles

¼ cup of whole-wheat flour

1 cup of whole-wheat bread crumbs

2 eggs

12 oz of mozzarella cheese

Approximately ¼ cup of olive oil for frying

26-oz jar of pasta sauce

¼ teaspoon of onion powder

¼ teaspoon of garlic powder

¼ teaspoon of salt or to taste

⅛ teaspoon of pepper

## DIRECTIONS:

1. Preheat the oven to 350°F.
2. Put the flour on one plate and the breadcrumbs on another plate.
3. In a small bowl, mix the eggs together with the seasoning.
4. Dip each eggplant in the flour, then the egg mixture, and then the breadcrumbs.
5. In a large skillet, fry both sides of each eggplant circle in the olive oil until golden brown, about 2 minutes each side.
6. In a 9 × 13-inch pan, layer ⅓ of the pasta sauce in the bottom of the pan, then half of the eggplant, and then half the cheese. Repeat this sequence. Put the remaining ⅓ of the pasta sauce on top of the cheese.
7. Bake in the oven for 35 minutes at 350°F.

**NUTRITIONAL INFORMATION**

Per serving: 40 g total carbohydrate, 461 cals, 24 g fat, 9 g saturated fat, 8 g fiber, 1108 mg sodium.

# FRIED EGGPLANT

**COOKING TIME** *5 minutes* ▪ **SERVES** *5*

- 1 medium eggplant, cut into ½-inch slices
- ¼ cup of whole-wheat flour
- 1 cup of whole–wheat breadcrumbs
- 1 egg
- ¼ teaspoon of garlic powder
- ¼ teaspoon of onion powder
- ¼ teaspoon of salt or to taste
- ⅛ teaspoon of pepper
- Approximately ½ cup of olive oil for frying

## DIRECTIONS:

1. Dip the eggplant slices into the flour.
2. In a small bowl, mix the egg, salt, pepper, garlic salt and onion powder.
3. Dip the eggplant slices into the egg mixture.
4. Then dip the eggplant slices in the breadcrumbs.
5. Fry the eggplant slices until golden brown on both sides, about 2 minutes each side.

**NUTRITIONAL INFORMATION**

Per serving: 25 g total carb, 333 cals, 24 g fat, 4 g saturated fat, 4 g fiber, 291 mg sodium.

# MICROWAVED MUSHROOMS

**COOKING TIME** *3 minutes* ▪ **SERVES** *4*

*This a great side dish for a quick dinner on the run.*

- 8 oz of mushrooms, sliced
- 2 tablespoons of olive oil
- ¼ teaspoon of garlic powder
- ¼ teaspoon of salt or to taste

## DIRECTIONS:

1. Place the mushrooms in a microwave dish and sprinkle them with oil, garlic powder and salt to taste.
2. Cover the dish and microwave on high for 2½-3 minutes.

**NUTRITIONAL INFORMATION**

Per serving: 2 g total carbohydrate, 73 cals, 7 g fat, 1 g saturated fat, 1 g fiber, 148 mg sodium.

# Spinach Kugel

**COOKING TIME** *40 minutes* ▪ **SERVES** *9*

*A kugel might seem an unusual way for promoting vegetables, but for many families ingenuity is the name of the game. A kugel is a sort of solid casserole, and kugels like this have been cooked in Europe for centuries. Cut-up squares are very handy for packed lunches and snacks.*

¼ cup of green pepper, chopped
1 cup of onion, chopped
½ cup of celery, chopped
1½ cups of raw carrot, grated
10-oz package of fresh spinach, chopped
3 eggs
3 tablespoons of olive oil
¾ cup of whole-wheat breadcrumbs or whole-wheat matzoh meal
1½ teaspoon of salt
⅛ teaspoon of pepper

## DIRECTIONS:

1. Sauté the green pepper, onion, celery and carrot in the oil for about 10 minutes, stirring occasionally.
2. Cook the spinach in a small amount of water until wilted, about 5 minutes, and then drain.
3. Combine the vegetables and add the eggs, salt, pepper and matzoh meal.
4. Place the mixture in a greased 9-inch square pan and bake in the oven at 350° F for 30 minutes.
5. Serve as squares, either hot or cold.

### NUTRITIONAL INFORMATION

Per serving: 16 g total carbohydrate, 88 cals, 5 g fat, 1 g saturated fat, 2 g fiber, 434 mg sodium.

# MICROWAVED ARTICHOKE WITH VINAIGRETTE DIP

**COOKING TIME** *7 minutes* ▪ **SERVES** *4*

*There is something about "doing things" to food that makes it attractive to kids. This recipe offers it all – cutting, pulling and dipping. If you are not into making vinaigrettes, use a bought Italian dressing.*

4 artichokes

**DIP:**

6 tablespoons of olive oil
2 tablespoons of white wine vinegar
½ teaspoon of Dijon mustard
1 clove of garlic, minced
1 teaspoon of sugar
¼ teaspoon of dried oregano
⅛ teaspoon of salt
⅛ teaspoon of pepper

## DIRECTIONS:

1. Wash the artichoke. Cut off the stem and peel off the smallest outer leaves.
2. Place the artichokes in a microwave-safe bowl. Cook on high for 7 minutes and then let the artichokes stand for 5 minutes with the cover on.
3. Meanwhile, mix the ingredients of the vinaigrette dip and place in a small container.

# BROCCOLI CORN BAKE

**COOKING TIME** *45 minutes* ▪ **SERVES** *9*

*This is more than just a vegetable recipe – it's a combination of wonderful tastes.*

1 16 oz-package of frozen broccoli flowerets or mixed broccoli/cauliflower flowerets
1 15 oz-can of creamed corn
½ small onion, finely minced
1 egg
¼ cup of whole-wheat breadcrumbs
2 tablespoons of olive oil
½ teaspoon of salt
Pepper to taste

## DIRECTIONS:

1. Preheat the oven to 350°F.
2. Defrost the vegetables and drain (but do not cook them).
3. Mix all the ingredients and pour into a greased 9-inch square pan.
4. Bake at 350°F for about 45 minutes.

**NUTRITIONAL INFORMATION**

Per serving: 14 g total carbohydrate, 90 cals, 4 g fat, 1 g saturated fat, 2 g fiber, 306 mg sodium.

# Coated Broccoli

**COOKING TIME** *20 minutes* ▪ **SERVES** *6*

*These vegetables will disappear in no time at all. Cauliflower can also be used instead of broccoli florets.*

4 cups of broccoli florets
⅔ cup of seasoned breadcrumbs
2 tablespoons of grated Parmesan cheese
2 eggs
1 tablespoon of milk
2 tablespoons of olive oil
⅛ teaspoon of salt or to taste

## DIRECTIONS:

1. Preheat the oven to 400°F.
2. Prepare 2 sealable plastic bags, one containing the breadcrumbs, cheese and salt, and the other containing the eggs and milk. Shake both bags well.
3. Add the vegetables to the bag containing the egg mixture, close, and shake to coat the vegetables well.
4. Now add the vegetables to the bag containing the breadcrumbs mixture, close, and shake to coat well.
5. Lightly coat a 15 × 10-inch baking dish with cooking oil spray. Place the vegetables onto the dish. Drizzle the oil over the vegetables.
6. Bake in the oven at 400°F for about 20 minutes, stirring twice.

**NUTRITIONAL INFORMATION**

Per serving: 13 g total carbohydrate, 127 cals, 6 g fat, 1 g saturated fat, 2 g fiber, 351 mg sodium.

# BROCCOLI WITH CHERRY TOMATOES

**COOKING TIME** *18 minutes* ▪ **SERVES** *8*

*The tastes of the cherry tomatoes and broccoli blend beautifully together in this winning recipe.*

2 bunches of broccoli, cut into florets

1 medium onion

1 pint of cherry tomatoes

3 cloves of garlic, chopped

4 tablespoons of olive oil

1 teaspoon of salt or to taste

## DIRECTIONS:

1. Preheat the oven to 450°F.
2. Mix the ingredients in a large bowl and toss to coat.
3. Spread the vegetables on a large cookies sheet.
4. Roast for 18 minutes, stirring once or twice.

**NUTRITIONAL INFORMATION**

Per serving: 7 g total carbohydrate, 93 cals, 7 g fat, 1 g saturated fat,2 g fiber, 313 mg sodium.

# ROASTED CHERRY TOMATOES

**COOKING TIME** *30 minutes* ▪ **SERVES** *4*

1 lb of cherry tomatoes, halved

2 garlic cloves, crushed

½ tablespoon of honey

3 tablespoon of olive oil

Salt to taste

Pepper to taste

## DIRECTIONS:

1. Place the tomatoes upside down in an oiled pan.
2. Pour the garlic, honey, olive oil, salt and pepper over the tomatoes.
3. Bake at 375°F for 30 minutes.

**NUTRITIONAL INFORMATION**

Per serving: 8 g total carbohydrate, 128 cals, 11 g fat, 2 g saturated fat, 1 g fiber, 6 mg sodium.

# Fried Green Tomatoes

**COOKING TIME** *20 minutes* ▪ **SERVES** *4*

*Do you have lots of green tomatoes in your yard? Try this recipe for something different.*

3 medium-sized firm green tomatoes
½ cup of whole-wheat flour
1 egg
⅓ cup of cornmeal
½ cup of dry whole-wheat bread crumbs
¼ cup of olive oil
¼ teaspoon of salt

## DIRECTIONS:

1. Cut the unpeeled tomatoes into ½-inch slices.
2. Sprinkle the slices with salt, and let the slices stand for 5 minutes.
3. In 3 separate shallow bowls place the flour, the egg, and the breadcrumbs mixed with the cornmeal. Beat the egg.
4. Dip the tomato slices into the flour, then the beaten eggs, and then the breadcrumb-cornmeal mix.
5. In a large skillet, heat the oil on medium heat.
6. Fry the coated tomato slices for about 3-5 minutes on each side until brown.
7. Drain on paper towels.

**NUTRITIONAL INFORMATION**

Per serving: 36 g total carbohydrate, 298 cals, 15 g fat, 2 g saturated fat, 4 g fiber, 273 mg sodium.

CHAPTER 4

# Classy Cold Salads

Eating salads is an important part of Mediterranean-style meal planning. It is also an excellent way for keeping the edge off your hunger when trying to control or lose weight. However, a salad consisting of a few chunks of tomato and cucumber is not going to keep your family happy for very long. This chapter is therefore about new ideas for increasing your stock of tasty salad recipes.

The Israeli Mediterranean diet is not a low-fat diet and there is no reason to use low-fat salad dressings or to be too stingy with the olive oil. Olive oil is an important ingredient of the Mediterranean diet and provides many health benefits because of its content of anti-oxidants.

# VINAIGRETTE

*I highly recommend having a good vinaigrette at hand. With this, a few cut-up vegetables can become an enticing salad in a matter of minutes. This vinaigrette has a delicate and subtle taste and is a pleasant alternative to a bought salad dressing. This recipe was previously used with the Microwaved Artichoke with Vinaigrette Dip recipe, but it is repeated here because of the importance of having a tasty and healthful salad dressing readily available.*

6 tablespoons of olive oil
2 tablespoons of white wine vinegar
½ teaspoon of Dijon mustard
1 clove of garlic, minced
1 teaspoon of sugar
¼ teaspoon of dried oregano
⅛ teaspoon of salt
⅛ teaspoon of pepper

# MANDARIN ORANGE SALAD

**COOKING TIME** *2 minutes* ▪ **SERVES** *9*

*Greens with citrus fruit are a wonderful combination for a salad.*

1 large head of leaf lettuce, cut into bite-sized pieces
1 cup of sliced celery
4 green onions, chopped
1 tablespoon of fresh parsley, chopped
¼ cup of slivered almonds
2 fresh mandarin oranges or 1 11-oz can of mandarin oranges in light syrup, drained

### DRESSING:

¼ cup of olive oil
2 tablespoons of red wine vinegar
¼ teaspoon of tarragon
½ teaspoon of salt or to taste
1½ tablespoons of sugar

## DIRECTIONS:

1. In a small skillet, toast the almonds until very lightly browned.
2. In a small bowl, mix the oil, vinegar, tarragon, salt and sugar.
3. Pour the dressing over the vegetables, fruit and almonds just before serving and toss the salad.
4. Serve chilled.

**NUTRITIONAL INFORMATION**

Per serving: 8 g total carbohydrate, 100 cals, 8 g fat, 1 g saturated fat, 2 g fiber, 145 mg sodium.

# Mediterranean Salad

**SERVES** *4*

*A plate of tomatoes, cucumbers and peppers is wholesome, but not too exciting. But chop these vegetables into small pieces and add some lemon juice, salt and pepper and you have an extremely tasty salad.*

1 cucumber
3 medium-size tomatoes
1 green pepper
2 scallions
1 clove of garlic, minced
½ cup of fresh parsley

**Dressing:**

2 tablespoons of lemon juice
½ teaspoon of salt or to taste
⅛ teaspoon of pepper or to taste

**DIRECTIONS:**

1. Cut all the vegetables into small dices no larger than ½ inch and combine together.
2. Add the parsley, oil, lemon juice, salt and pepper.

# Seven Layer Salad

**SERVES** *13*

*The kids will love "digging" into this incredibly good salad.*

1 iceberg lettuce, shredded (1)
1 green pepper, chopped (2)
1 10-oz box of frozen peas, defrosted (3)
2 stalks of celery, finely chopped (4)
1 red onion, finely sliced (5)
Approximately 1 cup of mayonnaise (6)
4 carrots, shredded (7)

**DIRECTIONS:**

1. In a large serving dish, layer each ingredient in the order listed.
2. Cover the entire salad with the shredded carrots.
3. Dig in through all the layers when serving.

**NUTRITIONAL INFORMATION**

Per serving: 7 g total carbohydrate, 155 cals, 14 g fat, 1 g saturated fat, 2 g fiber, 148 mg sodium.

# Apple Feta Salad

**COOKING TIME** *18 minutes* ▪ **SERVES** *6*

*This is a queen of salads!*

1 cup of walnut halves

1 tablespoon of sugar

⅛ teaspoon of pepper

1 head of romaine lettuce, torn into bite-sized pieces

1 head of red leaf lettuce, torn into bite-sized pieces

1 medium red apple, chopped

1 medium green apple, chopped

4 oz of feta cheese

2 tablespoons of olive oil

## Dressing:

6 tablespoons of olive oil

2 tablespoons of white wine vinegar

2 tablespoons of onions, very finely chopped

1½ teaspoons of Dijon mustard

2 cloves of garlic, minced

½ teaspoon of sugar

¼ teaspoon of dried oregano

⅛ teaspoon of dried parsley flakes

⅛ teaspoon of pepper

## DIRECTIONS:

1. Preheat the oven to 350°F.
2. In a medium skillet, toast the walnuts in the olive oil over medium heat. Sprinkle with sugar and pepper and stir until the walnuts are well coated.
3. Spread the walnuts onto a baking sheet and bake at 350°F for 15 minutes, stirring every 5 minutes. Cool on a wire rack.
4. In a large bowl, combine the romaine, red lettuce, apples and feta cheese. Set aside.
5. In a small bowl, mix the dressing ingredients.
6. Drizzle the dressing over the salad.
7. Sprinkle the salad with the sugared walnuts and serve immediately.

### NUTRITIONAL INFORMATION

Per serving: 14 g total carbohydrate, 308 cals, 28 g fat, 8 g saturated fat, 4 g fiber, 274 mg sodium.

# PORTABELLA MUSHROOM SALAD

**COOKING TIME** *7 minutes* ▪ **SERVES** *5*

*This salad won't hang around for long. Guaranteed!*

½ cup of a homemade vinaigrette (see beginning of this section) or bought Italian dressing
6 portabella mushrooms, sliced
4 cups of Romaine or leaf lettuce, cut into bite-sized pieces
½ cup (2 oz) of feta cheese
4 medium tomatoes, sliced

## DIRECTIONS:

1. Set oven control to broil. Spray the broiler pan rack with cooking spray.
2. Brush some of the vinaigrette on both sides of each mushroom. Broil the mushrooms 2 to 4 inches from the heat for 4 minutes. Turn and broil for another 3-4 minutes until the mushrooms are tender.
3. Slice the mushrooms when cool.
4. Crumble the cheese and mix with the greens, tomatoes and mushroom.
5. Drizzle the remaining dressing over the salad.

**NUTRITIONAL INFORMATION**

Per serving: 10 g total carbohydrate, 164 cals, 12 g fat, 2 g saturated fat, 4 g fiber, 574 mg sodium.

# AVOCADO WITH CITRUS SALAD

**SERVES** *6*

6 cups of torn salad greens
1 medium grapefruit, peeled and sectioned
2 navel oranges, peeled and sliced
1 ripe avocado, peeled and sliced
¼ cup of slivered almonds

### DRESSING:

½ cup of olive oil
3 tablespoons of sugar
3 tablespoons of vinegar
2 teaspoons of poppy seeds
1 teaspoon of finely chopped onion
½ teaspoon of ground mustard
½ teaspoon of salt

## DIRECTIONS:

1. Prepare the salad ingredients in a large bowl.
2. Prepare the salad dressing in a small bowl.
3. Mix the two together and chill before serving.

**NUTRITIONAL INFORMATION**

Per serving: 20 g total carbohydrate, 302 cals, 26 g fat, 4 g saturated fat, 4 g fiber, 200 mg sodium.

# SPANISH ORANGE AND AVOCADO SALAD

**SERVES** *4*

1 bunch of romaine lettuce, torn into bite-size bits

3 tangerines or Spanish Clementine oranges, peeled and separated into sections

2 small avocados or 1 large avocado, peeled and diced

1 small red onion, very thinly sliced (slice the red onion extremely thin, otherwise it may dominate the rest of the salad).

## DRESSING:

2 teaspoons of lemon juice

1 teaspoon of Dijon-style mustard

½ teaspoon of sugar

½ teaspoon of salt or to taste

¼ teaspoon of black pepper

Just under ¼ cup of olive oil

## DIRECTIONS:

1. Combine the lemon juice, mustard, sugar, salt and pepper in a small bowl. Slowly whisk in the olive oil until the dressing is thick and forms an emulsion (this dressing can be prepared in advance).
2. Just before serving, combine the lettuce, oranges, avocado and red onion.
3. Add the dressing and toss well to coat.

**NUTRITIONAL INFORMATION**

Per serving: 24 g total carbohydrate, 259 cals, 19 g fat, 3 g saturated fat, 9 g fiber, 329 mg sodium.

# Cucumber Salad

**SERVES** *7*

2 large peeled cucumbers or 1 seedless unpeeled English cucumber

¾ cup of onion, thinly sliced

1½ teaspoon of salt

### Dressing:

½ cup of boiling water

½ cup of white vinegar

½ cup of sugar

## DIRECTIONS:

1. Thinly slice the cucumbers.
2. Layer the cucumber and onion in a large bowl and sprinkle each layer liberally with salt. Leave it to sit for 30 minutes.
3. Rinse the vegetables with plenty of water and drain well.
4. Mix the water, sugar and vinegar in a small bowl until the sugar dissolves.
5. Pour the dressing over the vegetables.
6. Chill before serving.

**NUTRITIONAL INFORMATION**

Per serving: 18 g total carbohydrate, 75 cals, 0 g fat, 0 g saturated fat, 1 g fiber, 2 mg sodium.

# Health Slaw

**SERVES** *10*

*This is a colorful and popular salad that will keep nicely in the fridge for several days.*

1 carrot
1 green pepper
1 medium cabbage
1 onion
1 cucumber

### Dressing:

⅓ cup of sugar
½ cup of vinegar
½ cup of olive oil
¼ cup of water
1 tablespoon of salt or to taste

### DIRECTIONS:

1. Slice all the vegetables thinly (this is most conveniently done with a food processor) and place in a large bowl.
2. In a small bowl, mix the sugar, vinegar, oil, water and salt, and then mix this into the vegetables.

**NUTRITIONAL INFORMATION**

Per serving: 14 g total carbohydrate, 159 cals, 11 g fat, 2 g saturated fat, 3 g fiber, 730 mg sodium.

# Hearts of Palm Salad

**SERVES** *11*

4 avocados, peeled, pitted and diced
1 14-ounce can of hearts of palm, drained and sliced
½ cup of red onion, finely chopped
2 cups of grape or cherry tomatoes, halved
1 heaping tablespoon of mayonnaise
Juice from half of a lemon or 4½ teaspoons of lemon juice
Salt to taste
Pepper to taste

### DIRECTIONS:

1. Combine the ingredients in a large bowl.

**NUTRITIONAL INFORMATION**

Per serving: 12 g total carbohydrate, 161 cals, 12 g fat, 2 g saturated fat, 7 g fiber, 168 mg sodium.

# Sumi Salad

**COOKING TIME** *13 minutes* ▪ **SERVES** *14*

*This salad has a wonderfully crunchy taste.*

¼ cup of sliced almonds
¼ cup of sesame seeds
8 oz of angel hair pasta, broken into thirds
1 small head of red cabbage, shredded
6 scallions, sliced
1 8-oz can of sliced water chestnuts
½ teaspoon of olive oil

### Dressing:

¼ cup of sugar
1 teaspoon of salt or to taste
1 teaspoon of pepper
¾ cup of olive oil
¼ cup of cider vinegar

## DIRECTIONS:

1. Cook the pasta according to the packet instructions. Rinse with cold water.
2. In a small skillet, toast the almonds and sesame seeds in ½ teaspoon of oil. Set them aside.
3. Combine the pasta with the cabbage, scallions and water chestnuts.
4. In a small bowl, combine the dressing ingredients and pour the dressing over the pasta and cabbage mixture.
5. Chill the salad for a few hours.
6. Before serving the salad, sprinkle the almonds and sesame seeds on top.

**NUTRITIONAL INFORMATION**

Per serving: 22 g total carbohydrate, 264 cals, 19 g fat, 3 g saturated fat, 2 g fiber, 184 mg sodium.

# ASIAN SPAGHETTI SALAD

**COOKING TIME** *20 minutes* ▪ **SERVES** *13*

12-oz of thin spaghetti, uncooked
1 big bok choy, chopped
5 spring onions, chopped
¼ cup of sesame seeds
¾ cup of slivered almonds

**DRESSING:**

¼ cup of vinegar
½ cup of sugar
¼ cup of soy sauce
½ cup of olive oil
1 teaspoon of salt

## DIRECTIONS:

1. Cook the spaghetti according to the package directions.
2. Brown the sesame seeds without any oil for about 2 minutes.
3. Brown the slivered almonds with 1 teaspoon of oil for about 2 minutes.
4. Sauté the bok choy and onions with a small amount of oil until the bok choy is just beginning to wilt, about 3 to 4 minutes.
5. Mix the spaghetti, sesame seeds, almonds, sautéed bok choy and onion together.
6. Mix the dressing in a small bowl. Pour over the salad and mix well.

**NUTRITIONAL INFORMATION**

Serving size: 30g total carbohydrate, 262 cals, 14 g fat, 2 g saturated fat, 2 g fiber, 270 mg sodium

# Noodle Salad with Peanuts

**COOKING TIME** *13 minutes* ▪ **SERVES** *14*

*This splendid salad will get eaten very quickly by family members.*

1 lb of spaghetti

8 scallions, sliced thin

1 cup of chopped cilantro

1 ½ cups of lightly salted dry roasted peanuts, coarsely chopped

### Dressing:

¼ cup of sesame oil

¼ cup of soy sauce

2 tablespoons of sugar

1 ½ tablespoons of balsamic vinegar

1 teaspoon of salt

### DIRECTIONS:

1. Cook the spaghetti according to the package instructions.
2. Add the scallions, cilantro and peanuts to the spaghetti.
3. Prepare the salad dressing in a small bowl, mix well, and pour over the salad.
4. Toss the salad to coat thoroughly.

**NUTRITIONAL INFORMATION**

Per serving: 30 g carbohydrate, 259 cals, 12 g fat, 2 g saturated fat, 3 g fiber, 430 mg sodium.

# Spinach and Basil Pasta Salad

**COOKING TIME** *14 minutes* ▪ **SERVES** *8*

1 16-oz package of bow tie pasta
1 6-oz package of spinach leaves
2 cups of fresh basil leaves
½ cup of olive oil
3 cloves of garlic, minced
½ cup of pine nuts
¾ cup of grated Parmesan cheese
Salt and black pepper to taste

## DIRECTIONS:

1. Cook the pasta in boiled water in a large pot according to the package instructions. Rinse with cold water.
2. Toast the pine nuts in a small dry skillet on medium heat until brown, for about 3 minutes.
3. Toss the spinach and basil together in a large bowl.
4. Sauté the garlic in olive oil for 1 minute and then add it to the garlic and basil.
5. Add the drained pasta to the bowl with the spinach and basil and toss again.
6. Season with salt and pepper.
7. Sprinkle with Parmesan cheese and pine nuts when ready to serve.

### NUTRITIONAL INFORMATION

Per serving: 45 g total carbohydrate, 426 cals, 22 g fat, 4 g saturated fat, 3 g fiber, 148 mg sodium.

# Spinach Orzo Salad

**COOKING TIME** *9 minutes* ▪ **SERVES** *8*

*The spinach nicely sets off this salad. Orzo is a form of pasta and can be found in the noodle section in the supermarket. Unlike many green leaf salads, this one will keep well in the refrigerator for several days.*

8 oz of dried orzo

¾ lb of fresh spinach, torn into bite-sized pieces

⅓ cup of red onion, finely diced

1 small tomato, diced

¼ lb of feta cheese, coarsely crumbled

¼ cup of olive oil

1½ tablespoons of lemon juice

½ tablespoon of pepper

½ tablespoon of salt or to taste

**DIRECTIONS:**

1. Boil the orzo with 3 cups water and 1 teaspoon of salt for 9 minutes. Drain.
2. Allow the orzo to cool somewhat and then mix it with the vegetables.
3. Mix the oil, lemon juice, salt and pepper in a small bowl and add to the salad.
4. Sprinkle the feta cheese as a garnish on the salad.

**NUTRITIONAL INFORMATION**

Per serving: 24 g total carbohydrate, 162 cals, 4 g fat, 2 g saturated fat, 2 g fiber, 641 mg sodium.

# MEDITERRANEAN TABOULI

**SERVES** *10*

*This tasty Middle Eastern salad is easy to make and contains many health-promoting ingredients. The bulgur wheat contains fiber and is low-glycemic, and the lemon juice, tomatoes and olive oil provide plenty of antioxidants.*

1 cup of dry bulgur wheat

1½ cups of boiling water

½ cup of chopped scallions (include the green)

3 medium tomatoes, finely diced

1 cup of fresh parsley

2 teaspoons of salt or to taste

**DRESSING:**

¼ cup of lemon or lime juice

1 large garlic clove, minced or 1 heaping teaspoon of crushed garlic

½ teaspoon of dried mint

¼ cup of olive oil

## DIRECTIONS:

1. Combine the bulgur, boiling water and salt in a bowl. Cover and let stand for 15-20 minutes or until the bulgur is chewable.
2. Drain off any excess water on the bulgur with a dry paper towel.
3. Add the lemon juice, garlic, oil, and mint to the bulgur and mix thoroughly.
4. Refrigerate the bulgur for a few hours.
5. Just before serving, add the vegetables and mix gently.
6. This salad can also be garnished with feta cheese and olives.

**NUTRITIONAL INFORMATION**

Per serving: 12 g total carbohydrate, 104 cals, 6.0 g fat, 1 g saturated fat, 3 g fiber, 473 mg sodium.

# Bean and Corn Tabouli

**COOKING TIME** *20 minutes* ▪ **SERVES** *8*

¾ cup of bulgur wheat
15-oz can of corn
15-oz can of black beans
15-oz can of diced tomatoes
½ cup of red onion, fined chopped
3 cloves of fresh garlic
½ cup of fresh cilantro, chopped
4 tablespoons of lemon juice
2 tablespoons of olive oil
1½ tablespoons of diced jalapenos
1 teaspoon of cumin
¼ teaspoon of cayenne pepper
½ teaspoon of salt
⅛ teaspoon of pepper
1½ cups of boiling water

## DIRECTIONS:

1. Add 1½ cups of boiling water to the bulgur wheat and let sit for 15 minutes.
2. Drain off any excess water on the bulgur with a dry paper towel.
3. Add the other ingredients and toss to combine.

### NUTRITIONAL INFORMATION

Per serving: 33 g total carbohydrate, 186 cals, 4 g fat, 1 g saturated fat, 8 g fiber, 522 mg sodium.

# Bulgur, Garbanzo and Cucumber Salad

**COOKING TIME** *12 minutes* ▪ **SERVES** *6*

*This excellent tabouli recipe is well worth trying out!*

1 cup of dry bulgur wheat

1 ½ cups of boiling water

1 15.5-ounce cans of garbanzo beans, drained

1 ½-pint containers of small red or yellow cherry tomatoes, chopped in half

½ cup of diced unpeeled English cucumber

⅓ cup (packed) chopped of fresh dill

⅛ cup of white balsamic vinegar

½ tablespoon of ground cumin

3 tablespoons of olive oil

¼ cup of black olives, chopped

¼ cup of feta cheese, crumbled

Salt and pepper to taste

## DIRECTIONS:

1. Combine the bulgur, boiling water and salt in a bowl. Cover and let stand for 15-20 minutes or until the bulgur is chewable.
2. Make sure that most of the water is absorbed by the grain. If not, dry with a paper towel.
3. Transfer the bulgur wheat to a large bowl and add the garbanzo beans, tomatoes, cucumber and dill.
4. Whisk the vinegar and cumin in a small bowl and add in the oil, salt and pepper.
5. Pour the dressing over the bulgur.
6. Toss the salad with the olives and feta cheese.

### NUTRITIONAL INFORMATION

Per serving: 38 g total carbohydrate, 271 cals, 11 g fat, 2 g saturated fat, 8 g fiber, 400 mg sodium.

# Bulgur with Leek, Cranberries and Almonds

**COOKING TIME** *19 minutes* ▪ **SERVES** *11*

1½ cups of leeks, chopped (use only the white and pale green parts)

3 tablespoons of olive oil

2½ cups of chicken broth

1½ cups of dry bulgur wheat

⅓ cup of dried cranberries

⅓ cup of sliced almonds

Salt and pepper to taste

## DIRECTIONS:

1. In a large saucepan, sauté the chopped leaks in olive oil until tender, about 12 minutes.
2. Add the chicken broth and bring to a boil. Stir in the bulgur and boil for 5 minutes.
3. Add the dried cranberries and almonds.
4. Remove from the heat, cover, and let stand for 15 minutes.
5. Season with salt and pepper to taste.

### NUTRITIONAL INFORMATION

Per serving: 20 g total carbohydrate, 141 cals, 6 g fat, 1 g saturated fat, 4 g fiber, 22 mg sodium.

# FRUITED RICE SALAD

**COOKING TIME** *45 minutes* ▪ **SERVES** *8*

*Wild rice is not really rice but the seed of an aquatic grass. The wild rice, fruit and fruit juice all blend very nicely together.*

1 cup of uncooked wild rice (or brown and red rice blend)

2 Golden Delicious apples, chopped

1 cup of seedless red grapes, halved

1 cup of fresh parsley

1 cup of chives or green onions

1 cup of pecans, halved

### DRESSING:

¼ cup of olive oil

⅓ cup of orange juice

2 tablespoons of honey

1 teaspoon of lemon juice

## DIRECTIONS:

1. Cook the wild rice in 3½ cups of water with 1 teaspoon of salt for 45 minutes. Drain off any excess water. Allow to cool.
2. In a large salad bowl, combine the salad ingredients.
3. In a small bowl, combine the ingredients for the salad dressing and mix into the salad.
4. Chill for a few hours before serving.

### NUTRITIONAL INFORMATION

Per serving: 27 g total carbohydrate, 252 cals, 16 g fat, 2 g saturated fat, 4 g fiber, 9 mg sodium.

# Red Cabbage Salad

**SERVES** *14*

*Crunchy. Colorful. Tasty. This recipe will also keep well for several days in the fridge.*

1 16-oz bag of shredded purple cabbage or approximately half of a medium cabbage, shredded

⅓ cup of scallions, chopped

⅓ cup of pine nuts

1 8-oz bag of shredded carrot or 4 medium carrots, shredded

1 11-oz can of mandarin oranges (some of the juice is used for the salad dressing)

⅛ cup of craisins (sweetened dried cranberries)

**Dressing:**

4 tablespoons of brown sugar

½ teaspoon of pepper

¼ teaspoon of salt

4 tablespoons of wine vinegar

½ cup of olive oil

Dash of garlic powder

1 teaspoon of chicken bouillon granules

1 tablespoon of mandarin juice (from the opened can)

## DIRECTIONS:

1. Whisk together the dressing ingredients
2. Mix solid ingredients in a large bowl.
3. Pour in the dressing and mix well.
4. Serve chilled.

**NUTRITIONAL INFORMATION**

Per serving: 12 g total carbohydrate, 138 cals, 10 g fat, 1 g saturated fat, 1 g fiber, 145 mg sodium.

# Broccoli Craisin Salad

**SERVES** *5*

1 16-oz bag of frozen broccoli, thawed completely
1 small red onion, diced
½ cup of craisins
¼ cup of slivered almonds

**Dressing:**

½ cup of mayonnaise
1 tablespoon of sugar
1 tablespoon of vinegar
¼ tablespoon of salt
⅛ teaspoon of pepper

## DIRECTIONS:

1. Put broccoli, onion, craisins and almonds into a bowl.
2. Mix the dressing ingredients and pour over the salad. Toss to mix.

**NUTRITIONAL INFORMATION**

Per serving: 20 g total carbohydrate, 110 cals, 3 g fat, 0 g saturated fat, 4 g fiber, 134 mg sodium.

# Middle Eastern Carrot Salad

**COOKING TIME** *10 minutes* ▪ **SERVES** *10*

2 lb of carrots, sliced

**Dressing:**

5 cloves of garlic, minced
1½ teaspoons of cumin
2 teaspoons of paprika
Juice from 2 lemons or 6 tablespoons of lemon juice
¼ cup of olive oil
¼ cup of fresh parsley, chopped
Salt to taste

## DIRECTIONS:

1. Cook the carrots until they are tender but crisp.
2. Cool the carrots.
3. Combine the rest of the ingredients and pour over the cooled carrots. Mix.

**NUTRITIONAL INFORMATION**

Per serving: 10 g total carbohydrate, 89 cals, 6 g fat, 1 g saturated fat, 3 g fiber, 299 mg sodium.

# SWEET AND SOUR CARROT SALAD

**COOKING TIME** *15 minutes* ▪ **SERVES** *10*

2 lb of raw carrots, sliced
2 medium onions, sliced thin
1 large green pepper, sliced thin
¾ cup of distilled vinegar
½ cup of granulated sugar
½ cup of canola oil
1 cup of ketchup
1 teaspoon of yellow mustard

## DIRECTIONS:

1. Boil the carrots until soft, about 15 minutes. Cool.
2. Add the onions and pepper.
3. Mix the rest of the ingredients and pour over the carrots.
4. Mix gently and serve.

**NUTRITIONAL INFORMATION**

Per serving: 28 g total carbohydrate, 211 cals, 11 g fat, 1 g saturated fat, 3 g fiber, 338 mg sodium.

# BABY CARROT SALAD

**COOKING TIME** *12 minutes* ▪ **SERVES** *4*

1 lb of baby carrots
4 teaspoons of dried dill
6 cloves garlic, minced
1½ cups of water
¼ cup of balsamic vinegar, divided
1 teaspoon of salt
1 teaspoon of dried mustard
2 tablespoons of honey

## DIRECTIONS:

1. In a medium-sized pot, bring to a boil the water, 2 tablespoons of vinegar, salt, mustard, and honey, and stir until they dissolve.
2. Add the carrots, garlic and dill. Lower heat to a simmer.
3. Cook uncovered for about 10 minutes or until the carrots are as tender as you like them.
4. Cool to room temperature and add the remaining 2 tablespoons of vinegar.
5. Transfer to a container and chill.

**NUTRITIONAL INFORMATION**

Per serving: 20 g total carbohydrate, 85 cals, 0 g fat, 3 g fiber, 683 mg sodium.

# Carrots with Raisins

**SERVES** *5*

*This beats carrot sticks any day.*

½ lb of carrots, finely grated using a food processor
½ cup of raisins
¼ cup of sunflower seeds
2 tablespoons of mayonnaise

## DIRECTIONS:

1. Mix the contents of the salad together.

**NUTRITIONAL INFORMATION**

Per serving: 17 g total carbohydrate, 145 cals, 9 g fat, 1 g saturated fat, 2 g fiber, 63 mg sodium.

# Fried Eggplant Salad

**SERVES** *7*

1 large eggplant, cut into ½-inch slices
½ cup approximately of olive oil for frying
6 cloves of garlic, minced
½ cup of parsley, chopped
½ teaspoon of salt or to taste
½ teaspoon of black pepper
1 teaspoon of paprika
½ teaspoon of cumin
¼ cup of lemon juice
¼ cup of white vinegar
½ cup of water
Black olives (optional)

## DIRECTIONS:

1. Liberally salt the eggplant and put in a colander to drain. After 1 hour, rinse the salt off and dry the eggplant with paper towels.
2. Deep-fry the eggplant slices in hot oil on both sides over medium heat until slightly brown.
3. After frying, put the eggplant on a paper towel to absorb the extra oil.
4. In a medium-sized bowl, mix together the rest of the ingredients.
5. Dip the slices in this mixture and arrange in a salad bowl.
6. Pour any leftover mixture over the eggplant slices.
7. Cool in the fridge.
8. Garnish with black olives if desired.

**NUTRITIONAL INFORMATION**

Per serving: 6 g total carbohydrate, 164 cals, 16 g fat, 2 g saturated fat, 3 g fiber, 175 mg sodium.

# CHINESE EGGPLANT

**SERVES 5**

*Serving vegetables as hors d'oeuvre before a meal is common in Israel, especially in restaurants, and is a very good way of adding more vegetables to one's diet. Eggplant is often served.*

1 medium eggplant
1 tablespoon of olive oil
2 cloves garlic, minced
1 chili pepper, seeded and sliced
1 tablespoon of ginger, minced
1 scallion, sliced
1 tablespoons of soy sauce
1 tablespoon, vinegar
½ teaspoon sugar
Cooking oil spray

## DIRECTIONS:

1. Cut the eggplant into ¼-inch thick slices.
2. Cover a cookie sheet with parchment paper, place the eggplant slices on the parchment paper, and lightly spray the eggplant and parchment paper with oil.
3. Bake at 375°F for about 15 minutes until the eggplant is soft.
4. In a medium-sized skillet, sauté the garlic, pepper, sugar and scallion in the oil until they just start to brown. Add the soy sauce, vinegar and sugar.
5. Heat the mixture for 1 minute in the skillet.
6. Add the eggplant to the skillet and toss the eggplant to coat.
7. Serve hot or cold.

**NUTRITIONAL INFORMATION**

Per serving: 8 g total carbohydrate, 61 cals, 3 g fat, 0 g sat fat, 4 g fiber, 686 mg sodium.

# FOUR BEAN SALAD

**COOKING TIME** *5 minutes* ▪ **SERVES** *10*

*This four-bean salad is very easy to make. Just open the cans and pour them into a salad bowl. The green beans though need to be cooked.*

16 oz of frozen green beans
1 16-oz can of chick peas, rinsed and drained
1 16-oz can of kidney beans, rinsed and drained
8 oz of frozen corn, defrosted
½ of a large red onion, finely chopped
1 red pepper, chopped
½ cup of vinegar
¼ cup of canola oil (tastes better than olive oil for this salad)
1 teaspoon of oregano
1 teaspoon of crushed garlic
½ teaspoon of salt or to taste
¼ teaspoon of pepper

## DIRECTIONS:

1. Cook the green beans for 5 minutes in ½ cup of water, according to the package instructions.
2. Combine the ingredients in a large bowl.
3. Serve chilled.

**NUTRITIONAL INFORMATION**

Per serving: 23 g total carbohydrate, 173 cals, 7 g fat, 0 g saturated fat, 6 g fiber, 316 mg sodium.

# COLORFUL PEPPER SALAD

**COOKING TIME** *15 minutes* ▪ **SERVES** *4*

3 red, yellow or orange peppers, sliced lengthwise
1 tablespoon of olive oil
1 tablespoon of white vinegar
Salt to taste

## DIRECTIONS:

1. Sauté the peppers in the olive oil.
2. Cover the pan and steam the peppers for 10 minutes on a low heat, stirring occasionally.
3. Drain the peppers on paper towel.
4. Put the peppers in a serving bowl and add the vinegar and salt to taste.

**NUTRITIONAL INFORMATION**

Per serving: 3 g total carbohydrate, 33 cals, 2 g fat, 0 g saturated fat, 1 g fiber, 100 mg sodium.

# CAESAR SALAD WITH CROUTONS

**COOKING TIME** *20 minutes* ▪ **CROUTONS SERVE** *10*

*This is a very family-friendly salad – in other words it will get readily eaten. Because of the croutons and salad dressing, it also makes a filling snack. The croutons though get soggy if left too long on the salad.*

3 heads of Romaine lettuce, torn

### DRESSING:

4 cloves garlic, crushed
¾ cup of mayonnaise
1 tablespoon of lemon juice
1 teaspoon of Worcestershire sauce
1 teaspoon of Dijon mustard
Salt to taste
Pepper to taste

### HOMEMADE CROUTONS:

6 slices of whole wheat bread, cut into small cubes
¼ cup of olive oil
¼ cup of mayonnaise
1 tablespoon of green onion, finely chopped
1 garlic clove, minced
¼ cup of Honey Dijon Mustard
¾ teaspoon of dried oregano

### DIRECTIONS:

1. Preheat the oven to 350°F.
2. Heat the olive oil in a large pan and whisk in the other crouton ingredients until they are all well combined.
3. Add in the bread cubes and toss until well coated.
4. Transfer to a baking sheet and cook in the oven for 15-20 minutes.
5. Allow the croutons to cool before serving. They can also be stored in a container or frozen.
6. Combine the dressing ingredients in a small bowl and then mix into the lettuce pieces in a large bowl.
7. Serve chilled.
8. Add the croutons just before serving.

**NUTRITIONAL INFORMATION FOR THE CROUTONS**

Serving size: 10 croutons. Per serving: 6 g total carbohydrate, 85 cals, 7 g fat, 1 g sat fat, 12 g fiber, 110 mg sodium.

# TUNA SALAD WITH GRAPES AND ALMONDS

**COOKING TIME** *3 minutes* ▪ **SERVES** *5*

*This is an incredibly delicious salad.*

10-oz can of tuna in spring water, drained
⅓ cup of chopped scallions
1 cup of grapes, cut in halves
½ cup of celery, chopped
3 tablespoons of mayonnaise
1 teaspoon of lemon juice
¼ teaspoon of salt
⅛ teaspoon of pepper
¼ cup of slivered almonds

**DIRECTIONS:**

1. Toast the slivered almonds in a small dry skillet for a few minutes until they are just turning golden. Set aside 1 tablespoon of almonds.
2. Combine all the ingredients in a bowl and mix well.
3. Sprinkle the reserved almonds on top of the salad.

**NUTRITIONAL INFORMATION**

Per serving: 8 g total carbohydrate, 177 cals, 11 g fat, 1 g saturated fat, 1 g fiber, 438 mg sodium.

# CHICKPEA SALAD WITH RED ONION AND TOMATO

**SERVES 5**

1 15-oz can of chickpeas (garbanzo beans)
1 tomato, chopped
2 tablespoons of red onion, chopped
½ cup of parsley
3 tablespoons of olive oil
1 tablespoon of lemon juice
Salt and pepper to taste

**DIRECTIONS:**

1. Combine all the ingredients in a large bowl.
2. Chill for a while before serving.

**NUTRITIONAL INFORMATION**

Per serving: 24 g total carbohydrate, 195 cals, 9 g fat, 1 g saturated fat, 5 g fiber, 293 mg sodium.

# Quinoa Salad with Ginger Dressing

**COOKING TIME** *15 minutes* ▪ **SERVES** *6*

¾ cup of uncooked quinoa
1-2 cups of shredded red cabbage
1 red bell pepper, diced
½ red onion, diced
1 cup of shredded carrots
½ cup of chopped cilantro
¼ cup of diced green onions
½ cup of cashew halves

**Dressing:**

½ cup of peanut butter
2 teaspoons of freshly grated ginger or ½ teaspoon of ginger powder
3 tablespoons of soy sauce
1 tablespoon of honey
1 teaspoon of sesame oil
1 teaspoon of olive oil

## DIRECTIONS:

1. Cook the quinoa by bringing to boil 1½ cups of water and adding the quinoa, cover, reduce heat and simmer for 15 minutes. Remove from the heat and fluff the quinoa with a fork. Set aside.
2. To make the dressing, add the peanut butter and honey to a medium-size bowl suitable for microwaving and heat in the microwave for 20 seconds. Add in the ginger, soy sauce, vinegar, sesame oil and olive oil and stir until the mixture is smooth and creamy.
3. Add the dressing to the salad (can vary the amount of dressing used according to preference).
4. When cool, add the red pepper, onion, cabbage, carrots and cilantro into the quinoa.
5. Garnish the salad with the cashews and green onions.

**NUTRITIONAL INFORMATION**

Per serving: 30 g total carbohydrate, 7 g sugars, 282 cals, 15 g fat, 2 g saturated fat, 6 g fiber, 589 mg sodium.

# BEET SALAD

**COOKING TIME** *60 minutes* ▪ **SERVES** *4*

*Beets are a popular ingredient for hors d'oeuvres in Israel. They make sweet and tasty salads without having to add any sugar.*

1 large beet
1 large potato
½ medium red onion, diced
1 medium dill pickle, diced
1 teaspoon of vinegar
1 teaspoon of olive oil
Salt and pepper to taste

## DIRECTIONS:

1. Boil the beet for about 60 minutes until done, peel and dice.
2. Boil the potato for about 20 minutes until done, peel and dice.
3. Mix all the ingredients and serve chilled.

### NUTRITIONAL INFORMATION

Per serving: 20 g total carbohydrate, 100 cals, 1 g fat, 0 g saturated fat, 3 g fiber, 486 mg sodium.

# Chicken couscous

*In Mediterannean-style cooking different foods are mixed together within the same recipe. In this recipe, chicken pieces are served with whole-wheat couscous and vegetables The result is a delicious dish with very healthy ingredients.* *(Recipe on page 3)*

# Burrito Grande

*Ethnic recipes are a treasure trove of healthy dishes. In this wonderful family friendly, Mediterranean-style burrito recipe, whole-wheat tortillas (the grain) are served together with beans and vegetables.* ***(Recipe on page 25)***

# Beef Moussaka

*Red meat is not the healthiest of foods, but there is no reason to eliminate it entirely. When the chopped meat is eaten together with eggplant and tomato not only is a divine combination created but less chopped meat is eaten than if it were served alone.* *(Recipe on page 30)*

# Cauliflower Cheese Pie

*Family cooks – try and sneak in vegetables and whole grains into your family's diet whenever possible! With its whole-wheat pie crust and cauliflower, this cheese pie is definitely in the Mediterranean mode. Your family will love it.* *(Recipe on page 32)*

# Rice with Vegetables and Pecan

*Potatoes, except when roasted, lend themselves poorly to Mediterranean-style cooking. So experiment with other starches. For example, use brown rice rather than white rice. Add in vegetables, nuts and spices, as in this recipe, and you have an irresistible dish.* *(Recipe on page 41)*

# Quinoa with Roasted Brussels Sprouts, Leeks and Slivered Almonds

*Try out the whole grain recipes in this cookbook to find the ones your family likes. This quinoa dish containing Brussels sprouts, leek, almonds and raisins will likely be among them.* *(Recipe on page 51)*

# Roasted Vegetables with Chickpeas

*Roasting vegetables with olive oil is a delicious way for preparing them and provides additional super-healthful anti-oxidant. Health books in the past may have avoided a recipe such as this because of its fat content, but this is incorrect.* *(Recipe on page 57)*

# Sesame String Beans

*To ensure your family eats enough vegetables, make them tasty and attractive. A pile of boiled green beans on the plate is often not the answer - but a recipe like this will definitely get eaten.* *(Recipe on page 71)*

# Broccoli with Cherry Tomatoes

*Vegetables dishes need to be colorful and enticing. Eating at least four portions a day of vegetables is essential for weight control and for maintaining good health.* *(Recipe on page 79)*

# Mandarin Orange Salad

*Eating salads is an important part of Mediterranean-style meal planning. You will need delicious and innovative salad recipes – such as this one.* *(Recipe on page 82)*

# Salad Hors d'oeuvres

*Serving salad hors d'oeuvres before a main meal is very popular in Israel and is a splendid way for increasing your family's intake of vegetables. (Recipe on pages 83, 88, 100 and 129)*

# Tuna Salad with Grapes and Almonds

*This wonderful blend of fish, fruit and nuts can be a salad, a snack, or a main dish. Whichever way it is served, your family will love it.* (Recipe on page 106)

# Shakshuka

*What is an egg recipe doing in a health book? But why not? The notion that eggs promote heart disease is a myth. Eggs are a filling food and a good choice for breakfast. A shakshuka is a popular Israeli egg dish containing tomatoes and often other vegetables.* *(Recipe on page 114)*

# Split Pea and Barley Soup

*Serving soup as a first course is an excellent way for providing satiation from a main meal and preventing after-meal snacking. Soups also make nutritious snacks. This cookbook contains many superb soup recipes.* *(Recipe on page 133)*

# Salmon Pasta

*Pasta provides a useful base for Mediterranean dishes. Whole-wheat pasta is preferable to white pasta because of its fiber content. Blends of white and whole-wheat pasta are also becoming available in supermarkets and are a good second best. (Recipe on page 149)*

# Bran Muffins with Raisins

*Don't break your Mediterranean-style meal planning for dessert! These tasty and filling bran muffins contain lots of fiber and make a wonderful addition to a meal.* *(Recipe on page 163)*

CHAPTER 5

# Breakfast – an Essential Meal

Breakfast is an important meal – for everyone. Many kids have gotten into the habit of skipping breakfast and rolling directly from bed into the school bus. However, scientific studies consistently show that children who miss breakfast are more prone to obesity and do worse academically at school.

Unfortunately, many popular breakfast cereals are low in fiber and provide poor satiation. So how about making your own breakfast cereal? There is plenty of scope for creativity with homemade breakfast cereals. Nuts and dried fruit can be added, and berries and fresh fruit used as a topping to make a delicious breakfast.

Eggs also make a filling breakfast. This chapter contains three great egg recipes that include vegetables and whole grains.

Besides the recipes described here, other easy and healthful breakfast suggestions are: plain yogurt topped with berries, fruit or granola, and whole-grain toast with cheese or a healthy peanut butter.

# Crunchy Granola

**COOKING TIME** *25 minutes* ▪ **SERVES** *8*

*There is nothing like a homemade granola for breakfast. Add berries and fresh fruit, such as blueberries, strawberries, slices of apple and banana, and you have a delicious breakfast. Vary the fruits and nuts and you have a different breakfast each day!*

2 cups of Old Fashioned rolled oats
½ cup of shredded coconut
½ cup of wheat germ
½ cup of hulled sunflower seeds
¼ cup of honey
¼ cup of olive or canola oil
1 teaspoon of vanilla extract
½ cup of raisins

**DIRECTIONS:**

1. Preheat the oven to 325°F.
2. Spray a cookie sheet well with an oil spray, or even better place parchment paper on the cookie sheet since the ingredients in this recipe become very sticky because of the honey.
3. In a large mixing bowl, mix all the solid ingredients except for the raisins.
4. In a measuring cup, combine the oil, honey, and vanilla, and then work this mixture into the dry ingredients.
5. Spread the granola onto the cookie sheet or parchment paper and roast at 325°F for a total of 20-30 minutes.
6. Stir after 15 minutes or so, and add the raisins for the last 5 to 10 minutes of roasting.
7. When the mixture comes out of the oven, it is still very pliable. Dried fruit can be added at this time.
8. When the granola has cooled completely, store in an airtight container.
9. Serve in a bowl with milk.

**NUTRITIONAL INFORMATION**
**(without milk)**

Per serving: 35 g total carbohydrate, 259 cals, 12 g fat, 3.0 g saturated fat, 4.0 g fiber, 4 mg sodium.

# Maple Nut Granola

**COOKING TIME** *60 minutes* ▪ **SERVES** *12*

*This is another great tasting and healthy granola containing whole grain rolled oats.*

3 cups of Old Fashioned rolled oats
1 cup of walnuts, coarsely chopped
½ cup of almonds, sliced or slivered
¼ cup of whole-wheat flour
Pinch of salt
½ teaspoon of cinnamon
½ cup of maple syrup
⅓ cup of canola or olive oil
1 teaspoon of vanilla
¼ cup of raisins

## DIRECTIONS:

1. Preheat the oven to between 300° to 350°F.
2. In a mixing bowl, combine all the dry ingredients except for the raisins.
3. Add the liquid ingredients and mix until the dry ingredients are well coated.
4. Spread the mixture on a large oiled baking tray.
5. Bake for 45 minutes at 300° to 350°F.
6. Stir the granola occasionally.
7. Add the raisins to the hot or cold granola.
8. Serve in a bowl with milk.

**NUTRITIONAL INFORMATION**
**(without milk)**

Per serving: 31 g total carbohydrate, 264 cals, 14 g fat, 1 g saturated fat, 3.0 g fiber, 16 mg sodium.

# MUESLI

**SERVES 6**

*This is an excellent Muesli that is very easy and quick to make. Serve it with milk or yogurt and put berries and/or fruits on top. As with the previous granola recipes, there is plenty of scope for varying the ingredients and toppings to produce new and exciting tastes.*

2 cups of Old-Fashioned rolled oats
¼ cup of wheat germ
¼ cup of wheat bran
½ cup of raisins
¼ cup of brown sugar
¼ cup of chopped walnuts
¼ cup of raw sunflower seeds

## DIRECTIONS:

1. Combine all the ingredients in a large mixing bowl and mix well.
2. Store the muesli in an airtight container. (It will keep for up to 2 months at room temperature).
3. Serve with milk, together with fresh berries or sliced fresh fruit. For a smoother texture, allow the milk to soak into the cereal for ½ hour or so before serving.

**NUTRITIONAL INFORMATION**
**(without milk)**

Per serving: 32 g carbohydrate, 227 cals, 9 g fat, 1 g saturated fat, 5 g fiber, 4 mg sodium.

# SPANISH OMELET

**COOKING TIME** *10 minutes* ▪ **SERVES** *4*

*Strictly speaking, a Spanish omelet is a thick omelet stuffed with finely chopped potatoes and onions fried in olive oil. In this recipe, high-glycemic potato has been replaced by lower glycemic corn and other vegetables have been added. It's even better than the original!*

4 eggs
¼ cup of milk
¼ large green pepper, chopped
½ large onion, chopped
1 celery stalk, chopped
2 oz of frozen corn
1 tablespoon of olive oil
¼ teaspoon of salt or to taste
¼ teaspoon of pepper

**DIRECTIONS:**

1. Sauté the vegetables in the oil until softened. Transfer to a bowl.
2. Mix well the eggs, milk, salt and pepper, and fry until the mixture becomes slightly firm.
3. Add the vegetable mix to the eggs and continue cooking until the eggs are the appropriate consistency.

**NUTRITIONAL INFORMATION**
**(using whole milk)**

Per serving: 10 g total carbohydrate, 149 cals, 9 g fat, 2 g saturated fat, 1 g fiber, 232 mg sodium.

# SHAKSHUKA

**COOKING TIME** *15 minutes* ▪ **SERVES** *4*

*This is a very popular egg dish in Israel. The eggs stay intact rather than mushed up as in an omelet. The word shakshuka means "all mixed up" in Hebrew. That just about describes it. Za'atar is a mixture of ground-up dried spices used in the Middle East that usually contains thyme, oregano and marjoram with toasted sesame seeds and salt. If you don't have it on your spice rack, use thyme.*

3 tablespoons of olive oil
1 medium onion, chopped
4 tomatoes, chopped
5 medium mushrooms, chopped
1 cup of tomato sauce
½ teaspoon of salt
¼ teaspoon of pepper
4 eggs
½ teaspoon of paprika
1 teaspoon of crushed za'atar or dried thyme
Yellow cheese (optional)

**DIRECTIONS:**

1. Heat the oil in a deep frying pan or wide, flat pot. Fry the onion on high for about 3 minutes or until translucent.
2. Add the tomatoes and mushrooms and fry for another 3 minutes, stirring occasionally, until soft.
3. Add the tomato sauce, salt and pepper. Mix, bring to boil, and then lower to a medium flame and cook for another 7 minutes, stirring occasionally.
4. Break the eggs directly into the pan, spaced evenly around, and then sprinkle on the paprika and za'atar, (and cheese if using). Do not mix.
5. Cover and cook for another 2 minutes, depending on how you like the eggs – usually until the yolk is still mainly liquid (check with a fork).

**NUTRITIONAL INFORMATION**

Per serving: 12 g total carbohydrate, 214 cals, 15 g fat, 3 g saturated fat, 3 g fiber, 695 mg sodium.

# Shadowbox Egg

**SERVES** *1*

*This is a very kid-friendly way for introducing them to whole-grain bread for breakfast.*

1 egg

1 slice of whole-wheat or a healthy mix grain bread

1 tablespoon of olive oil

## DIRECTIONS:

1. Make a large hole in a slice of bread. If the slice of bread is big enough, use the edges of a glass cup.
2. Add the oil to a small skillet, place the bread in the skillet, and pour the egg into the hole.
3. Fry the bread and egg until the egg is just beginning to turn white and then flip the egg-bread combination.
4. Continue frying until the egg is cooked to your satisfaction.
5. Fry the bread taken from the hole in any remaining oil (optional).

**NUTRITIONAL INFORMATION**

Per serving: 12 g total carbohydrate, 258 cals, 19 g fat, 4 g saturated fat, 2 g fiber, 197 mg sodium.

# Strawberry Banana Smoothie

**SERVES** *2*

*A smoothie is a fine breakfast for a kid on the run. Put it in a container and it can be finished on the bus. The texture of the smoothie comes out best if the fruit is frozen before being added, but fresh banana also works well. A blender is needed for this recipe.*

½ cup of plain full-fat yogurt
½ cup of orange juice
1 cup of frozen strawberries
1 cup of frozen banana (1½ bananas)
1 teaspoon of sugar

## DIRECTIONS:

1. Puree all the ingredients in a blender until fully mixed.
2. Served chilled.

### NUTRITIONAL INFORMATION

Per serving: 34 g total carbohydrate, 164 cals, 3 g fat, 1 g saturated fat, 3 g fiber, 30 mg sodium.

CHAPTER 6

# Snacking to Health!

Snacks are often an unsupervised part of a child's diet, but this is a mistake. Eating healthy and filling snacks is important, especially for family members with a weight problem. Snacks made from highly-refined carbohydrate such as crackers, pretzels, cakes and cookies are neither healthy nor filling and may promote increased hunger later in the day.

A whole-wheat or whole grain sandwich makes an easy snack and some novel sandwich fillings are included in this section.

Here are some other ideas:

- Peanut butter without added sugar on whole-wheat or a healthy whole grain bread is always a useful standby.
- Whole-wheat pitas are easy to fill with salad and vegetables.
- Raw vegetables can be made extremely tasty with a dip. Middle Eastern foods such as hummus, tahini and baba ghanoush make excellent dips and can often be found in containers in supermarkets.
- A large pot of homemade chunky vegetable soup from which everyone can take seconds and thirds makes a very healthy and satisfying snack.

- Yogurt is a filling snack because of its protein and fat content. It also provides plenty of calcium and there is some evidence it may help improve bowel flora and therefore be helpful for weight control. There is no reason to buy low-fat yogurts, especially as these often contain added sugar. Add fruit slices, berries and granola and it is now fiber-rich!
- A cup of whole milk is a wonderful accompaniment for a snack. Milk consumption has fallen in the US and many individuals are no longer meeting their requirements for calcium. The recommendation of the American Academy of Pediatrics is that every child drink three glasses of milk a day.

The table below shows the recommended amounts of *elemental calcium* for children and adolescents:

| Age | Recommended daily intake of elemental calcium |
|---|---|
| 1 to 3 years | 500 mg |
| 4 to 8 years | 800 mg |
| 9 to 18 years | 1,300 mg |

An 8-oz cup of milk provides 300 mg of elemental calcium, 1 8 oz-cup of calcium-fortified orange juice about 300 mg, 8 oz of yogurt 350-400 mg and 1 oz of cheese 175-275 mg. A few non-dairy foods such as spinach also contain calcium, but the amount is small.

A useful exercise is to add up the amount of elemental calcium in your family's diet to see if your children reach the age-appropriate recommendation in this table. If not, a calcium supplement is advised and this should be discussed with your health provider.

# HOMEMADE TRAIL MIX

**SERVES** *10*

*Nuts should be high on any list of healthy foods. It is usually cheaper to make your own trail mix than to buy it at the store. Of course, other nuts and dried fruit besides those listed here can be used.*

½ cup of whole shelled almonds

½ cup of unsalted dry-roasted peanuts

½ cup of white raisins

½ cup of chocolate chips

4 oz of dried apricots or other dried fruit, chopped

**NUTRITIONAL INFORMATION**

Size per serving: 18 g total carbohydrate, 161 cals, 9 g fat, 3 g saturated fat, 2 g fiber, 3 mg sodium.

# CREAM CHEESE AND VEGETABLE WRAPS

**SERVES** *4*

*An attractive wrap can be an effective way for persuading family members to eat more vegetables. The instructions for making a wrap are described here. Experiment with different vegetables to find the combinations they like.*

4 10-inch whole-wheat/ mixed grain tortilla wraps

6 tablespoons of cream cheese

1 small carrot

¼ medium red onion

12 black olives

½ medium red pepper

¼ medium cucumber

**DIRECTIONS:**

1. Cut all the vegetables into very thin slices.
2. Spread the cream cheese thinly onto the wrap.
3. Place the vegetables in the form of parallel lines on the wrap.
4. Roll up the wrap parallel to the lines of vegetables. Then cut into desired lengths, such that each wrap contains a selection of all the vegetables.

**NUTRITIONAL INFORMATION**

Per serving: 45 g total carbohydrate, 337 cals, 14 g fat, 6 g saturated fat, 5 g fiber, 521 mg sodium.

# CHICKEN WRAPS

**COOKING TIME** *22 minutes* ▪ **SERVES** *8*

*Your family will rave about these wraps. They are very filling and make an excellent snack, or even a meal.*

- 3 boneless skinned chicken breasts, halved
- ½ cup of mayonnaise
- 6 tablespoons of honey mustard
- 1 tablespoon of red wine vinegar
- ¼ teaspoon of salt
- Dash of pepper
- 2 celery ribs, thinly sliced
- ¼ cup of red onion, chopped
- ½ cup of chopped cashews
- 8 6-inch whole-wheat or mixed grain tortillas

## DIRECTIONS:

1. Boil the chicken in enough water to cover for about 20 minutes, until no longer pink inside.
2. Remove the chicken from the pot and cut into bite-size pieces.
3. In a bowl, combine the mayonnaise, mustard, vinegar, salt and pepper. Stir in the chicken, celery, onion and cashews.
4. Spoon the mixture into each of the tortillas and roll up the tortilla.
5. Warm the tortillas for a few minutes in the oven.

### NUTRITIONAL INFORMATION

Serving size: 1 tortilla. 33 g total carbohydrate, 344 cals, 23 g fat, 3 gm sat fat, 5 g fiber, 773 mg sodium.

# VEGETABLE FOCACCIA

**COOKING TIME** *15 minutes* ▪ **SERVES** *12*

*Kids and adults alike will love this pizza-like dish. Guaranteed.*

1¼ cups of bread or white flour
1 cup of whole-wheat flour, or more if needed
1 package of quick-rise yeast (2 teaspoons)
1 teaspoon of salt
1 cup of warm water
1 tablespoon of canola or olive oil
2 teaspoons of cornmeal

### TOPPING:

3 medium tomatoes, chopped
5 fresh mushrooms, sliced
½ cup of chopped green peppers
¼ cup of chopped onion
3 tablespoons of olive oil
2 tablespoons of red wine vinegar
¾ teaspoon of salt
¼ teaspoon of garlic powder
¼ teaspoon of dried oregano
¼ teaspoon of pepper
½ cup of sliced black olives (optional)

## DIRECTIONS:

1. Preheat the oven to 475°F.
2. In a large mixing bowl, combine the flours, yeast and salt. Add the water and oil, and beat until smooth. Stir in enough additional flour to form a soft dough.
3. Turn onto a floured surface and knead until smooth and elastic.
4. Cover and leave for 15 minutes.
5. In a bowl, combine all the topping ingredients.
6. Coat a 15 × 10 × 1-inch pan with nonstick cooking spray.
7. Sprinkle with cornmeal.
8. Press the dough into the pan. Prick the dough generously with a fork.
9. Bake at 475°F for 5 minutes.
10. Cover with the vegetable topping.
11. Bake for 8-10 minutes longer or until the crust is golden.

### NUTRITIONAL INFORMATION

Per serving: 24 g total carbohydrate, 155 cals, 5 g fat, 1 g saturated fat, 4 g fiber, 360 mg sodium.

# Broiled Portabella Mushroom Sandwich

**COOKING TIME** *10 minutes* ▪ **SERVES** *4*

*This is a delicious sandwich recipe. It is best served warm – either freshly cooked or warmed in the microwave. Use a bought Italian dressing, or even better make your own vinaigrette (see Cool Salad section).*

4 fresh portabella mushrooms
1 medium onion, cut into ¼-inch slices
4 tomato slices
8 slices of whole-wheat or mixed grain bread
4 teaspoons of Italian dressing

## DIRECTIONS:

1. Brush the mushrooms and onion slices liberally with Italian dressing.
2. Broil the mushrooms and onion for 10 minutes, turning the mushroom over after 5 minutes.
3. Fill the sandwich with the mushroom, onion and slices of tomato.

**NUTRITIONAL INFORMATION**
**(for 1 sandwich made from 2 slices of bread)**

Per serving: 28 g total carbohydrate, 161 cals, 3 g fat, 1 g saturated fat, 4 g fiber, 336 mg sodium.

# GUACAMOLE

**SERVES** *2*

*Serve this tasty veggie snack with corn tortilla chips.*

2 ripe avocados
2 tablespoons of lemon juice
2-3 garlic cloves, minced
¼ teaspoon of salt or to taste
¼ teaspoon of chili powder
Black pepper to taste

**DIRECTIONS:**

1. In a large bowl, mash the avocados well, and combine with remaining ingredients.
2. Mix thoroughly until smooth.
3. Chill the guacamole and use soon after preparation, as it does not keep well beyond 24 hours.
4. Serve with corn tortilla chips.

**NUTRITIONAL INFORMATION**
**(not including the tortilla chips)**

Per serving: 10 g total carbohydrate, 155 cals, 13 g fat, 2 g saturated fat, 6 g fiber, 305 mg sodium.

# TUNA NOODLE SALAD

**COOKING TIME** *12 minutes* ▪ **SERVES** *4*

8 oz of dried Rotini noodles or other pasta
1 5-oz can of chunk light tuna in water
¼ cup of red onion, finely diced
1 medium celery stalk, diced
½ cup of defrosted frozen peas
2 tablespoons of mayonnaise
⅛ teaspoon of pepper
¼ teaspoon salt or to taste

**DIRECTIONS:**

1. Cook the pasta according to the package directions.
2. In a large bowl, combine all the ingredients together.

**NUTRITIONAL INFORMATION**

Per serving: 44 g total carbohydrate, 307 cals, 7 g fat, 1 g saturated fat, 1 g fiber, 328 mg sodium.

# FARFALLE AND ARTICHOKE SALAD

**COOKING TIME** *11 minutes* ▪ **SERVES** *8*

*This dish will disappear rapidly!*

16-oz packet of farfalle or bow-tie pasta
1 4-oz jar of pimentos, drained
½ cup of finely chopped red onion
½ cup of parsley, chopped
1 14-oz can of marinated artichoke hearts, cut into quarters

### DRESSING:

⅓ cup of olive oil
¼ cup of red wine vinegar
1 teaspoon of salt or to taste
⅛ teaspoon of pepper

## DIRECTIONS:

1. Cook the farfalle according to the package instructions. Allow to cool for 10 minutes.
2. Mix the salad dressing ingredients together
3. Add the pimento, artichokes, red onion and parsley to the salad dressing and pour onto the farfalle. Mix well.
4. Cool before serving.

### NUTRITIONAL INFORMATION

Per serving: 50 g total carbohydrate, 326 cals, 10 g fat, 1 g saturated fat, 7 g fiber, 337 mg sodium.

# QUICK CHILI

**COOKING TIME** *25 minutes* ▪ **SERVES** *11*

*This wonderful dish tastes equally good served cold as a salad, as a filling in a pita or taco, or served warm as a vegetarian main or side dish. When used as a pita or taco filling, cover with grated cheese and vegetables such as lettuce and chopped tomatoes and pour a taco dressing on top.*

1 tablespoon of olive oil
3 onions, chopped
1 carrot, chopped
2 cloves of garlic, minced
3-4 teaspoons of chili powder
1 teaspoon of ground cumin
1 28-oz can plus a 14-oz can of chopped tomatoes, with juice
1 teaspoon of brown sugar, packed
2 15-oz cans of red kidney beans, drained and rinsed (equivalent to 1⅓ cups of dried beans)
⅓ cup of bulgur

## DIRECTIONS:

1. Heat the oil over medium heat in large saucepan. Add the onions, carrots, garlic, chili powder and cumin, and sauté for 5-7 minutes until the onions and carrots are soft.
2. Add the tomatoes with their juice and the brown sugar and cook for 5 minutes over high heat.
3. Stir in the beans and bulgur and reduce heat to low.
4. Simmer the chili uncovered for 15 minutes or until thickened.

**NUTRITIONAL INFORMATION**

Per serving: 25 g total carbohydrate, 132 cals, 2 g fat, 0 gm sat fat, 6 g fiber, 519 mg sodium.

# BAKED SWEET POTATO

**COOKING TIME** *45 minutes* ▪ **SERVES** 6

*This sweet potato recipe can be served as a snack or as a starch or vegetable side dish. Sweet potatoes may well have health benefits not present in regular potatoes because of their anti-oxidant content. They also contain slightly more fiber.*

3 large sweet potato, cut into cubes
2 tablespoons of olive oil
1 tablespoon of brown sugar
1 teaspoon of chili powder
½ teaspoon of salt
¼ teaspoon of cayenne pepper

## DIRECTIONS:

1. Preheat the oven to 400°F.
2. Mix all the ingredients in a large re-sealable plastic bag.
3. Transfer all the ingredients to a greased 11 × 7-inch pan.
4. Bake uncovered at 400°F for 40-45 minutes until the potatoes are tender, stirring every 15 minutes.

### NUTRITIONAL INFORMATION

Per serving: 31 g total carbohydrate, 173 cals, 5 g fat, 1 g saturated fat, 4 g fiber, 271 mg sodium.

# POTATOES WITH VEGETABLE FILLING

**COOKING TIME** *86 minutes* ▪ **SERVES** *4*

*This is a great recipe. It's filling, contains vegetables and is quite delicious.*

4 large potatoes

1 cup of carrot strips

2 scallions, chopped

1 clove of garlic, minced

1 cup of thinly sliced red or green sweet pepper

1 cup of zucchini strips

1 tablespoon of olive oil, margarine, or butter

½ teaspoon of dry dill

½ teaspoon of dried oregano

1 teaspoon of salt, or to taste

Dash of pepper

½ cup of your favorite cheese, shredded

## DIRECTIONS:

1. Preheat the oven to 425°F.
2. Scrub and prick the potatoes and bake in the over at 425°F for 45 to 60 minutes until tender.
3. Cool for 10 minutes or so until the potatoes can be handled and then cut each potato in half.
4. Scoop out the potato pulp, leaving ¼–inch shell of the potato intact.
5. In a bowl, mash the pulp with a fork.
6. In a medium-sized skillet, sauté the carrot, sweet pepper, scallions, garlic and seasoning for about 5 minutes until tender but crisp.
7. Add the zucchini and cook for about 1 minute more until tender.
8. Stir the vegetables into the mashed potato pulp, and fill the potato shells with the pulp and vegetable mixture.
9. Place the potatoes on a baking sheet and bake in the oven at 400°F for 20 minutes.
10. After removing from the oven, sprinkle with the cheese so that it melts on the potatoes.

**NUTRITIONAL INFORMATION**

Per serving: 69 g total carbohydrate, 402 cals, 9 g fat, 4 g saturated fat, 8 g fiber, 749 mg sodium.

# Turkish Salad Dip

**COOKING TIME** *1 hour* ▪ **SERVES** *8 as a dip*

*Serve this as a dip with pita chips for a delicious and filling snack.*

- 4 fresh cloves of garlic, finely chopped
- 1 small onion, minced
- 1 15-oz can of diced tomatoes with garlic and onion
- ½ of a large red bell or green pepper, diced
- ½ teaspoon of chopped jalapeno or dash of cayenne pepper
- 4 tablespoons of olive oil, divided
- 1 tablespoon of paprika
- Dash of cumin
- ¼ teaspoon of salt or to taste

## DIRECTIONS:

1. In a 2-quart saucepan, sauté the garlic and small onion with 2 tablespoons of olive oil.
2. After 10 minutes, add the can of diced tomatoes and cook on high.
3. Once the mixture starts to boil, decrease the heat to a simmer and add the paprika, cumin, chopped jalapeno or dash of cayenne pepper, and salt to taste. Stir whenever possible.
4. Allow the mixture to simmer until most, but not all, the liquid has steamed off.
5. Then add 2 tablespoons of olive oil and stir.
6. Refrigerate for 1 hour and serve.

### NUTRITIONAL INFORMATION

Per serving: 7 g total carbohydrate, 91 cals, 7 g fat, g saturated fat, 1 g fiber, 368 mg sodium.

# HUMMUS WITH CILANTRO AND GINGER

**SERVES** *10*

*Hummus is often available in a tub in the supermarket. However, there is no comparison to this superb recipe. Serve it together with pita or whole-wheat crackers as a snack or hors d'oeuvre.*

1 15-oz can of chickpeas (garbanzo beans), drained and rinsed

½ cup of tahini

1 tablespoon of minced garlic

1 tablespoon of fresh ginger, minced

¼ cup of cilantro

½ lemon, juiced

1 teaspoon of salt

¼ cup of olive oil

½ cup of water

## DIRECTIONS:

1. Blend the chickpeas in a food processor until the texture is coarse.
2. Add the tehina, garlic, ginger, cilantro, lemon juice and salt.
3. Process for another 1 to 2 minutes.
4. Drizzle in the oil followed by the water with the processor still running.

### NUTRITIONAL INFORMATION

Per serving: 15 g total carbohydrate, 176 cals, 12 g fat, 2 g saturated fat, 3 g fiber, 389 mg sodium.

# Vegetarian Chopped Liver

**SERVES** *8*

*This dish can be served with whole-wheat crackers or bread as a healthy and filling snack or as an hors d'oeuvre.*

2 medium onions, chopped
1 tablespoon of olive oil
1 15-oz can of string beans, drained
3 hard boiled eggs
½ cups of chopped walnuts
1 cup of bran flakes or cornflakes
1 teaspoon of salt
¼ teaspoon of pepper

## DIRECTIONS:

1. In a skillet, fry the onions in the tablespoon of oil until lightly brown.
2. Place all the ingredients in a food processor and process the mixture until almost smooth.

**NUTRITIONAL INFORMATION**

Per serving: 4 g grain carbohydrate, 10 g total carbohydrate, 133 cals, 9 g fat, 1 g saturated fat, 3 g fiber, 501 mg sodium.

# A TROPICAL SMOOTHIE

**SERVES** *4*

*This smoothie made with a blender makes a wonderful and nutritious fruit snack that provides fiber and anti-oxidants. It can be made with water, fruit juice, milk or yogurt. Pre-freeze the fruits or use fresh fruits and ice. This recipe uses tropical fruits and water, has a subtle mango flavor, and can be made in a few minutes. Now that you have the gist, let the kids experiment with different fruits!*

1 large mango, peeled, cut into chunks, and frozen

2 bananas, peeled, cut into chunks, and frozen

1 cup of pineapple pieces, fresh or canned, frozen

1 cup of water

**DIRECTIONS:**

1. Place the fruit in a blender and blend until smooth. If necessary, cut the frozen fruit into smaller pieces for easier blending.
2. Drink immediately or place for a short while in the fridge.

**NUTRITIONAL INFORMATION**

Per serving: 31 g total carbohydrate, 121cals, 0 g fat, 0 g saturated fat, 3 g fiber, 2 mg sodium.

CHAPTER 7

# Satisfying Soups

Homemade soups are a perfect way for increasing your family's intake of vegetables. They are also very filling, especially thick soups and those containing whole vegetables. If family members are requesting seconds after eating a substantial meal, start the meal with a soup course so they feel more satiated. Homemade soups also make wonderful between-meal snacks. For all these reasons, a number of delicious soup recipes are included here.

# SPLIT PEA AND BARLEY SOUP

**COOKING TIME** *70 minutes* ▪ **SERVES** *9*

*This is an irresistible soup – and kids and adults will love it. It's also very filling.*

1½ cups of dried split peas
½ cup of uncooked barley
½ medium onion, chopped
1 large carrot, peeled and diced
1 stalk of celery, diced
1 large clove of garlic, diced
7 cups of chicken broth, divided
1 cup of water (or more if needed)
¼ teaspoon of oregano
Salt to taste
Pepper to taste

## DIRECTIONS:

1. In a large saucepan, combine the split peas, onion, carrot, celery, garlic and 6 cups of broth, and bring the ingredients to a boil.
2. Reduce the heat to low and simmer the mixture in an uncovered pan for 1 hour, stirring occasionally. If the liquid gets too low, add more water to prevent scorching.
3. Meanwhile, in a small covered saucepan, cook the barley in the remaining 1 cup of broth plus 1 cup of water over a low heat for 40 to 60 minutes or until the barley is tender.
4. When the vegetable mixture is done, purée it using an immersion blender.
5. Stir in the barley, herb seasoning and white pepper.
6. Heat the soup over a low heat, stirring often before serving.

**NUTRITIONAL INFORMATION**

Per serving: 25 g total carbohydrate, 156 cals, 2 g fat, 0 g saturated fat, 9 g fiber, 761 mg sodium

# Zucchini-Tomato Soup

**COOKING TIME** *20 minutes* ▪ **SERVES** *6*

*This is a very tasty, easy-to-make, low-carb soup.*

1 medium onion, chopped
2 cloves of garlic, minced
2 medium zucchinis, chopped
1 medium potato, sliced
2 cups of broth, divided
1 large tomato, chopped
1 cup of milk, rice milk, or soy milk
¾ teaspoon of basil
½ teaspoon of salt or to taste
¼ teaspoon of pepper

## DIRECTIONS:

1. In a large pot, combine the onion, garlic, zucchini, potato, and 1½ cups of broth. Bring to a boil and then cover and simmer for 15 minutes.
2. Add the tomato and simmer for 5 minutes longer.
3. Partially purée the mixture with an immersion blender, leaving some chunks of vegetable remaining.
4. Add the milk, basil, salt, pepper and remaining broth.
5. Warm the soup.

**NUTRITIONAL INFORMATION**
**(with whole milk)**

Per serving: 14 g total carbohydrate, 80 cals, 2 g fat, 1 g saturated fat, 2 g fiber, 540 mg sodium

# Cauliflower Soup

**COOKING TIME** *30 minutes* ▪ **SERVES 9**

*At first glance, this might not seem a very-interesting soup – but it tastes quite delicious.*

½ cup of chopped onion
2 ribs of celery, sliced
1 large carrot, sliced
1 medium garlic, minced
1 tablespoon of olive oil
1½ teaspoon of cumin
1 ½ teaspoon of curry
⅛ to ¼ teaspoon of cayenne pepper
1 large cauliflower, cut into flowerets
1 large red potato, diced
4 cups of chicken broth
2 tablespoons of almonds
1 tablespoon of lime juice
¼ teaspoon of salt or to taste
Black pepper to taste

## DIRECTIONS:

1. In a large pot, sauté the onion, celery, carrot and garlic with the olive oil for about 10 minutes.
2. Add the cumin, curry and cayenne pepper, and sauté for another 30 seconds.
3. Add the cauliflower, potato and broth and bring to the boil, and then simmer for 30 minutes.
4. Add the almonds and lime juice.
5. Purée all the ingredients.
6. Add salt and pepper to taste.

**NUTRITIONAL INFORMATION**

Per serving: 12 g total carbohydrate, 75 cals, 3 g fat, 0 g saturated fat, 2 g fiber, 469 mg sodium.

# EASY VEGETABLE SOUP

**COOKING TIME** *40 minutes* ▪ **SERVES** *6*

3 cups of chicken broth

1 cup of water

2 cups of canned diced tomatoes

1 onion, coarsely chopped

1 large or 2 small cloves of garlic, finely chopped

2 stalks of celery, finely chopped

2 carrots, peeled and sliced

1½ cups of fresh or thawed frozen corn kernels

3 medium zucchini, sliced

2 tablespoons of fresh parsley, chopped

½ teaspoon of chili powder

Pinch of cayenne

¼ teaspoon of salt or to taste

⅛ teaspoon of pepper

(Variations: sliced turnips, broccoli, asparagus, or green peppers can be added with the zucchini).

## DIRECTIONS:

1. In a large soup pot, combine the broth, water, tomatoes, onion, garlic, celery, carrots and seasonings. Bring to a boil, cover, and simmer for 30 minutes.
2. Add the corn, zucchini and parsley and continue to simmer for an additional 10 minutes.

**NUTRITIONAL INFORMATION**

Per serving: 22 g total carbohydrate, 124 cals, 2 g fat, 0 g sat fat, 4 g fiber, 600 mg sodium

# SPICY VEGETABLE SOUP

**COOKING TIME** *30 minutes* ▪ **SERVES** *6 cups*

*The spices give zest to this filling soup.*

- 2 large onions, chopped
- 2 cloves garlic, crushed
- 2 sticks of celery, chopped
- 2 cups of sweet potatoes, peeled and chopped
- 3 tablespoons of olive oil
- 1 medium green or red sweet pepper, chopped
- ½ of a 15-oz can of chopped tomatoes
- 1 15-oz can of cooked chickpeas
- 3 cups of chicken stock
- 2 teaspoons of paprika
- 1 teaspoon of turmeric
- 1 teaspoon of basil
- 1 teaspoon of salt
- Dash of cinnamon
- Dash of cayenne pepper

**DIRECTIONS:**

1. Sauté the onions, garlic, celery and sweet potatoes in the olive oil for about 5 minutes.
2. Add the seasonings and the stock and simmer for 15 minutes.
3. Add the remaining vegetables and chickpeas and simmer for another 10 minutes until the vegetables are tender.

**NUTRITIONAL INFORMATION**

Per serving: 38 g total carbohydrate, 267 cals, 9 g fat, 2 g saturated fat, 7 g fiber, 471 mg sodium.

# Red Lentil Soup

**COOKING TIME** *30 minutes* ▪ **SERVES** *7*

*A very enticing effect is created by the colors of the red lentils and red pepper in this very tasty soup.*

1½ cups of uncooked red lentils

6 cups of water

3 bay leaves

2 slices of fresh ginger, each about the size of a quarter

2 medium carrots, grated

1 cup of canned chopped tomatoes, un-drained, or 1 large fresh tomato, chopped

1 small sweet red or green pepper, finely chopped

1½ cups of onion or 1 large onion, finely chopped

4 cloves of garlic, chopped

2 tablespoons of olive oil

1½ teaspoons of ground cumin

1½ teaspoons of ground coriander

Pinch of cayenne pepper

2 tablespoons of fresh lemon juice

½ teaspoon of salt or to taste

Pepper to taste

## DIRECTIONS:

1. In a skillet, sauté the onions and garlic in the olive oil for about 10 minutes or until browned.
2. Add the cumin, coriander and cayenne and sauté for another minute. Set aside.
3. In a large pot, combine the water, lentils, bay leaves, ginger, carrots, tomatoes and pepper. Bring to a boil, stir, and then simmer covered for 20 minutes until the lentils are tender.
4. Remove the bay leaves and ginger from the soup.
5. Stir in the sautéed onions and garlic, and the lemon juice.
6. Add salt and pepper to taste.

**NUTRITIONAL INFORMATION**

Per serving: 33 g total carbohydrate, 212 cals, 5 g fat, 6 g fiber, 193 mg sodium.

# Sweet Potato Soup

**COOKING TIME** *60 minutes* ▪ **SERVES** *12*

4 large sweet potatoes, unpeeled, and quartered (take care with your fingers!)
1 large onion, chopped
3 cups of carrots or 6 large carrots, peeled, and chopped
1 cup of celery stalks or 2 stalks, chopped
5 cups of chicken broth
1 tablespoon of olive oil
½ teaspoon of dried oregano
½ teaspoon of dried thyme
1 pinch of nutmeg
½ teaspoon of ground cumin
1 teaspoon of salt or to taste
⅛ teaspoon of pepper or to taste

## DIRECTIONS:

1. Fill a large pot with enough water to cover the quartered sweet potatoes and add 1 teaspoon of salt to the water. Bring to a low boil and cook until tender, about 20 minutes.
2. Drain the water from the pot and remove the sweet potatoes.
3. When the sweet potatoes have cooled, remove the potato skins by hand, and put the sweet potatoes aside.
4. Sauté the carrots, onions and celery in a large (or the same) pot.
5. Add the broth, sweet potatoes and seasonings. Bring to a full boil and simmer for 40 minutes. It may be necessary to add up to 1 cup of water if the consistency is too thick.
6. With an immersion blender, purée the soup until it is almost smooth.

**NUTRITIONAL INFORMATION**

Per serving: 15 g total carbohydrate, 83 cals, 2 g fat, 0 g sat fat, 3 g fiber

# PUMPKIN AND CORN SOUP

**COOKING TIME** *15 minutes* ▪ **SERVES** *6*

2 tablespoons of olive oil

1 small onion, minced

1 10-oz package of frozen whole kernel corn

1 16-oz can of pumpkin

1 ½ cups of water

1 tablespoon of sugar

1 teaspoon of salt or to taste

⅛ teaspoon of ground cinnamon

2 chicken-flavored bouillon cubes

2 cups of milk

1 tablespoon of chopped parsley for garnish

## DIRECTIONS:

1. Cook the onion in the olive oil until tender over a medium heat.
2. Add the frozen corn and cook for 2 to 3 minutes until the corn is just tender.
3. Stir in the pumpkin, water, sugar, salt, cinnamon and bouillon until blended and the mixture begins to boil. Cook for 5 minutes to blend the flavors. Keep the lid on to stop splattering.
4. Stir in the milk and heat through. (Do not boil after adding the milk or the mixture will curdle).
5. Serve and garnish with chopped parsley.

**NUTRITIONAL INFORMATION**

**(with whole milk)**

Per serving: 26 g total carbohydrate, 185 cals, 87 g fat, 3 g saturated fat, 4 g fiber, 754 mg sodium

# PUMPKIN SOUP

**COOKING TIME** *25 minutes* ▪ **SERVES** *6*

1 lb of pumpkin, peeled, seeded, and cut into 1-inch cubes
3 cups of chicken broth
1 medium potato, peeled and diced
1 medium onion, peeled and chopped
¼ teaspoon of nutmeg
⅛ teaspoon of white pepper
⅛ teaspoon of salt

## DIRECTIONS:

1. In a large saucepan, combine the pumpkin, broth, potato and onion. Bring to a boil, reduce the heat, cover the pan, and simmer the vegetables for 20 minutes.
2. Puree the mixture using an immersion blender.
3. Heat the purée just to boiling point.
4. Add the nutmeg, pepper and salt.

NUTRITIONAL INFORMATION

Per serving: 21.8 g carbohydrate, 110 cals, 1.2 g fat, 5.8 g fiber, sodium 375 mg

# COLD BEET SOUP

**COOKING TIME** *75 minutes* ▪ **SERVES** *8*

*Beet soup or borscht is a popular East European dish that has a refreshing and sweet taste. The beets also provide plenty of anti-oxidant.*

2 lb of beets, peeled and cut into 1-inch pieces
1 cup of chopped onion
2 cups of thinly sliced celery
2 tablespoons of olive oil
2 teaspoons of sugar
Pepper to taste
1-2 tablespoons of red vinegar to taste
4 cups of chicken broth

## DIRECTIONS:

1. In a large soup pot, sauté the onion and celery together with the sugar and pepper for about 10 minutes until soft.
2. Add the beets, vinegar and broth, and simmer covered for 1 to 1¼ hours until the beets are very tender.
3. Purée the soup mixture.
4. Cover, refrigerate, and serve cold.

NUTRITIONAL INFORMATION

Per serving: 7 g total carbohydrate, 75 cals, 4 g fat, 1 g saturated fat, 1 g fiber, 77 mg sodium

# Gazpacho

**CHILLING TIME** *2 hours* ▪ **SERVES** *7*

*This cold soup is ideal for a hot summer day.*

4 cups of tomato juice
1 small onion, diced
2 cups of fresh tomatoes, diced
1 green pepper, diced
1 teaspoon of honey
1 clove of garlic, crushed
1 cucumber, diced
2 scallions, chopped
¼ cup of parsley, chopped
Juice of ½ lemon, or 1½ tablespoons of lemon juice
Juice of 1 lime, or 1½ tablespoons of lime juice
2 tablespoons of wine vinegar
1 teaspoon of tarragon
1 teaspoon of basil
Dash of cumin
½ teaspoon of salt
⅛ teaspoon of pepper
Dash of Tabasco sauce (optional)

**DIRECTIONS:**

1. Combine all the ingredients.
2. Blend the ingredients with an immersion blender, leaving enough solid vegetables for a chunky consistency. (Make sure to keep the blender vertical, otherwise the gazpacho will splash all over you)
3. Chill for at least 2 hours.

**NUTRITIONAL INFORMATION**

Per serving: 12 g total carbohydrate, 52 cals, 0 g fat, 2 g fiber, 187 mg sodium.

# CURRIED ZUCCHINI SOUP

**COOKING TIME** *34 minutes* ▪ **SERVES** *6*

1 large onion, thinly sliced
2 tablespoons of olive oil
2 tablespoons of curry powder
Salt to taste
4 small zucchinis
1 quart of chicken stock
1 sweet potato, or 1 potato plus 2 teaspoons of brown sugar

## DIRECTIONS:

1. Heat the oil in a large pot.
2. Stir in the onion, and add the curry powder and salt. Cook until the onion is tender, about 4 minutes.
3. Add the zucchini and cook until tender, about 10 minutes.
4. Pour in the chicken stock and bring to the boil.
5. Cover, reduce heat to low, and simmer for 20 minutes.
6. Bake the potato or sweet potato in the microwave and add to the soup mixture.
7. Remove the soup from the heat. Blend the soup until almost smooth.

**NUTRITIONAL INFORMATION**

Per serving: 15 g total carbohydrate, 140 cals, 7 g fat, g saturated fat, 2 g fiber, 248 mg sodium.

# MUSHROOM BARLEY SOUP

**COOKING TIME** *70 minutes* ▪ **SERVES 6**

*Delicious soups do not come any easier than this.*

1 pound of mushrooms, sliced
2 medium carrots
1 small tomato, chopped (or half a 15-oz can of diced tomato)
1 medium onion, chopped
2 ribs of celery, chopped
½ cup of uncooked barley
4 sprigs of parsley, finely chopped
¾ teaspoon of salt
¼ teaspoon of black pepper
3 cups of chicken stock
2½ cups of water

## DIRECTIONS:

1. Put all the ingredients in a large pot and bring to the boil.
2. Cover the pot, reduce heat, and simmer for 1 hour.

**NUTRITIONAL INFORMATION**

Per serving: 25 g total carbohydrate, 141 cals, 2 g fat, 0 g saturated fat, 5 g fiber, 499 mg sodium.

# WHITE BEAN AND MEATBALL SOUP

**COOKING TIME** *65-95 minutes* ▪ **SERVES 8**

*This is a filling and healthy way for serving meatballs.*

1 lb of ground beef
1 egg
½ cup of whole-wheat breadcrumbs
2 tablespoon of olive oil
3 carrots, sliced
2 stalks celery, sliced or chopped
1 onion, diced
2 cloves of garlic, minced
1 large potato, diced
1 cup of dried white beans, soaked overnight in water to cover, or 1 15-oz can of white beans
8 cups of vegetable broth
Salt and pepper to taste
1 cup of fresh spinach, chopped (optional)

## DIRECTIONS:

1. Mix the ground beef, breadcrumbs and egg together, and shape into small meatballs.
2. In a large frying pan, sauté the meatballs in 1tablespoon of olive oil until browned. Set aside.
3. In a large pot, sauté the onion, garlic, carrots and celery in 1 tablespoon of olive oil for a few minutes.
4. Add the broth, beans and potatoes, bring to a boil, cover, and simmer for 1 hour until they are all soft (or for 30 minutes if using canned beans).
5. Add meatballs to the pot of soup. Cook for another 30 minutes with added salt and pepper to taste.
6. Stir in the spinach at the end.

### NUTRITIONAL INFORMATION

Per serving: 35 g total carbohydrate, 334 cals, 14 g fat, 4 g saturated fat, 7 g fiber, 1062 mg sodium.

# Albondigas Soup

**COOKING TIME** *36 minutes* ▪ **SERVES 12**

*This soup is very quick to make and is almost a meal in itself. It is also very Mediterranean-like with its content of beef, veggies and grains. Your family is sure to love it.*

1 tablespoon of olive oil
1 large onion, chopped
1 large garlic clove, minced
3 quarts of chicken stock
½ cup of tomato sauce
½ pound of string beans, ends removed, and cut into 1 inch pieces, or frozen cut beans
2 carrots, peeled and sliced
1 lb of ground beef
⅓ cup of uncooked brown rice
1 raw egg
¼ cup of chopped parsley
1/ cup of chopped fresh mint leaves (or 1 tablespoon of dried mint)
1½ cups of fresh or frozen peas
1½ teaspoons of salt
¼ teaspoon of black pepper
1 teaspoon of dried oregano (or 1 tablespoon of fresh chopped oregano)
Dash of cayenne pepper

**DIRECTIONS:**

1. In a large pot, heat the oil over medium heat. Add the onion and cook for about 5 minutes until tender.
2. Add the garlic and cook a minute more.
3. Add the broth and tomato sauce, and bring to a boil. Then reduce the heat to simmer.
4. Add the carrots and string beans.
5. To prepare the meatballs, mix the rice into the meat, add the mint and parsley, and mix in the raw egg. Form the mixture into meatballs.
6. Add the meatballs to the simmering soup one at a time, cover, and simmer for ½ hour.
7. Add the peas towards the end of the ½ hour.
8. Add the oregano, salt and pepper, and dash of cayenne.

**NUTRITIONAL INFORMATION**

Per serving: 19 g total carbohydrate, 237 cals, 11g fat, 4 g saturated fat, 2 g fiber, 746 mg sodium.

# CHAPTER 8

# Encouraging Fish

Fish, particularly fatty fish, have very healthful properties, particularly for the cardiovascular system, because of their high content of omega-3 fat. For most families, fish has to be presented in the same way as vegetables – the dish has to look attractive and taste good – otherwise it won't get eaten.

A word of caution. Fish, especially fatty fish, are susceptible to contamination with pollutants and heavy metals, such as mercury. Therefore, if you eat local freshwater fish, check on its source and status.

The recommendations for women who are pregnant or who may become pregnant, nursing mothers and young children are to eat up to 2 servings per week of fish with a lower mercury content, such as canned tuna, salmon and Pollack, up to 1 serving per week of albacore canned tuna, as this could contain more mercury, and to avoid entirely fish that contain higher amounts of mercury (but which are generally rarely consumed anyway) such as king mackerel. However, even women who are pregnant should not avoid fish entirely, as there are benefits to the fetal brain from eating fish and fish oil. For everyone else, there are no limits to how much fish should be eaten, although it is a good idea to eat a variety of fish so that any risk is widely dispersed.

# HONEY SALMON

**COOKING TIME** *25 minutes* ▪ **SERVES** *2*

*It can sometimes be difficult to persuade non-fish lovers to change their ways. This quick and extremely easy recipe has almost a 100% success rate!*

12 oz of fresh salmon

1 ½ tablespoons of honey mustard

1 tablespoon of honey

## DIRECTIONS:

1. Preheat the oven to 350°F.
2. Cover the top of the salmon with the honey mustard and honey.
3. Place in the oven at 350°F and bake for 20-25 minutes until the fish is opaque.

**NUTRITIONAL INFORMATION**

Per serving: 11 g total carbohydrate, 458 cals, 25 g fat, 5 g saturated fat, 0 g fiber, 202 mg sodium.

# SALMON PIE

**COOKING TIME** *35 minutes* ▪ **SERVES** *8*

*This is a popular family recipe. The first four numbered directions are for a 2-crust pie.*

**PIECRUST:**

1 cup of whole-wheat flour
1 cup of white flour
1 teaspoon of salt
½ cup of canola oil
5 tablespoons of water

**FILLING:**

2 tablespoons of butter
2 tablespoons of whole-wheat flour
1 cup of milk
1 egg yolk, slightly beaten
1 14¾-oz can of pink salmon, drained, broken into pieces
¾ cup of frozen peas
4-oz can of pimentos, coarsely chopped
1 teaspoon of salt or to taste
¼ teaspoon of pepper

## DIRECTIONS:

1. Preheat the oven to 450°F.
2. In a large bowl, combine the flour and salt for the piecrust. Whisk together the oil and ice water until it has the appearance of whipping cream.
3. Add the dry ingredients. Mix well with a fork or pastry cutter.
4. Divide into two parts and roll out.
5. Line the pan with half of the pastry dough.
6. For the filling, melt the butter in a 2-quart saucepan. Blend in the flour and milk. Cook until thick, stirring constantly. Stir in the egg yolk, salmon, pimentos, peas and seasoning.
7. Pour the filling into the pastry-lined pan.
8. Cover with the remaining dough and seal the edges. Cut slits for the steam to escape.
9. Bake at 450°F for 10 minutes, and then at 400°F for 20-25 minutes until golden brown.

**NUTRITIONAL INFORMATION**

Per serving: 27 g total carbohydrate, 363 cals, 21 g fat, 5 g saturated fat, 3 g fiber, 350 mg sodium.

# SALMON PASTA

**COOKING TIME** *6 minutes* ▪ **SERVES** *4*

*This delicious Mediterranean-style dish is easy and quick to make and highly recommended.*

- 8 oz of uncooked linguine
- 2 salmon fillets (6 oz each), cut into 1-inch cubes
- 1 teaspoon of minced fresh rosemary or ½ teaspoon of dried rosemary
- 5 tablespoons of olive oil, divided
- 2 medium-sized tomatoes, chopped
- 5 garlic cloves, minced
- ½ teaspoon of salt or to taste
- ⅛ teaspoon of pepper

## DIRECTIONS:

1. Cook the linguine according to the package directions. Drain the linguine and place in a bowl.
2. Cut the salmon into 1-inch cubes, peeling off any skin.
3. In a large skillet, sauté the salmon cubes and rosemary in 2 tablespoons of oil for 5 minutes or until the salmon flakes easily with a fork.
4. Add the tomatoes, garlic, salt and pepper to the salmon and cook for 1 minute.
5. Add the salmon to the linguine and toss gently.
6. Drizzle the remaining 3 tablespoons of oil over the mixture (if you find this too oily, use only 2 tablespoons of oil).

### NUTRITIONAL INFORMATION

Per serving: 34 g total carbohydrate, 519 cals, 30 g fat, 5 g saturated fat, 2 g fiber, 380 mg sodium.

# MICROWAVED POACHED SALMON WITH SOUR CREAM SAUCE

**COOKING TIME** *14 minutes* ▪ **SERVES** *2*

4 6-oz salmon steaks
1½ cups of hot water
2 peppercorns
1 lemon, thinly sliced
1 bay leaf
1 teaspoon of instant minced onion
1 teaspoon of salt or to taste
⅓ cup of dry wine (optional)

**SAUCE:**

½ cup of sour cream
1 tablespoon of finely chopped parsley
1 teaspoon of lemon juice
½ teaspoon of dried dill weed
Pinch of white pepper

## DIRECTIONS:

1. In an oval microwave-baking dish, pour the water and wine. Add the peppercorns, lemon, bay leaf, onion and salt.
2. Microwave on High for approximately 5 minutes or until it reaches a full boil.
3. Carefully place the salmon steaks in the hot liquid. Microwave covered with plastic wrap on High for approximately 2 to 3 minutes or until the fish becomes opaque.
4. Let the steaks stand for about 5 minutes to finish cooking.
5. To prepare the sauce, mix all the ingredients in a small bowl. Cook on 80% power for 1 to 2 minutes or until hot.
6. Drain the salmon and serve with the heated sauce.

**NUTRITIONAL INFORMATION**

Per serving: 1 g total carbohydrate, 75 cals, 7 g fat, 4 g saturated fat, 0 g fiber, 20 g sodium.

# Baked Salmon with Rice

**COOKING TIME** *40 minutes* ▪ **SERVES** *4*

*Salmon is a very versatile fish in how it can be cooked, and is therefore a great fish for starting a let's-eat-more-fish campaign.*

1 cup of raw brown rice
2½ cups of water
1 lb of salmon fillets
¼ cup of orange juice
1 teaspoon of dried dill weed
1 teaspoon of dried rosemary
1 teaspoon of dried basil
1 teaspoon of ground mustard
1 teaspoon of lemon pepper

## DIRECTIONS:

1. In a small saucepan, bring 2½ cups of water to boil. Add the rice and stir. Reduce heat, cover, and simmer for 20 minutes. Set aside.
2. Preheat the oven to 350°F.
3. In a large baking pan, add enough water to just cover the bottom of the pan. Lay the salmon fillet in the pan, pink side up. Place cooked rice around the outside of the fish. Sprinkle the orange juice over the fish and rice.
4. In a small bowl, combine the dill weed, rosemary, basil, mustard and lemon pepper, and sprinkle over the fish and rice.
5. Cover with aluminum foil.
6. Bake in the preheated oven for 30-40 minutes or until the salmon is tender and flaky.

**NUTRITIONAL INFORMATION**

Per serving: 39 g total carbohydrate, 346 cals, 9 g fat, 1 g saturated fat, 2 g fiber, 53 mg sodium.

# GRILLED OR BAKED SALMON WITH VINAIGRETTE

**COOKING TIME** *20 minutes* ▪ **SERVES** *4*

*This is an easy gourmet dish. If you want to make it simpler, leave out the spinach and orange slices.*

4 6-oz salmon fillets
2 tablespoons of lemon juice
1 teaspoon of pepper
6 oz of fresh spinach
4 oranges, sliced

### VINAIGRETTE:

¼ cup of orange juice
2 tablespoons of olive oil
2 tablespoons of balsamic vinegar, preferably rice vinegar
½ teaspoon of honey mustard
½ teaspoon of pepper
1 clove of garlic, minced

## DIRECTIONS:

1. Drizzle the lemon juice over the salmon, and sprinkle with pepper.
2. Bake at 375°F for 15 to 20 minutes, or grill until done.
3. Arrange 4 plates with the spinach, orange slices and salmon, and pour the dressing on top.

**NUTRITIONAL INFORMATION**

Per serving: 30 g total carbs, 426 cals, 18 g fat, 3 g saturated fat, 8 g fiber, 117 g sodium.

# SALMON PATTIES WITH SPINACH

**COOKING TIME** *10 minutes* ▪ **YIELDS** *13 patties*

½ cup of dried couscous
⅔ cup of orange juice
1 14¾-oz can of red salmon, drained
1 10-oz package of frozen chopped spinach – thawed, drained, and squeezed dry
2 egg yolks, beaten
2 cloves garlic, crushed
3 tablespoons of olive oil
1 teaspoon of ground cumin
½ teaspoon of ground black pepper
½ teaspoon of salt or to taste

## DIRECTIONS:

1. Prepare the couscous according to the package directions, but instead of water use ⅔ cup of orange juice.
2. In a bowl, combine all the ingredients except for the olive oil and form into patties.
3. In a large skillet, heat the olive oil over medium heat and fry the patties until golden brown for about 8 to 10 minutes, turning once.

**NUTRITIONAL INFORMATION**

Per serving: 8 g total carbohydrate, 120 cals, 6 g fat, 1 g saturated fat, 1 g fiber, 132 mg sodium.

# GLAZED SALMON

**COOKING TIME** *10 minutes* ▪ **SERVES** *3*

3 (6-oz.) salmon fillets or steaks (about ¾-inch thick)
3 tablespoons of dark brown sugar, packed
4 teaspoons of Dijon mustard
1 teaspoon of rice vinegar
1 tablespoon of soy sauce

## DIRECTIONS:

1. Preheat the oven to 475°F.
2. Mix the glaze ingredients together in a small bowl. Pour over the salmon.
3. Bake at 475°F for 10 minutes.

**NUTRITIONAL INFORMATION**

Per serving: 14 g total carbohydrate, 413 cals, 23 g fat, 5 g saturated fat, 0 g fiber, 524 mg sodium.

# Salmon Kebabs

**PREPARATION TIME** *60 minutes* ▪ **COOKING TIME** *10 minutes* ▪ **SERVES** *4*

1 pound of salmon, cut into cubes
1 pint of cherry tomatoes
1 red onion
2 medium zucchinis
8 oz of small mushrooms
¼ cup of soy sauce
1 tablespoon of olive oil
1 tablespoon of grated fresh ginger
4 garlic cloves, chopped
2 tablespoons of sugar

## DIRECTIONS:

1. Mix the marinade of soy sauce, oil, cloves, garlic, ginger and sugar in a bowl.
2. Cut up the vegetables to a suitable size for kebabs.
3. Marinate the fish and vegetables for 30 to 60 minutes.
4. Place the fish and vegetables on the kebab sticks.
5. Heat oven to broil, and broil the kebabs for 10 minutes, turning once.

### NUTRITIONAL INFORMATION

Per serving: 20 g total carbohydrate, 284 cals, 11 g fat, 2 g saturated fat, 3 g fiber, 892 mg sodium.

# TUNA PATTIES

**COOKING TIME** *5 minutes* ▪ **SERVES** *10*

*This easy tuna recipe will likely be a big hit with the family.*

5-oz can of tuna in water
½ onion, chopped fine
½ cup of whole-wheat breadcrumbs, divided
1 egg
3 to 5 tablespoons of olive oil for frying

**DIRECTIONS:**

1. Mix the tuna, onion, and egg together in a bowl with ¼ cup of the breadcrumbs and make into patties.
2. Coat each patty with the remaining breadcrumbs.
3. Fry in the olive oil until slightly brown.

NUTRITIONAL INFORMATION

Per serving: 5 g total carbohydrate, 121 cals, 8 g fat, 1 g saturated fat, 1 g fiber, 188 mg sodium.

# TUNA PATTIES WITH MUSHROOM AND ONION

**COOKING TIME** *10 minutes* ▪ **SERVES** *4*

1 5-oz can of canned tuna in water
4 oz of mushroom, chopped
½ medium onion, chopped
1 egg
2 tablespoons of whole-wheat bread crumbs
3 tablespoons or more of olive oil for frying

**DIRECTIONS:**

1. In a small frying pan, sauté the mushroom and onion until soft, approximately 4 minutes, using 1 tablespoon of olive oil.
2. In a bowl, add this mixture to the other ingredients and form into 12 patties.
3. Fry the patties in as much of the oil as needed until lightly browned, turning once, about 3 minutes per side.

NUTRITIONAL INFORMATION

Per serving: 5 g total carbohydrate, 179 cals, 12 g fat, 2 g saturated fat, 1 g fiber, 170 mg sodium.

# MICROWAVED TUNA CASSEROLE

**COOKING TIME** *12 minutes* ▪ **SERVES** *4*

*Try out this recipe. It's a delicious way for eating fish.*

1 cup of raw rice, preferably brown rice

2 tablespoons of butter

2 tablespoons of whole-wheat flour

½ teaspoon of salt or to taste

¼ teaspoon of dry mustard

⅛ teaspoon of pepper

1 cup of milk

½ cup of shredded Cheddar cheese

1 6½-oz can of chunk light tuna, drained

1 stalk of celery, thinly sliced

¼ cup of chopped onion

½ medium green pepper, cut into ¼ × 1-inch strips

1 4-oz can of mushroom stems and pieces, drained (optional)

¼ cup of sliced almonds (optional)

**DIRECTIONS:**

1. Cook the rice according to the package instructions.
2. In a 1-quart casserole dish, melt the butter in the microwave on High for 30 to 45 seconds.
3. Blend in the flour, salt, mustard and pepper. Stir in the milk.
4. Microwave for 4½ to 7 minutes or until thickened, interrupting the microwaving to stir every minute.
5. Stir in the cheese until melted. Add the tuna, and mushrooms if desired, into the cheese sauce.
6. In a 2-quart casserole dish, place the celery, onion and green pepper and cover the dish. Microwave for 2½ to 3½ minutes on High or until tender-crisp.
7. Stir in the cheese sauce.
8. Microwave uncovered for another 2½ to 3½ minutes on High or until thoroughly heated.
9. Sprinkle with almonds (optional).
10. Serve over the rice.

**NUTRITIONAL INFORMATION (USING WHOLE MILK)**

Per serving: 45 g total carbohydrate, 429 cals, 18 g fat, 9 g saturated fat, 3 g fiber, 285 mg sodium.

# Fish Cheese Puff

**COOKING TIME** *30 minutes* ▪ **SERVES** *4*

*Cheese together with fish might seem an unusual combination, but they go well together in this and the previous recipe.*

1 lb of fillets (e.g. sole or flounder), with skin removed

½ cup of milk

½ cup of shredded Cheddar cheese

2 eggs, with the white and yolks separated

1 tablespoon of onion, finely chopped

¼ teaspoon of salt or to taste

## DIRECTIONS:

1. Heat the oven to 350°F.
2. Grease an 11 × 7-inch baking dish. Arrange the fillets, slightly overlapping. Set aside.
3. In a large mixing bowl, combine the milk, cheese, egg yolks, onion and salt. Set aside.
4. In a medium-size mixing bowl, beat the egg whites with a mixer at high speed until stiff, but not dry.
5. Gently fold the egg whites into the milk mixture. Spread the mixture evenly over the fillets.
6. Bake at 350°F for 25 to 30 minutes or until the fish is firm and opaque and just begins to flake and the puff is light golden brown.

### NUTRITIONAL INFORMATION

Per serving: 1 g total carbohydrate, 135 cals, 6 g fat, 3 g saturated fat, 0 g fiber, 333 mg sodium.

# Spanish Style Fish

**COOKING TIME** *40 minutes* ▪ **SERVES** *6*

*There's no "fishy taste" in this winning recipe.*

6 fish fillets (e.g. sole or flounder)
¼ cup of olive oil
1 large onion, chopped
1 green pepper, chopped
1 clove garlic, finely chopped
¼ cup of whole-wheat flour
2 cups of tomato juice
Salt to taste
Pepper to taste

**DIRECTIONS:**

1. Preheat the oven to 350°F.
2. Place the fish in a 9 × 13-inch pan.
3. In a medium-size skillet, sauté the onion, pepper and garlic in the olive oil.
4. Add the flour, tomato juice, salt and pepper.
5. Pour this mixture over the fish.
6. Bake the fish in the oven for 30-40 minutes at 350°F.

**NUTRITIONAL INFORMATION**

Per serving: 11 g total carbohydrate, 356 cals, 13 g fat, 2 g saturated fat, 2 g fiber, 237 mg sodium.

# ROLLED FISH

**COOKING TIME** *50 minutes* ▪ **SERVES** *4*

1 lb of fish fillets (e.g. sole or flounder)
1½ cups of chopped celery
1 large onion, chopped
⅓ cup of seasoned bread crumbs, preferably whole-wheat
8-oz can of tomato sauce
Salt to taste
Pepper to taste
8 oz of mushroom (optional)

## DIRECTIONS:

1. Preheat the oven to 350°F.
2. Sauté the celery, onion and mushroom together in a small skillet until they are soft.
3. Remove from the heat. Add breadcrumbs and season to taste.
4. Spread the mixture over the fillets. Roll up the fillets, and place a toothpick in the fish to hold them in shape.
5. Place the fish in a dish and pour the tomato sauce over the fish.
6. Bake at 350°F for 45 minutes.

**NUTRITIONAL INFORMATION**

Per serving: 15 g total carbohydrate, 161 cals, 3 g fat, 1 g sat fat, 4 g fiber, 733 mg sodium.

# LEMON GARLIC TILAPIA

**COOKING TIME** *35 minutes* ▪ **SERVES** *4*

*This fish recipe has a wonderful lemon tang.*

4 tilapia fillets
2 cloves garlic, minced
1 tablespoon of olive oil
3 tablespoons of fresh lemon juice
1 teaspoon of dried parsley flakes
Salt and pepper to taste

## DIRECTIONS:

1. In a small skillet, preheat the oven to 375°F.
2. Sauté the garlic in olive oil, about 1 minute.
3. Add the lemon juice and parsley, stir, and sauté a few minutes longer.
4. Place the tilapia in a slightly greased 9 × 13-inch dish. Spread the topping over the tilapia. Sprinkle with salt and pepper.
5. Bake at 375°F for 25-30 minutes.

**NUTRITIONAL INFORMATION**

Per serving: 1 g total carbohydrate, 116 cals, 5 g fat, 1 g saturated fat, 0 g fiber, 218mg sodium.

# Moroccan Fish

**COOKING TIME** *45 minutes* ▪ **SERVES** *5*

*The chickpeas nicely complement the fish in this delightful recipe.*

5 fish fillets
1 medium onion, chopped
3-4 cloves of garlic, left whole
2 tablespoons of oil
15-oz can of chopped tomatoes
½ cup of chopped red pepper
½ 15-oz can of chickpeas
2 tablespoons of tahini
Paprika
½ teaspoon of salt or to taste
Pepper
Cayenne pepper

## DIRECTIONS:

1. Sauté the onions and garlic in oil in a wide pot.
2. Add the chopped tomatoes, red pepper, chickpeas, tahini and seasonings.
3. Add a little water if needed, and bring to a boil.
4. Add the fish carefully. Reduce heat and simmer, covered, for about 35 minutes.

### NUTRITIONAL INFORMATION

Per serving: 22 g total carbohydrate, 245 cals, 11 g fat, 2 g saturated fat, 5 g fiber, 994 mg sodium.

## CHAPTER 9

# Tasty Desserts!

Desserts and a health book might seem a contradiction in terms, especially if they contain a hefty measure of sugar and are loaded with calories. Clearly, if you are trying to lose weight desserts should be avoided. However, for everyone else occasional cakes and cookies are part of family life. Nevertheless, an important point is being made in this section, namely that even cakes and cookies can be made in a way that maximizes healthful ingredients such as nuts, fruits and whole-wheat flour. If your family is sneaking from the cookie jar, at least make sure the cookies are as healthy as you can make them! However, even with the best of intentions one does come up against reality. It would be nice if one could bake cakes entirely with whole-wheat flour instead of white flour, but they often do not rise well when made like this and a mixture of white and whole-wheat flour has to be used instead.

A muffin for dessert is a very nice way of rounding off a meal. Because of their fiber content, muffins are quite filling and this helps prevent after-meal snacking. For this reason, a number of appealing muffins are included in this chapter.

# NUTTY FRUIT SALAD

**COOKING TIME** *3 minutes* ▪ **SERVES** *4*

*There are a number of ways for presenting fruits to your family. One way is just to hand them some fruit. Another way, and this has more likelihood of success, is to make a fruit salad. There are as many variations on this recipe as there are fruits and berries in the store, but this is a good one to start off with and you can branch out from here!*

1 cup of grapes, halved

2 oranges, cut into pieces

1 banana, sliced

2 kiwis, sliced

⅓ cup of walnuts, broken into small bits

⅓ cup of orange juice

¼ teaspoon of cinnamon

⅛ teaspoon of nutmeg

**DIRECTIONS:**

1. In a small skillet, toast the walnuts (without any oil) until they are just turning brown.
2. Mix all the ingredients, including the walnuts, in a large bowl.
3. Serve chilled.

**NUTRITIONAL INFORMATION**

Per serving: 32 g total carbohydrate, 189 cals, 7 g fat, 1 g saturated fat, 4 g fiber, 3 mg sodium.

# BRAN MUFFINS WITH RAISINS

**COOKING TIME** *20 minutes* ▪ **YIELDS** *12 muffins*

*Leaving a meal feeling even slightly hungry is an invitation for after-meal snacking. These tasty muffins contain fiber from bran and whole-wheat flour and can be extremely helpful for providing that full-up feeling (satiation) from a meal.*

1½ cups of wheat or oat bran

1½ cup of milk (or 1½ cups of rice milk for a dairy-free recipe)

1 egg

¼ cup of canola oil

½ cup of whole-wheat flour

½ cup of white flour

2½ teaspoons of baking powder

½ teaspoon of baking soda

½ cup of raisins

½ cup of granulated sugar

**DIRECTIONS:**

1. Preheat the oven to 400°F.
2. Mix the bran cereal and milk (or milk substitute) and let stand for 5 minutes.
3. Add the egg and oil.
4. To this mixture, add the flour, sugar, baking powder, baking soda and raisins.
5. Fill about 12 muffin cups three-quarters full and bake for 20 minutes at 400°F.

**NUTRITIONAL INFORMATION**

Per serving: 28 g total carbohydrate, 166 cals, 6 g fat, 1 g saturated fat, 4 g fiber, 176 mg sodium.

# BANANA MUFFINS

**COOKING TIME** *25 minutes* ▪ **YIELDS** *12 muffins*

1 cup of wheat or oat bran
1 cup of milk (or 1 cup of rice milk for a dairy-free recipe)
1 large mashed banana
1 egg
3 tablespoons of canola oil
½ cup of whole-wheat flour
½ cup of white flour
2 teaspoons of baking powder
½ teaspoon of salt
⅓ cup of granulated sugar
¼ teaspoon of cinnamon
½ cup of walnuts
½ cup of raisins (optional)

## DIRECTIONS:

1. Preheat the oven to 350°F.
2. In a large bowl, mix the beaten egg, bran, milk, mashed banana and oil. Let the mixture soak for 5 minutes.
3. Add the flour, sugar, baking powder, salt and cinnamon.
4. Add the walnuts and raisins (if desired).
5. Fill about 12 muffin cups three-quarters full and bake at 350°F for 25 minutes.

### NUTRITIONAL INFORMATION

**(without the raisins)**

Per serving: 22 g total carbohydrate, 158 cals, 8 g fat, 1 g saturated fat, 3 g fiber, 207 mg sodium.

# APPLE MUFFINS

**COOKING TIME** *20 minutes* ▪ **YIELDS** *12 muffins*

¾ cup of milk (or ¾ cup of rice milk with ¾ tablespoon of vinegar for a dairy-free recipe)

½ cup of maple syrup

2 eggs or egg whites

1 tablespoon of canola oil

½ cup of grated tart apple

½ cup of shredded carrot

¾ cup of whole-wheat flour

½ cup of wheat bran

¼ cup of all-purpose flour

3 tablespoons of granulated sugar

1 teaspoon of baking powder

1 teaspoon of baking soda

½ teaspoon of salt

½ teaspoon of ground cinnamon

## DIRECTIONS:

1. Preheat the oven to 375°F.
2. In a large bowl, beat the milk, syrup, eggs and oil until smooth.
3. Stir in the apple and carrot.
4. Combine the dry ingredients, and stir them into the milk mixture until it is just moistened.
5. Fill about 12 muffin cups three-quarters full and bake at 375°F for 20 minutes.

**NUTRITIONAL INFORMATION**

Per serving: 23 g total carbohydrate, 2 g fat, 0 g saturated fat, 270 cals, 2 g fiber, 233 mg sodium.

# PEAR MUFFINS

**COOKING TIME** *20 minutes* ▪ **YIELDS** *18 muffins*

4 large pears, peeled, cored, and chopped

1 cup of sugar

½ cup of canola oil

2 large eggs, beaten

2 teaspoons of vanilla extract

2 cups of whole-wheat flour

2 teaspoons of baking soda

2 teaspoons of ground cinnamon

1 teaspoon of ground nutmeg

1 teaspoon of salt

1 cup of raisins

1 cup of chopped walnuts

## DIRECTIONS:

1. Preheat the oven to 375°F.
2. Mix the pears and sugar in a medium bowl.
3. Blend the oil, eggs, and vanilla in a large bowl.
4. Combine the flour, baking soda, cinnamon, nutmeg and salt in another medium bowl.
5. Stir the pear mixture into the egg mixture and mix in the dry ingredients. Add the raisins and walnuts.
6. Divide the batter among about 18 muffin cups and fill about three quarters full. Bake at 375°F for about 30 minutes.

**NUTRITIONAL INFORMATION**

Per serving: 36 g carbohydrate, 247 cals, 11 g fat, 1 g saturated fat, 4 g fiber, 281 mg sodium.

# OATMEAL COOKIES

**COOKING TIME** *10 minutes* ▪ **YIELDS** *5 dozen cookies*

*These cookies contain whole-wheat flour, rolled oats and nuts. If your family likes eating cookies, try at least to maximize the healthy ingredients.*

1½ cups of whole-wheat flour
2 cups of rolled oats
½ teaspoon of baking soda
1 teaspoon of salt
½ teaspoon of ground cinnamon
½ teaspoon of ground nutmeg
1 cup of butter
¾ cup of granulated sugar
¾ cup of brown sugar
2 eggs, beaten
1 cup of chopped nuts
1 cup of raisins

## DIRECTIONS:

1. Preheat the oven to 350°F.
2. Place the raisins in hot water for 5 minutes. Drain.
3. In a large bowl, cream the butter with the sugar.
4. Add the remainder of the ingredients.
5. Drop the mixture onto a cookie sheet (keep the cookies small and separate as they tend to expand a bit).
6. Bake at 350°F for 10 minutes.

**NUTRITIONAL INFORMATION**

**(for a single 2" diameter cookie)**

Per serving: 11 g total carbohydrate, 88 cals, 5 g fat, 2 g saturated fat, 1 g fiber, 46 mg sodium.

# Fruit-Almond Crisp

**COOKING TIME** *50 minutes* ▪ **SERVES** *9*

### Topping:

½ cup of whole-wheat flour
1 cup of old-fashioned oats
⅓ cup of firmly packed brown sugar
¼ teaspoon of salt
1 teaspoon of ground ginger
½ teaspoon of ground cinnamon
⅓ cup of canola oil
½ cup of sliced almonds

### Filling:

¾ cup of granulated sugar
2 tablespoons of quick cooking tapioca or cornstarch
1 teaspoon of ground ginger
Pinch of salt
2½ lb of apricots or nectarines, pitted and diced

### DIRECTIONS:

1. Preheat the oven to 350°F.
2. To make the topping, in a medium bowl, stir together all the topping contents.
3. To make the filling, in a small bowl, stir together the sugar, tapioca, ginger and salt.
4. Place the apricots or nectarines in a large bowl and sprinkle with the sugar mixture and toss to distribute evenly.
5. Spread the fruit mixture in a greased 9-inch square baking dish. Sprinkle the topping evenly over the fruit.
6. Bake at 350°F until the topping is crisp and golden brown and the fruit-filling slowly bubbles, about 50 minutes.
7. Serve warm or cold.

**NUTRITIONAL INFORMATION**

Per serving: 52 g total carbohydrate, 317 cals, 12 g fat, 2 g saturated fat, 4 g fiber, 69 mg sodium.

# APPLE-CRANBERRY CRISP

**COOKING TIME** *50 minutes* ▪ **SERVES** *9*

2 lb of apples, peeled, cored and thinly sliced

¾ cup of fresh cranberries

¼ cup of sugar

3 teaspoons of ground cinnamon

1 teaspoon of ground nutmeg

⅓ cup of old-fashioned rolled oats

⅓ cup of whole-wheat flour

½ cup of packed light brown sugar

¼ cup of butter or margarine, cut into pieces

½ cup of chopped pecans

## DIRECTIONS:

1. Preheat the oven to 375°F.
2. Grease an 8-inch square baking dish.
3. In a large bowl, mix together the apples, cranberries, white sugar, cinnamon and nutmeg. Place this mixture evenly into the baking dish.
4. In the same large bowl you used previously, combine the oats, flour and brown sugar. Then mix in the butter with a fork until the mixture is crumbly.
5. Stir in the pecans.
6. Sprinkle this over the apple mixture.
7. Bake in the oven at 375°F for 40-50 minutes or until the topping is golden brown.

### NUTRITIONAL INFORMATION

Per serving: 49 g total carbohydrate, 279 cals, 10 g fat, 4 g saturated fat, 5 g fiber, 2 mg sodium.

# Baked Banana

**COOKING TIME** *1½ minutes* ▪ **SERVES** *1*

*This is a great way for using up bananas before they go too mushy.*

1 banana

½ teaspoon of canola oil

Pinch of cinnamon

**DIRECTIONS:**

1. Cut the banana into chunks and place in a bowl.
2. Sprinkle the cinnamon and oil on the banana and cover with plastic wrap.
3. Heat the banana in the microwave on High, about 1½ minutes for one banana (or 2½ minutes for 2 bananas) until soft and mushy.

**NUTRITIONAL INFORMATION**

Per serving: 27 g total carbohydrate, 125 cals, 3 g fat, 0 g saturated fat, 3 g fiber, 1 mg sodium.

# ZUCCHINI AND SWEET POTATO CAKE

**COOKING TIME** *80 minutes* ▪ **SERVES** *12*

*To reiterate the main message of this chapter – if you are making a dessert, such as a cake, try to use as many healthful ingredients as possible. This recipe contains vegetables, whole-wheat flour and nuts.*

1½ cups of sugar
¾ cup of canola oil
3 eggs
1 cup of zucchini, grated
1 cup of sweet potato, grated
1 cup of walnuts, chopped
1 cup of white flour
1 cup of whole-wheat flour
2 teaspoons of cinnamon
1 teaspoon of baking soda
¼ teaspoon of baking powder
¼ teaspoon of salt
½ teaspoon of canola oil
Pinch of cinnamon

## DIRECTIONS:

1. Preheat the oven to 325°F.
2. Spray a 9 × 5-inch loaf pan with non-stick spray.
3. In a large mixing bowl, whisk the sugar, oil, eggs and vanilla together.
4. Stir in the zucchini, sweet potato and walnuts.
5. In another large bowl, combine the flour, cinnamon, baking soda, baking powder and salt, and stir until the mixture is blended.
6. Add the zucchini/sweet potato mix and stir, but do not over-mix.
7. Pour the batter into the loaf pan.
8. Bake at 325°F for 75-85 minutes until done.

### NUTRITIONAL INFORMATION

Per serving: 44 g total carbohydrate, 386 cals, 22 g fat, 2 g saturated fat, 2 g fiber, 75 mg sodium. 8. Bake at 325°F for 75-85 minutes until done.

# ZUCCHINI CARROT CAKE WITH OATS

**COOKING TIME** *40 minutes* ▪ **SERVES** *12*

½ cup of Old Fashioned oats
1 cup of whole-wheat flour
1 cup of white flour
1 ½ cups of sugar
1 tablespoon of baking powder
1 ½ teaspoon of cinnamon
1 teaspoon of salt
3 large eggs
¾ cups of canola oil
1 cup of grated zucchini
1 cup of grated carrot
¾ cup of raisins

## DIRECTIONS:

1. Preheat the oven to 350°F.
2. Mix all the ingredients and pour into two 8" x 4-inch greased loaf pans.
3. Bake for 35-40 minutes.

### NUTRITIONAL INFORMATION

Per serving: 51g total carbohydrate, 357 cals, 16 g fat, 2 g saturated fat, 3 g fiber, 544 mg sodium.

# Fruit Cake

**COOKING TIME** *60 minutes* ▪ **SERVES** *8*

*This quick-to-make cake is quite delicious.*

⅜ cup of whole-wheat flour
⅜ cup of regular flour
¾ cup of sugar
1 cup of dried fruits (e.g. raisins, craisins (dried cranberries), dates and apricots)
1 cup of nuts (e.g. almonds, walnuts, and pecans)
3 eggs
¼ cup of water

## DIRECTIONS:

1. Preheat the oven to 300°F.
2. Mix together the dry ingredients. Then add the fruits and nuts.
3. In a separate bowl, mix the eggs and water.
4. Add the wet ingredients to the dry ingredients and pour into a greased loaf pan.
5. Bake at 300°F for 1 hour.

**NUTRITIONAL INFORMATION**

Per serving: 48 g total carbohydrate, 312 cals, 12 g fat, 2 g saturated fat, 4 g fiber, 32 mg sodium.

# Strawberry and Pear Purée

**SERVES** 6

*This is a delicious and classy way of adding more fruits to your diet. Use fresh or frozen fruits together with the strawberries.*

1 pint of fresh strawberries
4 fresh pears
Small amount of water

## DIRECTIONS:

1. Purée the ingredients.
2. Add water to adjust to the appropriate consistency.
3. Serve chilled.

**NUTRITIONAL INFORMATION**

Per serving: 23 g total carbohydrate, 87 cals, 0 g fat, 0 g saturated fat, 5 g fiber, 2 mg sodium.

# CHAPTER 10

# The Israeli Mediterranean Diet – Debunking the Myths and Moving Forward

What if I could sell you a formula scientifically shown to reduce the risks of heart disease, obesity, type 2 diabetes, Alzheimer's disease, some forms of cancer and other medical conditions?[1] Most people would give a bundle to know its contents. But the details of this formula have been known for many years and its benefits have been described in numerous scientific papers.

It's called the Mediterranean Diet.

And it's yours for the taking!

No other diet in the world has the health track record of the Mediterranean diet in combating most of the nutritionally linked medical conditions affecting America and other Western countries. And certainly not the low-fat diet, which has been America's favored diet since the 1960's and which has indirectly promoted the biggest health disaster in the history of nutrition – America's obesity epidemic.

Despite its name, there is no *single* Mediterranean diet. Different Mediterranean countries have their own unique dietary preferences. However, there are a number of common features:

- They contain a lot of vegetables

- They include fruits, nuts and seeds
- They contain whole grains
- They use healthful fats, such as olive oil
- They do not include drinks with added sugar
- Drinking wine often accompanies meals

But there is more to the Mediterranean diet than this. Anyone can put a few vegetables and bits of fruit on their plate, but this does not constitute a Mediterranean diet. *Rather, the Mediterranean diet is* a *construct of how to eat vegetables, fruits and whole grains together.*

Let me explain.

Americans and Europeans from non-Mediterranean countries typically place the starch, protein and vegetable portions of a meal as separate items on their plate. By contrast, Mediterranean people learned to put foods together in combinations – grains together with vegetables, and meat and fowl combined with grains and vegetables – and they thereby create mouth-watering dishes from otherwise ordinary, but healthy, ingredients. One reason they are able to do this is that they use starches such as spaghetti, couscous and rice that keep their form when mixed together with vegetables and meat.

Of course, Mediterranean countries are not the only places in the world that figured out how to put foods together in tasty combinations. Many other countries do this, which is why I call this *Mediterranean-style* meal planning.

Typically, Mediterranean diets are low in animal products, such as meat, eggs and milk, and because of this they are often low in fat. Mediterranean people ate like this because these animal products were not as readily available in countries in the Mediterranean basin as they are in the West.

Is it possible, I asked myself, to include moderate amounts of dairy, eggs and meat in Mediterranean-style meal planning and for this diet to still retain its health benefits? Such a diet would be a lot more acceptable to people living in Western countries than a conventional Mediterranean diet.

I am convinced it is.

To explain why this is the so, I will provide you with some background about myself and explain how I became interested in the fascinating field of nutrition. And why from there it was a short jump to the realization that the Mediterranean diet is the best diet for you and your family and for everyone else in the United States. I also discovered that preventive nutrition in the United States for over half a century has been based on total myths.

## America's nutrition crisis

I am a pediatric endocrinologist and have been a full professor of Pediatrics in several medical schools in the United States. A pediatric endocrinologist is a pediatrician who specializes in evaluating and treating endocrine, metabolic and nutritional problems of childhood and adolescence.

One of my areas of expertise is pediatric obesity.

America is presently in the midst of an epidemic of obesity the likes of which have never been seen before. Some 18% of American kids and 70% of American adults are now obese or overweight. However, these figures do not capture the full extent of the problem. Not only are there more obese people in this country than previously, but the obese are heavier than they were in the past. Massive obesity has become almost commonplace.

Unfortunately, with massive obesity comes a greater likelihood of medical complications from obesity. As a pediatric endocrinologist, a large part of my work is evaluating children and adolescents with obesity and assessing for these complications.

And I find them.

I commonly diagnose blood sugar abnormalities and even type 2 diabetes in my young obese patients. Some of these kids require pills and even insulin injections to keep their blood sugars under control. Pediatric obesity-related type 2 diabetes was almost unheard of when I first started in practice many years ago. It is a serious condition, often leading in adulthood to such problems as heart disease, amputations and kidney failure.

I frequently diagnose airway obstruction during sleep (obstructive sleep apnea) as a consequence of obesity. When severe, this leads to daytime sleepiness and learning and behavior problems that are a disaster for schoolwork and academic success.

I also regularly identify fatty liver and liver inflammation in obese children on the basis of abnormal liver blood tests. Some of these children – and currently we have no reliable way of identifying which ones – will go on to develop severe liver disease during adulthood and may even require liver transplantation later in life.

Obese children and adolescents are also at risk for developing cardiovascular disease in adulthood. Cardiovascular disease is a major complication of obesity and often has its beginnings in young people. The amount of cardiovascular disease in the United States has fallen from the giddy heights it reached in the 1950's but it is still the number one killer in this country.

Nothing like this was supposed to happen. According to the script written in the 1960's, if everyone ate less saturated and total fat, LDL-cholesterol levels would come down and fewer people would develop heart disease. Eating less calorically dense fat-containing foods would also help prevent obesity, since dietary fat contains on a weight basis more than twice as many calories as carbohydrate or protein.

However, the more obese children I treated the more I realized that this emphasis on dietary fat was a tremendous mistake. Not only was it failing to solve the problem it was designed to fix but it was likely making matters worse!

A low-fat diet is a high-carbohydrate diet. By fixating on fat and failing to stress the importance of eating the *right type of carbohydrate*, the low-fat campaign of the 1960's was inadvertently encouraging Americans to eat more and more poor-quality carbohydrate. It turns out that a high-carbohydrate diet containing poor quality carbohydrate is one of the worse diets anyone could have devised. Yet this is precisely the type of diet that millions of Americans are eating in the mistaken belief that it's a healthy one!

**It is not dietary fat that promotes heart disease and obesity in most people but poor quality carbohydrate.**[2]

Poor quality carbohydrate is very easy to identify – it contains a lot of sugar and is highly refined.

But what constitutes the far preferable "good quality" carbohydrate?

I was so intrigued by this question that I decided to review the scientific literature on the associations between the properties of carbohydrate and disease; and I published my findings as a review article.[3] The work I did for this review was to change my entire perspective on preventive nutrition.

Two factors in particular stood out as being important in relation to weight control and cardiovascular disease – one was the amount of dietary fiber in carbohydrate-containing foods and the other was the anti-oxidant they contained.

Both of these, of course, are prominent constituents of the Mediterranean diet.

# THE MEDITERRANEAN DIET

What accounts for the health benefits of the Mediterranean diet?

A number of factors seem to be responsible. The Mediterranean diet contains a lot of dietary fiber. As will be explained in chapter 12, fiber is an important factor for controlling hunger and preventing excessive weight gain.

The Mediterranean diet also contains a lot of low-glycemic carbohydrates and these are helpful for preventing high blood sugars. *High-glycemic carbohydrates* are carbohydrates that are rapidly absorbed from the gut resulting in higher peaks of glucose in the blood. *Low-glycemic carbohydrates* are carbohydrates that are absorbed more slowly, leading to lower peaks of blood glucose. This is illustrated in the figure below that compares blood glucose levels after eating two carbohydrates – high-glycemic white bread and low-glycemic white pasta.

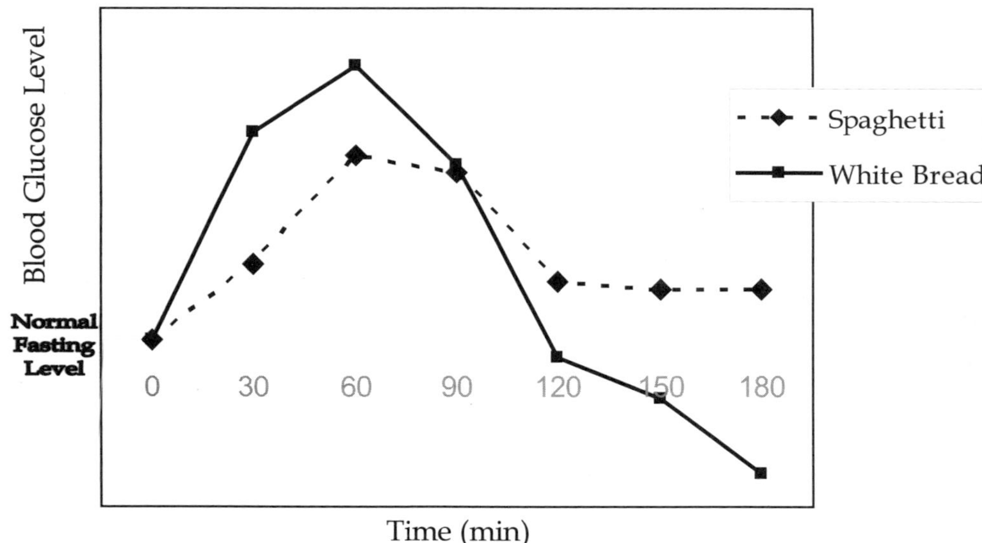


Note the high peak of glucose levels with high-glycemic white bread compared to the lower and more prolonged peak with low-glycemic spaghetti. Glucose levels may even dip below normal with high-glycemic foods.

This figure shows that blood glucose levels rise higher after eating high-glycemic bread than after eating low-glycemic white pasta. Pasta is made from semolina, and semolina is made from durum wheat. Durum wheat is a hard wheat that is broken down only slowly in the gut and its slow absorption of glucose accounts for its low glycemia.

A lot has been written in health books about the glycemia of carbohydrates and the subject may well have been overplayed. It is doubtful, for example, that high-glycemic carbohydrates are a major cause of the obesity epidemic in this country. Nevertheless, the glycemia of carbohydrates is important with respect to diabetes control and heart disease prevention and may have a role in appetite regulation.[3]

The Mediterranean diet is also rich in anti-oxidants, and this factor alone may be responsible for many of the health benefits of this diet.

Let me explain what anti-oxidants are about, since this is such an important subject. Every minute of the day our body produces *free oxygen and nitrogen radicals* as a result of normal cellular metabolism. These molecules contain extra electrons, and these extra electrons are potentially damaging to cell components. However, our bodies also produce natural *antioxidants* that can donate extra electrons and thereby neutralize these supercharged molecules.

Scientists often talk about *oxidative stress*. Oxidative stress is a biochemical stress that occurs whenever more than normal amounts of free oxygen radicals are produced in the body in response to nutritional and other biochemical stresses. This could include, for example, eating large amounts of trans fats or consuming a high-fructose or high-fat containing diet.

Fortunately, many of the natural foods we eat contain anti-oxidants that can supplement the body's natural defenses against oxidative stress. The fruits, vegetables, whole grains and herbs contained within the Mediterranean diet are chock full of anti-oxidants.

The study of individual Mediterranean foods, particularly olive oil and wine, has taught us a lot about the importance of natural anti-oxidants for health.

From scientific studies we know that the health benefits of olive oil derive not from its predominant fat, which is monounsaturated oleic acid, but from its phenolic anti-oxidants.[4]

A meta-analysis of 32 long-term studies with over ¾ million volunteers demonstrated that using olive oil significantly reduces all-cause mortality, cardiovascular events and stroke when comparing the top versus bottom third of olive oil consumption.[4] A meta-analysis is a means of gathering together the results of many similar studies and analyzing them together as if they were one giant study. Because of the large number of subjects analyzed, a meta-analysis permits definitive conclusions to be made that might otherwise be tentative if a smaller number of subjects had been studied.

These results are astounding for just one food alone. Use olive oil and you will likely prolong your life!

Drinking red wine also has significant health effects due to its content of an anti-oxidant called resveratrol.[5] Moderate wine drinkers live longer than non-wine drinkers, even when the non-wine drinkers drink other forms of alcohol. A meta-analysis of 26 long-term studies showed that wine's benefit on vascular disease follows a J-shaped curve. Drink too little and there is no benefit. Too much alcohol is harmful. The plateau, i.e. the most beneficial amount, coincides with 150 mL of wine a day.

These Mediterranean foods are, of course, not the only foods that contain anti-oxidants. There are thousands of antioxidants contained within plants, and scientists are just beginning to understand how these compounds help prevent cardiovascular disease and many other medical conditions.

The Mediterranean diet is a super-healthy diet. The novelty of this book is that it proposes that it is possible to include within this diet moderate amounts of animal products such as dairy, white meat and eggs with no loss in health benefits. This type of Mediterranean diet is more Western-like and therefore more palatable to people living in the United States and other Western countries than a traditional Mediterranean diet.

But are not saturated fat and dietary cholesterol harmful to health?

To answer this question we will need to debunk the myths that have pervaded Western preventive nutrition for over half a century.

## DEBUNKING THE MYTHS

In June 2014, the cover page of Time Magazine had the following headline – "Eat butter. Scientists labeled fat the enemy. Why they were wrong."

This headline, as well as the inside story, were based on very solid science. A meta-analysis had analyzed 49 long-term studies that included over ½ million participants and concluded that neither saturated fat nor polyunsaturated fat influence cardiovascular disease.[6] In the words of its authors:

> *"Current evidence does not clearly support cardiovascular guidelines that encourage high consumption of polyunsaturated fatty acids and low consumption of total saturated fats."*

Incredible as it may seem, this study (as well as other similar studies) tell us that over 50 years of nutritional recommendations to limit saturated and total fat for preventing heart disease have no scientific support. In other words, they are a total myth.

A low-fat diet does indeed reduce blood cholesterol levels slightly and it was logical to assume that as a result of this it would also reduce cardiovascular disease. But it is not so. When enough studies were done to examine the effectiveness of a low saturated fat diet in preventing heart disease, scientists found no benefit at all.

In fact, the very opposite may be the case. Another study showed that not only is a low-fat diet ineffective in preventing cardiovascular disease but it may make matters worse![7] This study looked at whether it makes any difference what type of carbohydrate does the replacing when cutting back on fat. It turns out it makes a lot of difference. Replacing saturated fat with "high-glycemic carbohydrate" actually leads to an *increase* in cardiovascular risk.

Do these studies mean that meat and full-fat dairy can be included in a health-promoting diet?

The answer is they most definitely can.

Whole milk is loaded with saturated fat and for many years has been considered a not particularly healthy drink. However, there is almost no scientific evidence that milk *or* dairy fat in usual amounts promote heart disease or obesity.

Prior to the days when lower fat milks were advised, a number of studies examined whether drinking milk was associated with cardiovascular disease and not a single study found this to be the case.[8]

But what about the obesity-promoting effects of whole milk? Because of its fat content and because fat contains more than twice as many calories per gram than carbohydrate or protein, whole milk is a calorically- dense food. If obesity was just a matter of calories, then whole milk should be quite a fattening food.

I was so intrigued by this assumption (since I suspected it was wrong) that I reviewed every scientific paper I could find that had examined the effect of milk on body weight in children and my findings were published in a scientific paper.[9]

I discovered that most investigators agree that drinking milk presents no risk for obesity, and in fact milk seems to be helpful in preventing excessive weight gain. But what about low-fat milk – is it better at controlling body weight than whole milk? The reality is that not a lot of research has been done on low-fat milk (since everyone assumes it must be helpful for weight control). But surprise – the studies that have been done invariably show that drinking low–fat milk in childhood is associated with *more* weight gain than whole milk![10]

Now a few studies like this do not prove that low-fat milk leads to excessive weight gain, since it may be that children who use low-fat milk are those most prone to gain too much weight, but they do indicate that low-fat milk is not helpful for weight control – and there is a lingering suspicion it may make matters worse.

How could this possibly be?

Unfortunately, the inappropriate campaign against dairy fat inadvertently encouraged people to turn to other types of drinks, such as sweetened soda and juices – drinks that do have an obesity promoting effect. Breakfasts and snacks containing no milk or low-fat milk may also be less filling than those containing whole milk. In turns out that the advice to use only low-fat milk may have been promoting obesity rather than preventing it!

Writing in the prestigious journal JAMA Pediatrics, two well-regarded nutrition experts, Ludwig and Willett, had the following comment to make about dairy fat:

> *"The recommendation to replace whole milk with reduced-fat milk lacks any evidence basis for weight management or cardiovascular disease prevention ..."*[11]

It turns out that the data linking dietary cholesterol to heart disease is also far from convincing. A high cholesterol intake, say from eating lots of eggs, can raise blood cholesterol levels slightly in some people (so called "hyper-responders"), but there is no evidence that this leads to an increase in heart disease. One analysis of 17 long-term studies found no association between egg consumption and risk for coronary disease and stroke.[12] The only exception was for diabetics, in whom a small increase in risk was evident. The relevance of this remains unclear.

Reflecting this knowledge, an article in a reputable medical journal had the following to say about eating eggs:

> *"The results of clinical trials, as well as epidemiological survey data, demonstrate that [egg] consumption has little relationship to hypercholesterolemia or coronary heart disease incidence. Recommendations that egg consumption be restricted by the general population are not supported by the experimental data, and ... limits a valuable and affordable source of high quality nutrition from the diet."*[13]

People with high cholesterol levels and those with diabetes may wish to be cautious about their daily egg intake, but for everybody else there is no reason at all to restrict eggs – although there is no reason to eat them to excess either.

What about meat - since red meat in particular can contain a substantial amount of saturated fat? Many people are careful about how much fatty red meat they eat since they assume it's unhealthy because of its saturated fat content. A large intake of red meat is indeed unhealthy, but it has nothing to do with how much saturated fat it contains. Eating a lot of red meat increases mortality from many diseases and this is related to the heme iron content of unprocessed red meat and the nitrites and nitrates in processed red meat.[14] Nitrates and nitrites are additives used in meat processing. This increased mortality from many diseases is due to oxidative stress.

This is not a reason to avoid red meat completely, but if you eat a lot of meat it is a reason to limit it. Many Americans eat far more red meat than they need to and should cut back to no more than a few days a week. Fish and poultry, on the other hand, have a protective influence, and these and vegetable protein should be eaten instead.

We can now summarize the main points raised in this section:

- There is no evidence that whole milk or full-fat dairy products increase risk for cardiovascular disease.
- Milk may have a protective effect against excessive weight gain and there are concerns that this protection may be lost using low-fat milk.
- Poultry is not an unhealthy food, but red meat is.
- Eating a moderate amount of eggs does not lead to cardiovascular disease, except perhaps in diabetics.

Because of all this new evidence, a committee of scientists was formed to advise the US Department of Agriculture and Department of Health and Human Services. This committee stated categorically that dietary cholesterol should no longer be considered a "nutrient of concern." It also stated that decreasing dietary fat does not lower cardiovascular disease risk.[15]

There is also no evidence that a healthy diet has to be low in fat. A low-fat diet may be lower in calories, but there is no evidence that it leads to better long-term weight control.

Admittedly, many Mediterranean diets are low in fat. Nevertheless, this is not invariably so. The Spanish Mediterranean diet contains significantly more fat than the Italian Mediterranean diet because of its high content of olive oil (about 40% of total energy versus <30%). Despite this, the Spanish Mediterranean diet has been shown to be an extremely healthy diet, probably because it uses a lot of olive oil and olive oil is loaded with healthful anti-oxidants.[16]

This does not mean, of course, that everyone should indulge in lots of cream, butter and ice cream. A high-fat diet is not a healthy diet. Plus, these foods contain a lot of calories. Everything needs to be in moderation.

When I first conceptualized the idea of blending together a Mediterranean diet with a Western-type diet containing animal-derived foods, I assumed I would have to design it from scratch – since such a diet exists nowhere in the world.

But I was wrong. It does exist – in a country on the Mediterranean coast called Israel.

## The Israeli Mediterranean Diet

I discovered the Israeli Mediterranean diet strolling through the Mahane Yehuda market, the famous fruit and vegetable market in Jerusalem, eating in friends' homes in Israel, eating at restaurants in Jerusalem, and looking at what people were eating as I walked past the numerous restaurants lining Jerusalem's streets.

Israelis eat a somewhat Western-style diet. They eat a fair amount of eggs. Red meat is not eaten as often as it is in America since it's expensive. Nevertheless, chicken and limited amounts of red meat are often part of Israeli meal planning. Israelis eat a significant amount of dairy in the form of milk, cheese, leben (soured milk products) and yogurt.

The diet of health-conscious Israelis is also very Mediterranean-like in that it contains lots of vegetables, fruits, nuts and spices. Many Israelis eat their meals in a very Mediterranean way with veggies and fruits mixed together with grains and meat. Fresh fruits are bought in season. Plates of vegetables are often served as hors d'oeuvres, and olive oil is used extensively for salad dressings and cooking, including for roasting vegetables.

Similar to the Spanish diet, the typical Israeli Mediterranean diet is not low in fat, since olive oil, dairy, eggs and poultry are not restricted. This provides a lot of potential for extremely tasty cooking.

Diets low in fat and containing only good-quality carbohydrate are often somewhat tasteless, since they lack creaminess, greasiness and sweetness – all the tastes that make food enjoyable! Because of this, a good quality low-fat diet can be difficult to adhere to over the long-term. However, tasteless food is not a problem at all with the Israeli Mediterranean diet since it is not a low-fat diet.

Statistics tell us this diet works. Heart disease is not the primary cause of death in Israel as it is in America. Israelis also have a high life expectancy compared to many other countries in the world. Obesity has crept into Israel as a result of adopting Western food habits such as drinking soda and eating highly refined snack foods and other refined starches but it is nowhere near the problem it is in America.

A good-quality Israeli Mediterranean diet is a wonderful model for how Mediterranean and Western culinary cultures can be blended together. As such, it is an ideal solution for you and your family. I am also convinced it is a very feasible solution to the nutritional problems of the United States and other Western countries.

## SUMMING UP

It's an incredible situation when one thinks about it. Countless people in the United States adopted low-fat meal planning on the assumption they would obtain health benefits from doing so. However, because of the large amount of poor-quality carbohydrate they were eating, they were actually worse off than if they hadn't bothered. A low-fat, high-carbohydrate diet containing a lot of sugar and highly refined carbohydrate promotes obesity, diabetes and heart disease – all the problems they were trying to avoid!

Clearly, people living in Western non-Mediterranean countries need to change their diets. Unfortunately, platitudes by the government and health experts that everyone should eat more veggies and fruits have not been overly successful. Many people in the United States are still on almost veggie-free diets. What families need is a program that tells them why they need to change, directs them on what they need to change, and provides enticing recipes on how to do it. This is what this cookbook is all about.

This book makes no claim that a healthy Israeli Mediterranean diet is a better diet than a traditional Mediterranean diet low in animal products. I cannot make this claim since there is no research data to support it. It is possible that a traditional Mediterranean diet has a slight health advantage over the diet described here, since it may contain more vegetables and whole grains.[17] However, what I am claiming is that since many animal products are not intrinsically unhealthy, any health disadvantage will be slight to non-existent provided other aspects of this diet are adhered to. This diet should also be more acceptable to Western cultures than a traditional Mediterranean diet since no radical changes in food preferences are needed.

The emphasis of the Mediterranean diet I am recommending is on carbohydrate quality:

- It uses vegetables, fruits, whole grains and beans as in the traditional Mediterranean diet.
- Soda and other sweetened drinks are very much discouraged.
- Highly-refined snack foods are discouraged.
- Olive oil is the preferred oil and its use is not restricted.
- Animal products such as eggs, meat and dairy are included in moderation, and red meat in limited amounts.

This diet will help alleviate many of the health problems afflicting Western nations, such as obesity, diabetes, hypertension and cardiovascular disease.

Nevertheless, many people have health problems that require special emphasis above and beyond the advice given in this chapter:

- In chapter 11, I probe why the American diet promotes obesity and how to reduce hunger and prevent excessive weight gain by increasing dietary fiber.

- I describe in chapter 12 a simple and effective method for losing weight based on cutting back or "regulating" carbohydrates.
- In chapter 13 I review why the Mediterranean diet is effective in preventing and treating heart disease, and discuss in greater detail the role of natural food-based anti-oxidants and healthy fats.
- I explain in chapter 14 why understanding the glycemia of carbohydrates can be helpful for people with type 2 and type 1 diabetes and borderline blood sugar abnormalities.

Let me end this chapter by saying that I practice what I preach. I admit it – I love eating! Mealtime for me is an important event. I enjoy quality foods – foods containing vegetables, fruits and grains – and I find Mediterranean-style cooking a wonderful way for combining these foods together. Living in Israel is a culinary delight for me since in-season fresh fruits and vegetables are so readily available. This is not to say these foods are unavailable in America, but in America there is no culture of eating them. I don't look for low-fat items, but I don't overdo the fat either. If my whole-wheat fruit-filled apple pie dessert calls for a topping of cream, I have no guilt feelings about putting cream on top. I drink whole milk. The Mediterranean-style dishes I eat contain liberal amounts of antioxidant-rich virgin olive oil. I also frequently drink a dry red wine with my main meal of the day. Not only does it add texture to the meal but it is also a wonderful source of helpful antioxidants.

Like many men my age, I need to be careful about how much food I eat; otherwise I put on belly fat. So I weigh myself every week or so and if the scale tells me to cut back, I eat less carbs – less desserts, less snacks and less starches. This way I bring my weight back into line. It always works for me. How to make this method work for you is discussed in chapter 12.

I am really fortunate to have a wife who loves cooking, and we both look for new and tasty dishes to add variety to our mealtimes. The results of our efforts are in this cookbook. Some of these recipes are Israeli, many are not; but they are all in a Mediterranean-style mode. By this I mean ethnic recipes that incorporate features of Mediterranean cooking, even though their origin is not necessarily from the Mediterranean basin.

This cookbook though is a lot more than just our favorite recipes. Working with obese families, I have come to appreciate that just telling families to eat more veggies, fruits and whole grains is insufficient. Many people have no idea where to start and are dubious that family members will follow through. I realized I had to provide models for these families for different mealtimes. This is how this cookbook came into being and why it is written in the way it is.

We truly hope you will appreciate these delicious and healthy recipes as much as we do.

Bon appetite!

# CHAPTER 11

# Prevent Excessive Weight Gain by Controlling Your Hunger

It seems obvious. You need to control your weight? So eat less food!

But the matter is not quite as simple as it might seem. There are two important steps in weight control and weight loss – not one. Certainly, you need to eat less food. But there is another equally important step and this is to *change the type of foods* that made you overweight in the first place. Without this change, weight control over the long term is going to be very difficult.

It was the parents of my obese patients who provided me the clue as to how obesity may progress, and this in turn led me to a new approach to weight control.

Time and again I kept hearing from the parents of my young patients that their overweight offspring were excessively hungry much of the time and insufficiently satisfied from the food they were eating. Shortly after finishing a meal they were requesting seconds and the parents were in a constant struggle to restrain them from overeating.

I was so intrigued by what they were telling me that I decided to do a survey to find out how common this phenomenon was. My suspicions were confirmed. It was extremely common! In a scientific paper I wrote based on this survey, I reported that 62% of my young, obese patients admitted to being "always" or "often abnormally hungry" compared to just 21% of my normal-weight patients.[1]

This was only a small survey in one pediatric endocrine practice in Pennsylvania, but I am convinced that this is a widespread problem and that many overweight people in this country have a problem with increased hunger.

Having gained this insight, I was intrigued to see how everything fits together.

It explains why so many people in this country, and much of the world for that matter, are becoming fat. The food they are eating is failing to control their hunger adequately.

It explains why obesity has become such an intractable problem for so many people. Their hunger is not a "behavioral" or "educational" problem – but a physiological one – and abnormal physiological urges are not easily resolved with counseling about how much food they should be eating.

It explains why *portion control,* i.e. eating appropriate portion sizes, has become a buzzword in this country. But why should so many people in America need *training* on how to eat appropriate portion sizes? How bizarre. It never used to be like this. People knew instinctively how much to eat! Something has happened in this country – and this is likely increased hunger.

It explains why sugar-containing drinks are a leading cause of obesity. If you drink a lot of sweetened soda, the chances are high you will gain too much weight.[2] Unlike solid foods which increase satiety from one meal to the next, sugar-containing drinks, such as soft drinks, many fruit juices, power drinks, sugared iced tea and beer, have a limited effect on satisfying hunger. This means you can drink x number of calories from a sugar-containing drink and as far as the body's hunger mechanisms are concerned, it's almost as if you drank water. A typical 8 oz. can of regular soda contains between 120 to 170 calories, so that whenever you drink a can of soda you are adding close to an *extra* 120 to 170 calories to your diet *above* your usual caloric intake. Drink a few cans of soda every day and this adds up to a lot of extra calories.

It also explains why low-fat diets have such a poor track record over the long-term. Low-fat diets can work well over the short-term, but over time their effectiveness wanes. This is because low-fat diets are also high-carbohydrate diets, and if that extra carbohydrate is poor quality carbohydrate it can lead to increased hunger.

I was coming to a new understanding. If I wanted to help my patients keep their weight under control for more than just a few weeks, I had to help them control their hunger.

Focusing on abnormal hunger is a new and exciting paradigm for understanding why obesity occurs and how it should be treated. Not everyone with a weight problem has a problem with excessive hunger, but it is an important problem for a lot of people and it invariably accounts for failure of weight loss efforts in unsuccessful dieters.

Your nutrition counselor may well have told you that only one thing is important in weight control – how many calories you eat. But this is incorrect. It is also important that your hunger is well controlled from one meal to the next. If you are insufficiently satisfied from your meals or feel hungry before your next meal is due you are setting yourself up for extra snacking, difficulty in controlling your weight and unsuccessful weight loss efforts.

**Hence, the first important snippet of this chapter – if you have a weight problem, change your diet to one that will decrease your hunger.**

But how do you do this?

The rest of this chapter will explain how.

## Understanding hunger

There are two aspects to hunger – *satiation* and *satiety*. Satiation is the feeling of fullness after eating a meal. If satiation is inadequate, you will soon be requesting seconds because you are insufficiently satisfied from the meal you have just eaten. Satiety describes how long you can last from one meal to the next. If your satiety is abnormal, you will begin feeling hungry before the next meal or snack is due and when it does arrive you may well overeat because you are so ravenous.

Hunger is controlled by hormones made in the upper part of the gut. These hormones are secreted in response to food and they inform specialized centers in the brain that enough food has been eaten and no more is needed for a while. Many of these satiety hormones are inappropriately low in obesity and controlling your body weight would be a lot easier if their levels were to increase.

The release of gut satiety hormones is influenced by the breakdown products of the protein and fat you have just eaten. This is why meals containing a lot of protein or fat have an appetite suppressing effect. Satiety hormones are also secreted in response to carbohydrate breakdown products. However, the lining of the gut only possesses the enzymatic apparatus for breaking down sugars and highly refined carbohydrate and their breakdown products have only a limited influence on satiety.

This is where gut bacteria come in. Even the most hygienic person has trillions of bacteria in his or her gut. Much of our stool, for example, consists of mashed up bacteria. One of the functions of these bacteria is to break down what would otherwise be indigestible complex carbohydrates, and their decomposition products are very effective at stimulating satiety hormones and thereby influencing satiety.[3]

If you eat mainly refined carbohydrate, most of it will be absorbed in the upper part of the gut and the satiety effect from this food will be limited. However, if you eat more natural complex carbohydrate, say from veggies and whole grains, then some of this carbohydrate will get broken down by bacteria in the lower part of the bowel, the type of bacteria in your gut will change to bacteria more favorable to health, the amount of satiety gut hormones secreted by the gut will increase, and the food you eat will produce more satiety and less hunger.

And this entire process is related to the amount of fiber in your diet.[4]

## More about dietary fiber

Fiber is part of the cell walls of plants and is found in large amounts in whole grains, vegetables, fruits and beans. How full or *satiated* you feel from a meal is very much related to the volume and bulk of that meal; and fiber provides some of this bulk. The amount of fiber in one's diet also influences how long you can last out from one meal to the next, i.e. your *satiety*.

Eat more fiber-containing foods and you will soon notice that you feel less hungry between meals – although the full effect of eating fiber-containing foods occurs when the microbes in your gut have changed to ones that cope better with the healthier foods you are now eating and this may take a while.

Fiber also has other beneficial effects besides its effect on hunger. High-fiber meals keep blood sugars lower. High-fiber diets are also associated with less heart disease and a lower incidence of insulin resistance and the metabolic syndrome.[5] The metabolic syndrome is a cluster of biochemical and physiological abnormalities associated with an increased risk for cardiovascular disease, type 2 diabetes and stroke.

It all fits together. Americans are eating more sugars and highly refined carbohydrates than in the past and because of this their diets are not as filling. They are therefore eating more. Part of the blame for this must surely go to the health experts who told us that to prevent obesity all we had to do was to eat less fat. But low-fat diets are high-carbohydrate diets, and if the carbohydrate replacement is high in sugars and highly refined carbohydrate and low in dietary fiber, this provides poor satiation and satiety and promotes overeating. Of course, physical activity is also important for weight control and health, but bad nutrition has been the primary driving force for much of our current obesity epidemic.

Mediterranean diets are high in fiber, low in glycemia and low in sugar-containing drinks and this diet alone will prevent much of the population from gaining excessive weight.

However, people living in Western countries are in a very obesity-promoting environment and if you or family members are gaining weight excessively, or are already overweight and need to lose some, then a Mediterranean diet may not be quite enough. More attention needs to be paid to hunger – and this means eating more fiber.

Eating more fiber does not automatically lead to weight loss – although it often does. However, it is an essential first step in preventing excessive weight gain, making weight loss easier, and making sure that any of that weight loss is not regained.

How much fiber should you eat? A common recommendation is 25 g a day for children and about 30 g a day for adults. 25 g of fiber is equivalent to 2 fruits, 3 veggies, 4 slices of whole-wheat bread, 1 cup of brown rice, ½ cup of legumes and ½ cup of granola or bran flakes. This may sound like a lot of veggies and whole grains and may be difficult for some families. But it *is* achievable and is a useful target to aim for. However, in the final analysis, *any* increase in fiber above the average for a Western diet (which is about 15 g a day in the US) is worth striving for.

The rest of this chapter will tell you how to do this.

## Eat the right type of bread!

Bread is a major component of many people's diets and it is important that the bread you buy for your family is not only tasty but filling. Whole grain bread contains a significant amount of fiber and is more filling than white bread.

A typical cereal grain consists of three parts – the germ that provides nourishment for the seed, the endosperm that provides the seed with energy for growth, and bran that forms its outer protective shell (see the diagram below). Most of the fiber from grain comes from the bran. White flour is made from grain in which the bran has been removed by milling, whereas in whole-wheat flour the bran is left intact. This is why whole-wheat flour contains a lot more fiber than white flour (see table 1).

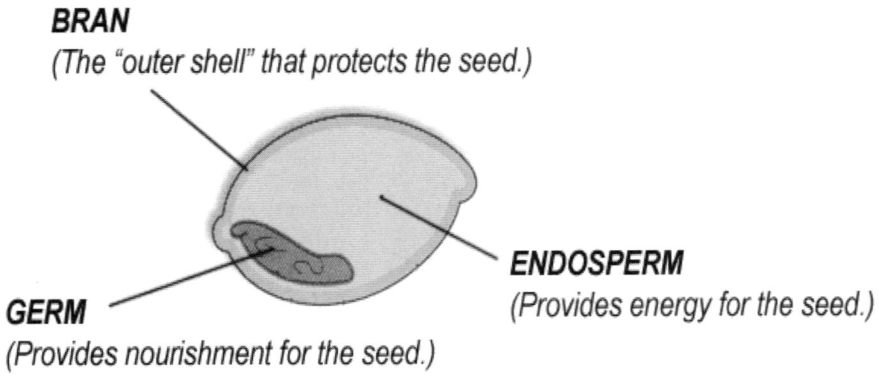

**BRAN**
*(The "outer shell" that protects the seed.)*

**ENDOSPERM**
*(Provides energy for the seed.)*

**GERM**
*(Provides nourishment for the seed.)*

Whenever a food manufacturer uses the term "*whole-wheat*" it is obliged to be very precise and "whole-wheat" bread must contain 100% whole-wheat flour. The legal definition of a "*whole grain*" product is less precise and depends on the country in which the food is bought, but is usually at least 8 g of whole grain for 30 g of food product. The bottom line is that foods labeled "whole-wheat" and "whole grain" can usually be relied upon to contain a significant amount of fiber.

Note, though, that breads and starches containing a lot of *intact seeds* are even better at controlling hunger than whole-wheat breads.[6]

This is where the terminology can get a bit confusing, so follow along with me. Breads containing different types of grains are often called "*multigrain breads*." Unfortunately, the term multigrain is used rather freely in the food industry. These "multiple" grains do not have to be whole grain or even intact seeds, so that the term multigrain may mean no more than that the bread contains different grains. Such bread offers no special health benefits.

It gets even more confusing than this. If a baker puts a lot of intact seeds into dough containing only whole-wheat flour, the bread may not rise well for baking and the baker may need to add white flour to the mixture. Because the dough now contains white flour, the bread no longer meets the definition of "whole-wheat." Nevertheless, provided there are lots of intact seeds in the bread

and it contains a reasonable amount of whole-wheat flour, this type of multigrain bread may be an excellent choice, even if it is not labeled as a whole grain product.

The bottom line is that you need to be a careful consumer with respect to multigrain breads, since this type of bread varies a lot in how much whole grain flour and fiber it contains. So read the label carefully and make sure it contains plenty of fiber. We will meet the same problem with multigrain breakfast cereals and many of these also provide no special health benefits.

The following table shows the fiber content of some typical breads and flour. This and the following tables are not meant to endorse any particular brands and the brand names are for illustration only. Constituents also change and you should check the brand website to be sure the information of interest to you is accurate and up-to-date before making any changes to your diet.

**Table 1. The nutritional content of typical breads and flour**

**Breads:**

| Type of bread | Manufacturer | Amount | Calories | Sugars (g) | Carbohydrate (g) | Fiber (g) | % Fiber |
|---|---|---|---|---|---|---|---|
| **High Fiber** | | | | | | | |
| 100% multigrain bread | Sarah Lee | 1 slice | 45 | 1 | 9.5 | 2.5 | 26.3 |
| 100% whole wheat natural whole grain | Pepperidge Farm | 1 slice | 100 | 3 | 20 | 4 | 25 |
| 15 grain whole grain bread | Pepperidge Farm | 1 slice | 100 | 3 | 20 | 4 | 25 |
| 100% Whole Wheat | Wonder | 1 slice | 80 | 3 | 12.5 | 2 | 16 |
| 100% whole wheat bread | Sarah Lee | 1 slice | 60 | 1 | 10 | 1.5 | 15.6 |
| 100% whole wheat bread | Natures Pride | 1 slice | 110 | 4 | 21 | 3 | 14 |
| **Low Fiber** | | | | | | | |
| Jewish Rye Real Seeded | Arnold | 1 slice | 80 | 1 | 15 | 1 | 6.5 |
| Enriched White bread | Wonder | 1 slice | 50 | 1.5 | 10 | 0.5 | 5 |
| Hearty White Farmhouse bread | Pepperidge Farm | 1 slice | 110 | 4 | 22 | 1.0 | 4.5 |

**Flour:**

| Type of flour | Manufacturer | Amount | Calories | Sugar (g) | Carbohydrate (g) | Fiber (g) | % Fiber |
|---|---|---|---|---|---|---|---|
| **High Fiber** | | | | | | | |
| Wheat Bran | Arrowhead Mills | 1 cup | 182 | 0 | 30 | 18 | 60 |
| Whole wheat flour | | 1 cup | 400 | 0 | 88 | 16 | 18 |
| Oat bran flour | Hodgson | 1 cup | 440 | 0 | 92 | 12 | 13 |
| **Low Fiber** | | | | | | | |
| White flour (All Purpose) | | 1 cup | 455 | 0 | 95 | 3 | 3 |

To understand these tables, look first at the column labeled "Fiber (g)". This is the amount of fiber contained within a serving size (which is in the "Amount" column). There is obviously a big difference between the 2 to 4 g of fiber in a slice of whole-wheat bread compared to 0.5 g of fiber in a slice of white bread.

Now look again at Table 1 and you will see a column on the far-right labeled "% Fiber". This is also a helpful column since it tells you what percentage of the carbohydrate in the food is fiber, since fiber is also a carbohydrate. This column is useful for comparing the fiber content of foods when the only information available to you is from different serving sizes, for example comparing a thick versus a thin slice of bread.

You can calculate the % fiber yourself for any food from its food label. Take the fiber content in grams for the serving size listed on the label, divide this figure by how much carbohydrate it contains in grams and then multiply the result by 100. This is the "% fiber".

**To increase your fiber intake, choose a high-fiber bread in which at least 10% of the carbohydrate is fiber.**

## Choose the Right Type of Breakfast and Breakfast Cereal!

Starting the day with a fiber-rich breakfast cereal is an excellent way to control hunger, since its favorable influence on hunger can last the entire morning and even beyond into the early afternoon.

An interesting study performed in Boston tells us why it is so important to eat good quality breakfasts and good quality snacks.[7] Adolescent volunteers for this study were fed three types of breakfasts and lunches – low-glycemic, intermediate-glycemic and high-glycemic. An explanation of carbohydrate glycemia was provided in chapter 10, but in brief it is the extent to which a carbohydrate leads to higher or lower post-meal blood sugars.

These researchers found that adolescents who ate high-glycemic meals felt hungrier and ate significantly more food later on in the day than those who ate the low-glycemic meals. The intermediate-glycemic meals had an effect somewhere in between.

This Boston study demonstrates well that what you eat at mealtime substantially impacts how hungry you feel afterwards. Eat a high-glycemic breakfast and it is likely you will be hungrier at lunchtime. This will lead you to grab the nearest high-glycemic food available – which of course will make you hungrier later on. In this way, a hunger cycle is perpetuated day after day.[8] Foods that are low-glycemic usually, although not always, contain more fiber. Most high fiber foods are also low-glycemic.

Many popular breakfast cereals are high-glycemic and low in whole grains and fiber and when eaten alone for breakfast or eaten as snacks are likely to predispose to increased hunger later on in the day. Rice Krispies, for example, contains almost no fiber. It is worthwhile, therefore, putting effort into finding high-fiber breakfast cereals that you and your family will enjoy.

Table 2 below compares some typical breakfast cereals. The nutritional information has been calculated in terms of 1 cup, although this may not be the portion size listed on the cereal box. This table also has a % fiber column, so you can see which cereals have the greatest amount of fiber relative to their starch and sugar content.

**Aim for a high-fiber breakfast cereal with a "% fiber" content of 15% or more.**

**Table 2. Nutritional information for some high and low-fiber breakfast cereals (without milk)**

| Cereal | Manufacturer | Amount | Calories | Sugars (g) | Carbs (g) | Fiber (g) | % Fiber |
|---|---|---|---|---|---|---|---|
| **Higher in fiber relative to total carbohydrate content** | | | | | | | |
| Fiber One | General Mills | 1 cup | 120 | 0 | 50 | 28 | 56 |
| All Bran | Kellogg's | 1 cup | 160 | 12 | 46 | 20 | 43 |
| Bran Flakes | Post | 1 cup | 133 | 6.5 | 32 | 6.5 | 20.5 |
| Honey Sunshine | Kashi | 1 cup | 133 | 8 | 33 | 6.5 | 20 |
| Raisin Bran | Kellogg's | 1 cup | 190 | 18 | 46 | 7 | 15 |

| CEREAL | MANUFACTURER | AMOUNT | CALORIES | SUGARS (g) | CARBS (g) | FIBER (g) | % FIBER |
|---|---|---|---|---|---|---|---|
| **Moderate in fiber relative to total carbohydrate content** | | | | | | | |
| Total Whole Grain | General Mills | 1 cup | 133 | 7 | 29 | 4 | 14 |
| Cheerios | General Mills | 1 cup | 103 | 1 | 21 | 3 | 14 |
| Wheat Chex | General Mills | 1 cup | 108 | 3 | 24 | 3 | 12.5 |
| Wheaties | General Mills | 1 cup | 110 | 4 | 24 | 3 | 12.5 |
| Fruit Loops | Kellogg's | 1 cup | 110 | 10 | 25 | 3 | 12 |
| Instant Oatmeal | Quaker | 1 packet | 128 | 9 | 27 | 3 | 11 |
| Kix | General Mills | 1 cup | 88 | 2 | 20 | 2 | 10 |
| **Lower in fiber relative to total carbohydrate content** | | | | | | | |
| Cocoa Puffs | General Mills | 1 cup | 133 | 13 | 30.5 | 2.5 | 8.5 |
| Life Cereal Original | Quaker | 1 cup | 160 | 8 | 33 | 2.5 | 8 |
| Puffed wheat | Quaker | 1 cup | 50 | 0 | 22 | 1 | 4.5 |
| Corn flakes | | 1 cup | 101 | 3 | 24 | 1 | 4 |
| Rice Krispies | Rice Krispies | 1 cup | 108 | 3 | 24 | 0 | 0 |
| Kellogg's Special K | Kellogg's | 1 cup | 120 | 4 | 23 | 0 | 0 |

OK, so you are not over-thrilled with the high-fiber cereals in this list. Is there any way to make these fiber-rich cereals more appetizing?

There certainly is!

- Add fruits such as apple or pear slices, or berries such as strawberries, blueberries or raspberries to your cereal. You will be surprised at what a difference it makes. You will also be adding more fiber!
- Consider adding a small amount of a high-fiber breakfast cereal, such as Fiber One, All Bran or Bran Flakes, to your child's usual breakfast cereal so that he or she gets accustomed to a high-fiber cereal and the transition thereby becomes easier.

An egg for breakfast can also be helpful in controlling subsequent hunger, since this also is a filling food.

But what about its cholesterol? Suffice to say, that the harmful effects of eggs have been considerably overplayed and chapter 10 discusses that there is no evidence that eggs promote cardiovascular disease. For this reason, a moderate amount of eggs can be safely included in Mediterranean meal planning.

Whole milk also provides satiety and is a tasty and healthful addition to breakfast. A number of studies in adults and children have shown that dairy can be helpful in weight control.[9] The experts are still debating why this is so. Milk may influence satiety because of its protein content.[10] Another possibility is that dairy products favorably influence the type of bacteria that live in one's gut.[11] Fermented milk products such as yogurt may be particularly helpful in this respect and should be included in a weight control diet.

All children and adolescents should drink at least 2 cups of milk a day for the following reasons (the recommendations for adults are more controversial):

- Milk is a good source of the calcium needed for bone health.
- All milk sold in the US is fortified with vitamin D. Everyone needs vitamin D in order to absorb calcium from his or her diet. Much of our vitamin D comes from sunlight exposure, but in winter especially this may be limited. A high percentage of the US population has suboptimal levels of vitamin D and this is particularly so in the overweight. Note that yogurt is an excellent source of calcium but is rarely fortified with vitamin D.

The following is a helpful way to add both dairy and fiber to your breakfast:

- To a small container of full-fat yogurt add fruits such as grapes and pears and sprinkle granola on top. The combination is delicious.

From a consideration of calories alone, skipping breakfast sounds like a non-fail way for controlling one's weight. However, studies have shown that people who skip breakfast gain *more* weight than those who eat breakfast.[12] How could this be? One possibility is that non-breakfast eaters soon become hungry and this leads to snacking and inappropriate food choices later on in the day.

**So, avoid skipping breakfast. It encourages weight gain and is a bad idea.**

## EAT ONLY FIBER-RICH SNACKS!

If you have a weight problem, cutting out low-fiber, highly refined snack foods is a must. Snacks are meant to curb hunger, but this type of snack does a poor job at doing this. As mentioned above, high-glycemic foods, and this includes many manufactured snack foods, lead to hunger later on in the day. Many popular snack foods also contain lots of sugar and calories. These types of snacks should be cut out entirely.

Many kids are left to their own devices when it comes to snacks, but this is a mistake since many popular snack foods contain nothing but poor-quality carbohydrate.

**If a family member has an obesity problem, look particularly at the snacks he or she is eating and make sure they eat only high-fiber snack foods.**

If you are able to, it's a good idea to make your own snacks for your family, since you can then control how much sugar and fiber they are eating. Check out the chapter "Healthy snacks" in the recipe section of this cookbook for helpful ideas on preparing family snacks.

**Table 3. The nutritional content of some high and low-fiber snack foods**

| SNACK FOOD | MANUFACTURER | AMOUNT | CALORIES | SUGARS (g) | CARBS (g) | FIBER (g) | % FIBER |
|---|---|---|---|---|---|---|---|
| **High Fiber** | | | | | | | |
| FiberPlus Anti-oxidants Protein Bar Peanut | Kellogg's | 1 granola bar | 170 | 9 | 18 | 7 | 39 |
| Chewy Bars Oats and Chocolate | Fiber One | 1 granola bar | 140 | 10 | 29 | 9 | 31 |
| **Moderate Fiber** | | | | | | | |
| Trail Mix Chewy Granola Bars | Kashi | 1 granola bar | 140 | 6 | 20 | 4 | 20 |
| Original 7 Grain | Kashi | 15 crackers | 120 | 4 | 19 | 3 | 16 |
| Triscuit Baked Whole Grain Wheat Original | Nabisco | 6 crackers | 120 | 0 | 20 | 3 | 15 |
| **Low Fiber** | | | | | | | |
| Chewy Granola Bars – Peanut Butter Chocolate Chip | Quaker Oats | 1 granola bar | 100 | 7 | 17 | 1 | 8 |
| Honey Whole Wheat Pretzel Stick | Trader Joe's | 10 sticks | 110 | 3 | 24 | 1 | 4 |
| Honey Wheat Braided Twists | Rold Gold | 8 pretzels | 110 | 3 | 23 | 1 | 4 |
| Ritz Crackers | Nabisco | 5 crackers | 79 | 1 | 10 | 0 | 0 |

Here are some ideas for fiber-rich snacks that you and your family may find useful:

- Bake bran muffins for your family. The bran muffin recipes in this cookbook contain a significant amount of fiber and are very filling. They are also extremely tasty!
- Prepare a container of nuts and raisins. As you can see from table 4, nuts are rich in fiber.

Table 4. The nutritional content of nuts

| Type of nut | Amount | Calories | Sugars (g) | Carbohydrate (g) | Fiber (g) | % Fiber |
|---|---|---|---|---|---|---|
| **High Fiber** | | | | | | |
| Pecan halves (raw) | 1 cup | 684 | 4 | 14 | 10 | 69 |
| Almonds (slivered) | 1 cup | 621 | 4 | 23 | 13 | 56 |
| Walnuts (pieces) | 1 cup | 785 | 3 | 17 | 8 | 49 |
| Peanuts (raw) | 1 cup | 828 | 8 | 24 | 12 | 47 |

## Don't skimp on vegetables!

From the "% fiber" column in Table 5 it can be seen that vegetables are usually rich in fiber – and many are extremely rich. They may also contain antioxidants and this helps keep cardiovascular disease at bay. Unfortunately, many children, and even families, have given up on non-starchy vegetables. This is a big mistake and parents should make sure this does not happen.

**Aim for *at least* four vegetable portions a day.**

Table 5. The nutritional content of vegetables

| Type of vegetable | Amount | Calories | Sugars (g) | Carbohydrate (g) | Fiber (g) | % Fiber |
|---|---|---|---|---|---|---|
| **High Fiber** | | | | | | |
| Broccoli (boiled) | 1 medium stalk | 50 | 3 | 9 | 6 | 65 |
| Spinach (boiled) | 1 cup | 41 | < 1 | 7 | 4 | 63 |
| Celery (raw and chopped) | 1 cup | 16 | 2 | 3 | 2 | 53 |
| Snap beans raw | 1 cup | 34 | 2 | 8 | 4 | 48 |
| Brussel sprouts (raw) | 1 cup | 38 | 2 | 8 | 3 | 42 |
| Cauliflower (raw) | 1 medium head | 144 | 11 | 29 | 12 | 40 |
| Carrot (boiled) | 1 carrot | 16 | 2 | 4 | 1 | 36 |
| Green peas (boiled) | 1 cup | 134 | 10 | 3 | 9 | 35 |
| Cucumber | 1 medium peeled | 24 | 3 | 4 | 1 | 32 |
| Tomato | 1 large raw | 33 | 5 | 7 | 2 | 30 |
| Lettuce | 1 head | 49 | 1 | 7 | 3 | 25 |
| **Moderate Fiber** | | | | | | |
| Corn on the cob (frozen) | 1 ear | 123 | 5 | 29 | 4 | 12 |
| Sweet potato (boiled without skin) | 1 medium | 115 | 9 | 27 | 4 | 14 |
| Potato (flesh plus skin) baked | 1 medium | 154 | 3 | 34 | 3 | 9 |
| Potato (flesh) boiled | 1 medium | 144 | 1 | 33 | 3 | 9 |

**For controlling weight and keeping chronic diseases at bay, adding vegetables to your family's meal plans is a must.**

The following vegetables are high in fiber and can make a useful addition to family meal planning:

- Avocados (10-13 g per avocado)
- Sweet potatoes (5.9 g per cup)
- Artichoke (10.3 g per artichoke)
- Sweet corn (4.3 g per cup)

But how does one persuade family members to eat more vegetables, especially those who have gotten used to a veggie-free diet?

I am always reminding veggie-deprived families that vegetables have to be presented in an attractive way to encourage family members to eat them. A dollop of broccoli or cabbage on a plate is not going to do it. However, cooking Mediterranean style is an excellent way for turning the situation round. In Mediterranean-style cooking, vegetables are combined with meat, fowl, grains and other vegetables to make wonderfully appetizing combinations (see "Eating Mediterranean-style" in the recipe section).

Remember, also, that there are other ways to cook vegetables besides boiling them – roasting vegetables with olive oil in the oven, for example. For other ideas, turn to "Jazzing up Vegetables" in the recipe section.

## MAKE YOUR MEALS MORE FILLING!

Many commonly eaten starches are not particularly high in fiber (see Table 6). White rice, for example, contains almost none. This may be one reason so many people feel like snacking only a few hours after eating a large meal.

**Table 6. The nutritional content of some starches**

| TYPE OF VEGETABLE | AMOUNT | CALORIES | SUGARS (g) | CARBOHYDRATE (g) | FIBER (g) | % FIBER |
|---|---|---|---|---|---|---|
| High Fiber | | | | | | |
| Whole wheat pasta spaghetti | 1 cup | 174 | 1 | 37 | 6 | 17 |
| Medium Fiber | | | | | | |
| Mashed potato (with whole milk or butter) | 1 cup | 237 | 3 | 35 | 3 | 8.5 |
| Brown rice (cooked) | 1 cup | 218 | | 46 | 4 | 8 |
| Pasta spaghetti (cooked) | 1 cup | 220 | < 1 | 43 | 3 | 6 |
| Low Fiber | | | | | | |
| White rice (cooked) | 1 cup | 205 | < 1 | 45 | 0 | < 1 |

Here are some hints for increasing the fiber content of your main starches:

- Change from regular to whole-wheat pasta. As you can see from Table 5, whole-wheat pasta contains twice as much fiber as regular pasta. Admittedly, it may be an effort to persuade your family to change from regular to whole-wheat pasta since whole-wheat pasta has its own distinctive taste. However, you will find whole-wheat pasta recipes in the recipe section of this cookbook in which the taste of the whole-wheat pasta is hidden by other ingredients in the recipe. Newer brands of pasta are also becoming available in supermarkets that are a blend of whole-wheat and white pasta but that taste like white pasta. Using this type of pasta can be a useful way for making a gradual changeover to whole-wheat pasta.
- Switch from white to brown rice. Brown rice contains a significant amount of fiber, whereas white rice contains almost none.
- Try out unusual starches such as quinoa. You will need good recipes to get you started and the section in this cookbook entitled "Experimenting with Grains" is tailor-made for you.

Is there anything else that can be done to increase the fiber content of your starch dishes? There most certainly is – Mediterranean-style meal planning! By this I mean adding vegetables, nuts, beans, and fruits to your starch dishes.

Tables 4 and 7 show that nuts and beans are excellent sources of fiber.

**Table 7. The nutritional content of beans**

| Type of bean | Amount | Calories | Sugars (g) | Carbohydrate (g) | Fiber (g) | % Fiber |
|---|---|---|---|---|---|---|
| **High Fiber** | | | | | | |
| White beans (boiled) | 1 cup | 254 | | 46 | 19 | 40 |
| Red kidney beans (boiled) | 1 cup | 218 | < 1 | 38 | 17 | 43 |
| Chickpeas (boiled) | 1 cup | 269 | 8 | 45 | 13 | 28 |
| Black beans (boiled) | 1 cup | 241 | < 1 | 45 | 10 | 22 |
| Baked beans (canned) | 1 cup | 239 | 23 | 54 | 10 | 19 |

## Start your meal with a soup!

Thick liquids add volume and bulk to your meals, and starting a meal with a soup, especially a chunky or thick soup, is an excellent way for feeling more satiated after eating.

I have noticed that few families these days begin their meal with a soup course. Starting a meal with a soup, preferably a home-made one, can be very helpful for controlling excessive hunger, especially for family members who are always requesting seconds or who feel like snacking almost as soon as they have finished their main meal. I did not make this up – it has been shown in scientific studies.[13] Soups also make filling snacks. For dealing with a confirmed veggie-hater in your family, preparing soups is also an excellent way for starting a veggie campaign.

**Hint: Make a big pot of chunky vegetable soup at the beginning of the week for your family and encourage everyone to help themselves for seconds and snacking.**

## Don't forget fruits and berries:

Many fruits and berries are excellent sources of fiber.

**Snippet – aim for three portions a day of fruits or berries.**

**Table 8. The nutritional content of fruits**

| | Amount | Calories | Sugars (g) | Carbohydrate (g) | Fiber (g) | % Fiber |
|---|---|---|---|---|---|---|
| **High Fiber** | | | | | | |
| Orange | 1 fruit | 62 | 12 | 15 | 3 | 21 |
| Pear (raw) | 1 medium | 96 | 16 | 26 | 5 | 20 |
| Apple (with skin) | 1 medium | 72 | 14 | 19 | 3 | 17 |
| Banana (raw) | 1 medium | 105 | 14 | 27 | 3 | 12 |
| Plum | 1 fruit | 30. | 7 | 9 | < 1 | 11 |
| Raisins seeded (Dole) | 1 cup | 520 | 116 | 124 | 8 | 7 |
| Water melon | 1 cup diced | 46 | 9 | 12 | < 1 | 5 |
| Grapes (seedless) | 1 cup | 106 | 24 | 28 | 1 | 5 |

**Table 9. The nutritional content of berries**

| | Amount | Calories | Sugars (g) | Carbohydrate (g) | Fiber (g) | % Fiber |
|---|---|---|---|---|---|---|
| **High Fiber** | | | | | | |
| Blackberries (raw) | 1 cup | 62 | 7 | 14 | 8 | 55 |
| Raspberries (raw) | 1 cup | 64. | 5 | 15 | 8 | 54 |
| Strawberries (whole) | 1 cup | 47 | 7 | 11 | 3 | 26 |
| Blueberries (raw) | 1 cup | 83 | 14 | 21 | 4 | 17 |

Much of the fiber in a fruit is in its peel, so if possible try not to peel it. An apple with its peel, for example, contains 4.4 gram of fiber, but without only 2.1 gram. A fruit peel with a bright color may also be high in anti-oxidants. Pulp-free fruit juices are poor sources of fiber, since it is the pulp that contains the fiber.

What else can you do if your family is not keen on eating fruits? Here are some suggestions:

- Make homemade fruit-salads with fruits and nuts.
- Let the kids cut up and arrange pieces of fruit for an attractive fruit plate. The greater their involvement with a meal the more likely they are to eat it.
- Put berries and pieces of fruit on your breakfast cereal or on top of unsweetened plain yogurt.
- Search for exotic fruit such as mangoes, kiwis and pineapple and serve them for dessert.
- Make salads that contain a mixture of vegetables and fruits (see "Classy Cold Salads" in the recipe section.
- Make a smoothie from blended fruit (see the Strawberry Banana Smoothie recipe in "Breakfast – an Essential Meal" recipe section, and A Tropical Smoothie in the "Snacking to Health!" recipe section)

## What about fiber from a bottle?

The suggestions described up to now are not the only way for increasing your fiber intake. You can buy it in a bottle and it works just as well. For example, take one tablespoon of Metamucil with a large glass of water or a chewable fiber tablet half an hour before a meal. Metamucil is made from the husk of a seed and has a fiber content 14 times that of oatmeal.

If these products contain so much fiber, why did I leave this information to the end??

There are several reasons. Firstly, eating quality food is more enjoyable than gulping down a glass of fiber. Secondly, it is far preferable to make changes in the foods you eat and to get accustomed to these changes rather than to drown poor-quality food with a glass of a fiber supplement. Thirdly, fiber supplements may not be as health promoting as whole grains and vegetables as they may not contain as much anti-oxidant. Nevertheless, if you feel that adding a fiber supplement is the only way for controlling your hunger, try it. In general, liquid preparations work better than a tablet.

## What about diet drinks?

I am often asked this question – what about diet drinks? Diet drinks contain zero calories and should therefore lead to zero weight gain. However, the reality is more complicated than this. Studies have compared people who drink diet drinks with those who do not and they invariably find that the diet drinkers gain more weight! No one knows why this is so. It may be that individuals who drink diet drinks are those most liable to gain weight. However, it cannot be totally excluded that diet drinks in some way promote obesity. One possible reason is that sugar craving may be an acquired sensation and diet products do nothing to dampen that craving.

A new study provides yet another reason why diet drinks are not the best of choices. This study found that experimental animals and adults who drink diet drinks experience a change in their bowel bacterial flora and this change is associated with higher blood sugars, although not to the point of diabetes.[14]

In sum, the data regarding diet drinks is not reassuring. There is no evidence that they help control excessive weight gain and there is a bit of evidence that they may be deleterious to health, although this needs further study.

But what else is there to drink if diet drinks and sugar-containing drinks are to be avoided? The answer is to get used to other options such as water, milk, coffee and tea (with a minimum of sugar), and flavored water and seltzers. For those who find it hard to survive without carbonated drinks, adding a small drop of fruit juice to seltzer for flavoring can be a satisfying option.

## Is physical activity helpful?

Contrary to what many people believe, increasing physical activity is not a very effective way for melting away lots of body fat, unless one engages in marathon-like activities. This is because the extra calories burned off by occasional physical activity is quite small relative to the amount of calories used each day for normal living – to keep the heart pumping and the lungs breathing.

However, there is more to it than this. Regular physical activity decreases fat within the abdominal cavity and this is the fat most responsible for many of the adverse effects of obesity. Physical activity also makes weight loss efforts that much easier. The bottom line is that exercise is extremely beneficial for health.

However, as for changing one's diet, increasing physical activity needs thought and perseverance. Buying an exercise bike to hang clothes on or to gather dust provides no benefit to health. For a family with an obese child, going out with him or her on family walks and arranging other physically active family activities should be high on a weekly list of things to do.

For an overweight adult, arranging an exercise program at work can be very effective, since work is such a large chunk of one's day. This can include walking up the stairs to one's office rather than taking the elevator, arranging with colleagues to have an exercise machine for communal use, and going for a jog during the lunch break. You will be surprised at how many of your coworkers will want to join you for a lunch time jog once you announce your intentions and how mentally refreshing such a break can be.

**Increasing physical activity is extremely important for health and for reducing your risk of heart disease, diabetes and obesity.**

## Slow down how fast you eat!

Many people with obesity eat faster than normal. No one knows for sure why this is so, but it could be due to increased hunger. In my research study of obese children, I found a very strong relationship between hunger and speed of eating.[1] Hungry children are anxious to get at food and they finish it up quicker!

Interestingly, researchers have found that when fast eaters are trained to eat slower, long-term weight loss is achieved.[15] For overweight people who eat quickly, this is worth trying. Don't nag your spouse or child continuously as this can be self-defeating – but reminding them occasionally to taste and appreciate the food they are eating can be very helpful.

## Summing up

These are the main points raised in this chapter for decreasing hunger and preventing excessive weight gain:

- Cut out all sugar-containing drinks
- Cut out low-fiber containing snacks
- Eat whole-wheat or whole grain breads
- Use high-fiber starches for meals

- Eat high-fiber breakfast cereals
- Eat at least 4 portions of veggies and 3 portions of fruits a day
- Drink whole milk or dairy equivalents daily, especially fermented milk products such as yogurt
- Plan an exercise program
- If you are a fast eater, try eating slower

Changing diet has to be a family affair. If one overweight child is singled out, it is very unlikely that much will be accomplished. But why should family members who are slim have to give up on their favorite (bad) foods? The answer is that a good diet should not only be for those who are gaining too much weight but for all family members. Families should work together towards good health, just as they work together towards other important goals.

Are there any negatives to the high-fiber approach described here? Fiber is not inert and its bacterial fermentation produces gas. Sometimes, this can be unpleasant. If it becomes a problem, back down on the fiber for a while and then re-introduce it back, but using lesser amounts. Fiber also draws water into the colon and you may need to drink more on a high-fiber diet. If you do not do this, constipation may result.

In conclusion, paying attention to your family's sense of fullness and hunger is an important step in weight control. This can be achieved by increasing dietary fiber. Increasing fiber also provides many other health benefits such as reducing the risk of insulin resistance and heart disease.[5]

If your weight problem is mild and stable, an Israeli-type Mediterranean diet plus keeping to the advice in this chapter may be all that is needed to control your body weight.

However, if you need to lose weight or have continuing weight gain despite keeping to the advice in this chapter, additional measures are going to be needed. Food intake needs to be reduced and *carbohydrate regulation* is an easy and effective way for doing this.

Read on!

## CHAPTER 12

# Lose Weight by Regulating Carbs!

I am now going to tell you about a simple, effective and healthy way for losing weight. It's called "*carbohydrate regulation*" and entails reducing the amount of sugars and starches you eat. As I will explain shortly, this is different from low-carb dieting.

**But before you begin, remember that the first step for achieving weight loss is to change the types of foods that made you overweight in the first place.**

If you continue eating as you have been eating up to now, you are likely setting yourself up for long-term failure.

Be sure, therefore, before starting on this weight loss program to read the previous chapter on how to control hunger by increasing fiber intake.

With this step alone many people experience some weight loss. You may have to go no further than this!

There are also two other steps to consider before beginning serious dieting.

One of these is to figure out your weight loss goal.

Many people assume that they need to become slim to reduce the metabolic abnormalities associated with their obesity and to obtain the full health benefits of weight loss. But this is not true at all.

**For obese adults and children, a weight loss of 10% of current weight is usually sufficient to improve, and even eliminate, mild metabolic ab-**

**normalities such as mildly elevated blood sugars, mild hypertension, mild hypertriglyceridemia and the hormonal abnormalities associated with polycystic ovary disease.**

A 5% weight loss may also do wonders, although not necessarily as effectively as 10%.

To calculate a 10% weight loss, divide your current weight by 10. Assuming a 1 to 2 pounds weight loss per week, you can also figure out how long it will take you to get to your weight loss goal. Attempting a weight loss greater than 10% is certainly achievable, and may be highly desirable, but will take that much longer.

Why is slimness not a requirement for metabolic health? The reason is that the fat store most responsible for the metabolic abnormalities of obesity is the fat inside your abdomen and around your gut – so-called *visceral fat*. Much of the remaining fat in your body is *subcutaneous fat*. Visceral fat is far easier to get rid of by weight loss and exercise than subcutaneous fat, and much of that 10% weight loss will be coming from visceral fat.

Most obese men have increased visceral fat stores. This is why obese men usually have bulging abdomens. Many obese women, on the other hand, carry their fat around their hips and have predominantly increased subcutaneous fat. Subcutaneous fat is less harmful to health but a bit more difficult to get rid of by dieting and exercise. Nevertheless, many obese women also have increased visceral fat stores and will benefit considerably from a 10% weight loss. So also will obese children of either sex, since visceral fat is increased in childhood. Only in adolescence does one start to see young females with fat stores that are predominantly subcutaneous and around their hips.

Your next decision is to decide what weight loss plan you are going to use.

**The most effective and simplest way for adults and children to lose weight is to use *carbohydrate regulation*.**

Let me now tell you how I discovered this weight loss method, what it entails, and the advantages it has over other weight-loss methods.

## "Carbohydrate regulation"

As a pediatric endocrinologist, I care for youngsters with type 1 diabetes. Young diabetics are very aware of what they eat. They have to be, since all the carbohydrate they eat needs to be covered by insulin. The majority of type 1 diabetics do this by counting in grams the amount of carbohydrate in their meals and snacks and they then base their insulin dose on this figure.

Like other kids, young diabetics can gain too much weight; but I noticed something very interesting. I could hold a detailed conversation with my diabetic patients about their food intake, since they knew exactly how much they were eating, and I would then suggest to them to cut back on the amount of carbohydrates they were eating at certain meals or snacks. This did not mean they would do exactly as I suggested but many did and these youngsters were able to control their body weight very effectively.

Why, I reasoned, could not everyone who needs to lose weight use this method?

The answer is they can. And it works equally well.

I call this method of weight loss *carbohydrate regulation,* since the amount of carbohydrate one eats is fine-tuned to produce the amount of weight loss needed.

The essential features of carbohydrate regulation are as follows:

- Drinks and foods with a high sugar content are eliminated.
- Highly refined starches such as cakes, cookies, many snack foods, white bread and white rice are avoided.
- All starches – even good quality ones – are reduced ("regulated")
- Hunger is alleviated by eating extra vegetables, fruits and seeds.
- Animal protein and fat from meat, eggs and dairy can also be used to alleviate hunger, but not to the extent that one slides into a high-protein or high-fat diet.

As you use this method, you will soon appreciate how easy, flexible and effective it is. Most importantly, it allows you to achieve weight loss in a *gradual* and controlled way. And because vegetables and fruits are not restricted, you can continue eating in a Mediterranean way without having to make major changes in your usual meal planning.

I have been advocating carbohydrate regulation for many years, but I am certainly not the only physician to do so. The more physicians I talk to, the more I realize how many have changed to this method because of their frustration with other ways of losing weight.

What are these other weight loss methods and why is their effectiveness so limited?

A very popular weight-loss method is *calorie counting*. Obesity is the result of eating too many calories – so just cut back on them. A problem with this method is that it does not on its own direct you to improve the quality of the foods you eat. Another is that it pushes you in the direction of reducing dietary fat, since fat contains more than twice as many calories as the equivalent weight of carbohydrate or protein. Because of this, calorie-based dieting usually ends up as low-fat dieting.

So what could be wrong with low-fat dieting? There is after all a wealth of scientific literature attesting to the effectiveness of low-fat diets for *short-term* weight loss.

This is exactly the problem – the weight loss is short-term. Skimping on fat means increasing your intake of carbohydrate, and unless this carbohydrate is good-quality carbohydrate it leads to increased hunger. Because of this, the *long-term* success of low-fat diets is dismal, except for people with considerable will power.

Another frequently taught weight-loss method is *portion control*. The theory behind this is that people have gotten used to heaping up their plates with piles of food and they need to be "taught" what constitutes appropriate serving sizes for the foods they eat. Countless dietitians have achieved excellent short-term results with this method. However, this method does not attempt to balance food intake with weight loss, provides no encouragement for improving carbohydrate quality, and like most other methods its effectiveness wanes over time.

Then what about *very low-carb dieting* that plunges you immediately into severe carbohydrate restriction and drastic weight loss?

At first glance, it sounds very tempting. Lose a lot of weight quickly and then get on with life. It is also a tremendous morale booster to watch excess fat melt away. You can do it!

Unfortunately, there are some major downsides. During severe weight loss, metabolic responses are set in motion that try to push your weight back to where it was previously. What is happening in scientific terms is that your *basal metabolic rate* is decreasing. Basal metabolic rate is the energy expended by your body just to keep it ticking – your lungs breathing and your heart pumping. Because of this change in basal metabolic rate, the calories needed to keep you at your new weight are now less than previously. Therefore, to keep your weight steady, you now need to eat *less food than you did prior to dieting.* This can be quite challenging and is one reason why most dieters find that over time their body weight creeps back to where it was before they embarked on their crash diet – and precious little has been achieved. Some people even overshoot and end up heavier than before dieting. This leads to the well-known "yo-yo" effect.

Another problem with low-carb dieting is that much of its short-term success is due to the mild ketosis it induces. A severe reduction in carbohydrate intake leads to an increase in ketone production, and the increased ketones in the blood are quite effective at suppressing appetite. However, once one changes to the weight maintenance phase of this diet and begins increasing carbohydrate intake, the ketosis disappears and so does its appetite suppressing effect. Hunger returns and so does overeating – and one is back to square one.

Low-carb diets also entail an increase in either dietary protein or fat to replace some of the carbohydrate eliminated. Over the short term, there is little harm in doing this. However, obesity is not a short-term problem. This is why everyone who is overweight needs to be on a weight control plan that can be continued for years, and even for a lifetime.

Low-carb high-fat and high-protein diets are not prescriptions for long-term health.[1] High-fat diets are unhealthy for arteries and this may promote heart disease. Individuals with obesity are at some risk for kidney disease and there is a theoretical concern that the use of high protein loads may put extra strain on the kidneys and increase this risk. Over the short-term, researchers have been unable to demonstrate any health problems from high-protein diets, but no long-term studies have been performed to provide similar assurance. High-protein and high-fat diets also do not provide the vegetable and fruit-based anti-oxidants that protect the body against heart disease and other medical conditions. And finally, there is a limit as to how long one can enjoy eating large amounts of steaks and eggs. For a few weeks perhaps – but a lifetime is pushing it!

There is a commonly held misconception that our hunter ancestors ate predominantly meat and that a carnivorous diet is the most natural way of eating. But this is not true. While it is true that our primitive ancestors did not cultivate grains and vegetables, they certainly picked them and they constituted a large part of their diet.

To summarize, in *carbohydrate regulation*:

- Carbohydrates are regulated to provide a *gradual* weight loss without any major shifts in energy balance.

- There is no major change in the amount of protein and fat in your diet, so you can continue eating delicious meals in an Israeli Mediterranean way.
- The increased intake of vegetables and fruits leads to an exceptionally healthy diet that you can continue using for the rest of your life.
- Carb regulation can fit easily into family meal planning, since no special diet is needed for family members who need to lose weight.

**So, don't go too fast. Lose weight gradually using the carb-regulated plan outlined in this chapter.**

Depending on how much weight you need to lose, a timeframe of three to six months, or even longer, may be realistic. Remember – it took time to gain all that weight and it's going to take time to get rid of it.

**A very workable plan is to lose one to two pounds a week.**

Is there any scientific evidence that weight loss on the background of a Mediterranean diet is effective? Evidence comes from a study done in Israel reported in the prestigious New England Journal of Medicine.[2] Three hundred and twenty-two moderately obese adult men and women were randomized to three weight loss diets – a Mediterranean diet moderate in fat, a low-carb high-fat diet, and a low-fat diet. On average, subjects in all three groups lost weight over 24 months, but the least successful diet was the low-fat diet. The winner in terms of weight loss achieved was the low-carb diet. But – and it's an important but – this group regained much of their weight loss and by 16 months those on the Mediterranean diet and low-carbohydrate diet were at an identical weight.

There are a number of important take-home messages from this study. Firstly, low-fat dieting is an inferior method for attempting weight loss; secondly, much of the effort from low-carb dieting is usually wasted since a lot of the weight loss is regained; and thirdly, the Mediterranean way is a healthy way for successful weight loss.

## "Carbohydrate regulation" – the details

*Carb regulation* entails cutting back on sugars and starches and eating veggies and fruits instead. Veggies and fruits are not calorically dense and contain satiety-producing fiber.

This is how it works:

**The following foods are eliminated**:

***Drinks containing a lot of sugar such as:***

- Soda
- Fruit juices
- Iced tea
- Beer

***Foods containing a lot of sugar such as:***

- Candies
- Fruit rollups
- Sugar-containing granola bars
- Canned fruit
- Dried fruit
- Breakfast cereals with a high sugar content

***Highly-refined starches such as:***

- White bread
- White rice
- Low-fiber breakfast cereals
- Most prepared snack foods

***At the same time, the following starchy carbohydrates are "regulated":***

- Whole-wheat bread
- Pasta
- Couscous
- Brown rice
- Breakfast cereals
- Potato
- Potato chips
- Beans

***The following foods are encouraged in order to relieve hunger:***

## Carbohydrates:

- Vegetables (other than potato)
- Sweet potato
- Corn
- Fresh fruits
- Nuts in moderation
- Seeds
- Tofu
- Hummus
- Tahini
- Non-sweetened peanut butter (this food also contains a significant amount of protein)

## Protein-containing foods – in moderation:

- Fish
- Fowl, such as unprocessed chicken and unprocessed turkey
- Eggs
- Up to 3 cups of milk a day
- Yoghurt and sour milk products

## Fat-containing foods – in moderation:

- Butter
- Cheese
- Margarine
- Oils
- Non-sugar containing salad dressings

As you begin using this weight loss plan, you will soon appreciate how easy it is to master, as the number of carbohydrates needing regulation is not that great.

Another big plus of this weight-loss plan is that it avoids periods of hunger. Few adults, much less kids, have the ability to stay hungry for very long, which is why it is important that vegetables, fruits and seeds are not restricted.

A small increase in fish, cheese, fowl and beef is fine in this weight-loss plan, particularly when starting out, with fish at the top of the list because of its healthful omega-3 fat content. Protein, in particular, has a significant satiety effect which can be very helpful for weight loss. Extra fat has also has a satiety effect. Nevertheless, be careful not to slide into a long-term high-protein or high-fat diet based on animal-based products, since this is not a prescription for good health. Extra protein and fat from vegetable-based foods, however, say from humus, tahini, nuts and seeds, is fine.

Do check out the veggie-containing recipes for salads, cooked vegetables and veggie-enriched grain recipes in this cookbook. Even when dieting for weight-loss, it is important that everyone in your family enjoy the food you are preparing for them.

A very helpful step before starting weight loss is to record over a 3-day period *all* the *carbohydrates* you eat. Do this as the day proceeds rather than late at night as it is very easy to forget later on what you have eaten, especially your snacking.

Examine your record carefully and separate off all the non-starchy veggies and fruits. You will be making no changes in these foods and will probably be increasing them. Next, identify the desserts and snacks you will be forgoing and which starches you will be cutting back on.

Interestingly, researchers have found that the very act of tracking one's food intake can lead to weight loss. A lot of the time we eat mindlessly. In effect, this is carb control by awareness – being aware of what you are eating. You may have to go no further than this!

It goes without saying that the plan described here will only work if there are enough appropriate food choices available in the house. If the only items in the pantry are cakes, cookies and potato chips – then this is what will get eaten. Your job as a parent is to ensure that only good food choices are available.

I rarely see this in America, but in Europe where I grew up it is common practice for the hostess or host to portion out the main part of the meal onto people's plates in the kitchen. Open dishes are still available on the table, but these are usually side dishes such as bread or salads. It would be quite impolite to request more of the main dish from a hostess unless she specifically asks if anyone wants seconds. Putting all the dishes of food on the table from which everyone can help him or herself is very much an American way. If you are the main meal preparer for the home you may well consider using this European model. You can limit the carbs for those family members who need carb regulation, while leaving out bowls of vegetables, salads and fruits on the table for the whole family. They will soon get the message!

Weigh yourself once a week to be sure your weight is heading in the right direction. Do this before rather than after eating and at a consistent time of the day. If a bathroom scale was not previously in your thoughts, now is the time to go out and get one.

For many people, what I have described up to now is all you will need to do to obtain a satisfactory weight loss of 1 to 2 pounds per week. If your initial carbohydrate restriction leads to insufficient weight loss, then just cut back more on the carbs.

Nevertheless, there are individuals who need a more disciplined system. It may also be that the weight loss you have achieved so far is insufficient. If this is the case, your carbohydrate will need to be regulated more precisely. The best way to do this is by *counting carbs.*

## "Carb counting" for weight loss

*Counting carbs* is not at all complicated. Many type 1 diabetics do this routinely whenever they eat to figure out their pre-meal insulin dosing and as a result they become very proficient at it.

The first step is to do another 3-day food record of *all the carbohydrates* you are eating on your current diet and then to calculate your average daily intake of carbohydrate in grams.

To help you with this step, chapter 16 at the end of this book contains a list of commonly eaten foods together with their carbohydrate and fiber content. You may also consider using technology to help you by installing an app on your smart phone to work out the carbohydrate content of the foods you eat. Several apps are available to do this. Kids and tech-oriented adults will find these a lot of fun.

For manufactured foods there is no choice but to read the food label. On the back of each food package you will find a table with the nutritional content per *portion size*. This table tells you what constitutes a portion size and provides its nutritional content, including how many grams of carbohydrate it contains.

**The amount of carbohydrates in grams you will be eating will be 10% less than what you are currently eating. Focus particularly on sugar and starch containing foods, since these are the carbs you will be reducing first. Veggies and fruits are only restricted if weight loss is insufficient.**

Once you have figured out your total daily carb allocation, decide on how to divide it up.

Someone with a carb allocation of 140 gram may well consider dividing it as follows:

**40 gram for breakfast**

**40 gram for lunch**

**20 gram for a mid-afternoon snack**

**40 gram for dinner**

In theory, it is possible to chop up your carb allocation into frequent small snacks rather than a few large meals. However, the disadvantages of doing this usually outweigh the advantages. Firstly, you would need to have plenty of healthy snacks readily available and many families will find this a challenge. Plus, if everyone in the family is snacking at different times of the day, family support is lost. Therefore, most families will do better on the conventional three meals a day with just one or two snacks.

Over the next few days, see how the allocation you have chosen fits your schedule. It is certainly permissible to "borrow" carbohydrates from one meal to the next, as long as your daily total remains unchanged. Nevertheless, it is preferable to decide on one allocation scheme fairly soon and to stick to it. The more borrowing you do, the greater the chances this plan will fall by the wayside.

Most people are fairly consistent in the types and amounts of carbohydrates eaten from day to day, and you will probably soon remember the figures for the foods you eat most often.

What should you do if your weight does not decrease sufficiently? It can happen. If this is the case, take off another 10% from your daily allocation of carbohydrate. If needs be, continue decreasing in 10% increments every week or so until your weight is heading in the right direction.

Dieters on this plan will need encouragement and support from their families to keep on track. Family members, whether overweight or normal weight, can provide this support by eating Mediterranean-style meals. They taste good and are super-healthy. This way, everyone in the family will be eating the same foods, while those needing weight stabilization or weight loss will be restricting their total carbohydrates.

**Try to keep this a family-together diet program!**

## PEDIATRIC CONSIDERATIONS

Many obese children and adolescents will find engaging in serious weight loss too much of a challenge. If this is so, and especially if they have no complications from their obesity, a very acceptable goal is to slow down their *normal* rate of weight gain so that a slimming out occurs over time as they grow. This type of *weight stabilization* requires less food restriction than for weight loss, although it is still a significant commitment of effort.

For weight stabilization you should aim for just that – to keep your child's weight stable with no further weight gain. Boys and girls normally gain about 4 to 7 pounds a year from about age 6 until the beginning of puberty. Weight gain is about 20 pounds a year for boys during the peak growth spurt and 18 pounds a year for girls. Normal weight gain slows down after menarche, although weight gain continues until late adolescence. Because growth is so rapid during puberty, more flexibility with weight stabilization is appropriate, and significant slimming can be achieved despite a small yearly weight gain.

**If this also is too challenging, then at the very least make sure your child is eating the healthiest diet possible so as to prevent future complications from their obesity.**

It is also very important to follow your child's weight carefully to be sure that their weight gain over time is not excessive. In other words, their weight should not be deviating further from their weight percentile on the growth chart. If it is deviating, then you have no choice but to take more intensive action. Weight gain is normal during childhood – but your child should not be getting fatter.

There is another point worth making. Some parents assume that as their child gets older, and particularly as he or she hits puberty, that a natural slimming out will occur. It can happen. Unfortunately, the odds are against it and many chubby children get even chubbier as they go through puberty if no attention is paid to their diet.

## Summing up

You now have before you the details of one of the simplest of all weight-loss plans. It works. It provides long-term benefits to health. If your weight-loss goal is big, it will take you many months to achieve. But it could save your life.

# CHAPTER 13

# Go Mediterranean and Save Your Arteries – and Your Life!

Obesity is a major risk factor for cardiovascular disease. For this reason, the nutritional prevention of cardiovascular disease needs to be part of the treatment plan for everyone with a weight problem.

More than this – heart disease is the leading cause of death in America and much of the Western world, so that preventing heart disease by nutritional means should be a priority for everyone and not just the obese. This is particularly the case for those with a family history of coronary artery disease, since cardiovascular disease often runs in families.

Be aware, though, that there is currently considerable ferment in the field of nutrition as old ideas about preventing heart disease are being thrown out the window and new ones coming to the fore.

Nutrition in this country has been governed for over half a century by the notion that LDL-cholesterol, the so-called "bad cholesterol", is the primary villain in cardiovascular disease and that it can be de-fanged by diet. Eat less saturated fat and cholesterol, the nutrition experts advised, and LDL-cholesterol levels will come down and so will your chances of developing heart disease.

We now know that this model was widely off the mark:

- Cutting back on saturated fat is not associated with less heart disease.

- Eating less cholesterol-containing eggs has no influence on heart disease.
- Although a high LDL-cholesterol level is an important risk factor for heart disease, important conditions leading to cardiovascular disease such as diabetes, obesity and smoking are not associated with high LDL-cholesterol levels.

However, a new nutritional model has been waiting in the wings and is now ready for prime time. It's called the Mediterranean diet.

## Cardiovascular disease and the Mediterranean diet

We have been aware for many years that the French suffer from less cardiovascular disease than Americans even though they eat more saturated fat and have similar blood cholesterol levels. This *French paradox* fitted poorly into the blame-your LDL-cholesterol-model and was therefore conveniently ignored.

The first attempt to unravel the mystery was the Lyon Diet Heart Study carried out in Lyon, France.[1] The French eat a Mediterranean diet. The researchers therefore posed the question – is a Mediterranean diet enriched in omega-3 fat (more about this fat in a moment) better at preventing heart disease than a Western fat-restricted diet? Volunteers for this study had already suffered from a heart attack and were therefore at high risk for future cardiovascular events.

The results were astounding. Within 4 years, cardiovascular events were reduced by 30% and death by 70% for those on the Mediterranean diet compared to volunteers on the low-fat diet. In most successful cardiovascular studies, the protective effect of an intervention such as a drug is usually fairly modest and takes years to become evident. Not so in this study. Subjects on the Mediterranean diet were already experiencing less cardiovascular problems soon after joining the study, demonstrating that this diet was having an immediate effect. Its benefit also had nothing to do with blood lipid levels, since blood lipids were similar in the two groups.

Another recent Mediterranean diet study obtained equally impressive results.[2] This study randomized a large number of Spaniards at risk for heart disease to three diets – a Mediterranean diet containing extra-virgin olive oil, a Mediterranean diet supplemented with nuts, and a non-Mediterranean diet with advice on reducing dietary fat. Both Mediterranean diets were fairly liberal in dietary fat because of their use of olive oil and nuts. Over almost 5 years, subjects on both Mediterranean diets significantly reduced their risk of major cardiovascular events by 30% compared to those on the low-fat diet.

These and similar studies have demonstrated conclusively that the Mediterranean diet is far more effective in preventing the progression of cardiovascular disease than a diet low in total and saturated fat.

Why is this diet so effective?

It is probably due to a number of factors working in combination. As discussed in chapter 1, the Mediterranean diet is typically high in dietary fiber and low in glycemia (i.e. it keeps blood sugars low), and both these factors are related to the development of coronary disease. The Lyon Heart Study also tried to imitate a diet once popular in Crete, a Greek island known for its low incidence of heart disease; and the Crete diet contained a lot of omega-3 fat. Omega-3 fat is found particularly in fish and certain plants. For this reason, all the volunteers on the Mediterranean diet in the Lyon Heart Study received a margarine enriched in omega-3 fat. The Mediterranean diet is also loaded with of *anti-oxidants* – and this accounts for a large part of the health benefits of the Mediterranean diet.[3]

## ANTI-OXIDANTS AND THE MEDITERRANEAN DIET

The Bible describes "seven agricultural species" uniquely adapted to the climatic conditions of Israel. These are olives, grapes, pomegranates, figs, dates, wheat and barley.[4] These are all Mediterranean foods and they are all rich in antioxidants.

A significant part of the health benefit from the Mediterranean diet likely comes from its content of olive oil and the anti-oxidants it contains. As discussed in chapter 1, olive oil reduces overall mortality and prevents heart disease and stroke. About 75% of the fat in olive oil is *mono-unsaturated fat.* In the past, this was thought to be the ingredient that accounted for most of olive oil's health promoting effects. However, we now know that this fat provides no particular cardiovascular protection, and it is the high content of anti-oxidant polyphenols in olive oil that make it such a healthy food.[5]

Be aware, though, that not all olive oil sold in the stores is rich in antioxidants. *Extra-virgin olive oil* has the highest content of polyphenols. *Pure olive oil,* or regular olive oil, is a mixture of extra virgin olive oil and olive oil that has been processed, either by heat, chemicals or filtration. During the purification process a lot of the antioxidants are removed. *Light olive oil* is not light in fat (all olive oils contain the same amount of fat) but olive oil that has been finely filtered and is *light* in impurities. The impurities removed include its anti-oxidants.

**Extra-virgin olive oil is preferable to other types of olive oil. It has a richer taste and higher content of antioxidants.**

There is no reason to be skimpy with olive oil when preparing a meal for your family – although there is no reason to drown the food either. Dressing salads with an olive oil-containing salad dressing, sautéing with olive oil, and roasting vegetables with olive oil are all wonderful ways to make vegetables more appetizing and to simultaneously add extra anti-oxidants to your diet.

Wine is another food often consumed as part of a Mediterranean diet and it also has considerable health promoting properties.[6] The most important anti-oxidant in wine is a chemical called resveratrol, and this chemical has many impressive properties related to inflammation, cancer and allergy when studied in the test tube.

Note though that whereas red wine has a high content of resveratrol, white wine contains very little. This is because resveratrol is found in the grape skins. When white wine is manufactured the skins are removed, whereas they remain in the fermentation process when making red wine and the alcohol leaches out the resveratrol from the skins. Grape juice has a high resveratrol content but it is not absorbed well by the gut in this form and free resveratrol levels in the blood do not increase much after drinking grape juice.

It is unlikely you will ever see official health recommendations for everybody to drink red wine, since it is illegal for anyone under age 21 to possess alcoholic drinks in the United States, although states have exceptions for religious purposes and with family members. There is also the potential for abuse and it is an inappropriate drink for pregnant women. Nevertheless, for responsible adults, wine is an excellent tonic for health and longevity – as well as adding depth and richness to a meal.

Of course, these plants mentioned in the Bible are not the only source of anti-oxidants. There are literally thousands of antioxidant compounds within plants from all over the world; and scientists are just beginning to understand how these compounds favorably influence many medical conditions.

In general, vegetables, fruits, berries,whole grains and herbs are good sources of antioxidants. Many of the chemicals that provide natural coloring to fruits and vegetables are antioxidants. The antioxidants in grains are found within their cell walls and are removed during milling. This is why whole grain cereals and whole grain breads contain more antioxidants than white bread.[7]

Nuts also contain anti-oxidants. Walnuts in particular have a high content. Not surprisingly, studies have shown that eating nuts protects against cardiovascular disease.[8]

**Nuts (non-sugared and non-salted) make excellent snacks and are much healthier than fiber-free snack foods, such as pretzels and crackers.**

Other foods often discussed in health magazines because of their high anti-oxidant content include cocoa and chocolate, tomatoes, coffee, tea and herbs. However, there are almost certainly numerous other super-healthy foods that have not yet been identified.

The nutritional experts from over half a century ago made a terrible mistake. By focusing on lowering saturated fat, total fat and dietary cholesterol they encouraged people to eat more carbohydrate than previously. Much of this carbohydrate was refined carbohydrate and often contained a lot of sugars. It contained very little fiber, was high-glycemic, and had very little anti-oxidants. Understandably, it did nothing to prevent cardiovascular disease and may even have promoted it.

However, anti-oxidants are not the only the nutritional factor that influences cardiovascular disease. Dietary fats, fructose and salt are also important – and these will now be discussed. Physical activity, which also is of considerable importance, was discussed in the previous chapter.

## Understanding fats

Advice in the past regarding dietary fat was very simple. Restrict it – particularly saturated fat.

We now know that this advice was unhelpful, since total and saturated fat do not promote heart disease. Moreover, certain fats are *beneficial* to health and it is far better to have these in rather than out of one's diet.

Firstly, some chemistry. A fat molecule consists of a long chain of carbon atoms joined together by chemical bonds. Fats are distinguished by their chain length (i.e. how many carbon atoms they contain) and the type of chemical bond between the carbon atoms. Bonds can be either a single-carbon bond that is *saturated* with two hydrogen atoms, or a double-carbon bond that is *unsaturated* and contains only a single hydrogen atom. A *saturated fat* is one in which all the available carbon bonds in the chain are saturated with two hydrogen atoms. Because of the configuration of the hydrogen atoms, these chains of fat are straight, without kinks, and they therefore align easily with each other; and this is why they readily solidify at room temperature. A *mono-unsaturated* fat is a fat in which all the carbon bonds in the chain are saturated *except for one double-carbon bond* that is unsaturated. A *polyunsaturated fat* is a fat in which there is *more than one unsaturated-carbon bond* within the carbon chain. The presence of unsaturated bonds in mono-unsaturated and polyunsaturated fats produce kinks in the molecule. The fat chains cannot neatly align with each other and these fats tend to be liquid at room temperature.

A particularly healthy *polyunsaturated fat* is *omega-3 fat,* so called because one of its unsaturated carbon bonds is three carbons distant from one end of the carbon chain.

Omega-3 fats have many favorable effects related to the cardiovascular system: they lower blood triglyceride levels, improve blood vessel wall functioning, reduce blood vessel inflammation and thin the blood.

Important sources of *omega-3 fat* are fatty fish and certain plants. Much of the fat eaten by Eskimos is from whale, seal and fish, all of which are high in omega-3 fat. Because of this, the Eskimos are remarkably free from cardiovascular disease. Japanese living in coastal fishing villages also have a low incidence of heart disease because of their high intake of sea foods.

**Include fish at least twice a week in your family's meal planning, and even more if you can.**

The American diet tends to be very beef-centric. As a result, many families are unfamiliar with fish and the kids are put off by its appearance and smell. It's a good idea, therefore, to put effort into finding fish recipes that will appeal to your family. Some excellent fish recipes are included in the recipe section of this book. This section also contains information about when to be worried about mercury and other heavy metal contamination.

Useful facts about omega-3 fat in fish include the following:

- Oily fish such as salmon, herring, mackerel, anchovies and sardines are particularly good sources of omega-3 fat.

- Tuna contains omega-3 fat, but in lesser amounts than these other fish.

Plant sources of omega-3 fat include dark leafy vegetables such as Romaine lettuce and spinach, members of the cabbage family such as cauliflower, broccoli, Brussels sprouts and bok choy, and winter squash such as acorn squash, butternut squash and pumpkins. Other sources of omega-3 fat include flax, sunflower, safflower and pumpkin seeds, as well as oil made from these seeds. Canola, soybean and walnut oil also contain substantial amounts of omega-3 fat.

**Using a canola-based margarine and canola-based mayonnaise are excellent ways to increase your family's omega-3 fat intake.**

## SATURATED FAT – NOT SO HARMFUL AFTER ALL

Saturated fat is found in meat, lard, dairy foods, tropical vegetable oils such as coconut and palm kernel oil, and coca butter.

Saturated fats raise blood cholesterol levels slightly, but as discussed in chapter 10 of this book there is no evidence they promote heart disease. Therefore, whole or 2% milk, high-fat cheese and full-fat yogurt can be safely included in Mediterranean-type meal planning.

Does this mean that everyone can indulge in lots of cream and butter? The answer is – not so fast! A high-fat diet is not a healthy one for the vascular system. Fat also contains lots of calories and can lead to weight gain. Nevertheless, a *moderate* intake of saturated fat from animal or plant sources does not promote vascular damage or lead to excessive weight gain and can be safely included in a Mediterranean diet.

## THE VILLAIN ON THE BLOCK – TRANS FAT

The mind boggles when one thinks about it. Half a century ago, health experts began recommending a food that actually promoted the very disease it was thought to guard against!

The low-fat campaign of the 1960's encouraged use of margarine made from vegetable oils to replace butter and other animal fats and this margarine contained a manufactured form of fat called *trans fat.* Trans fat is made by adding extra hydrogen industrially to the unsaturated double-carbon bonds of vegetable oil and thereby *partially hydrogenating* the fat molecule.

It took clever detective work by suspicious nutrition scientists to figure out that trans fats are damaging even in small amounts and are extremely harmful to health. This is because the added hydrogen molecules are in a *trans* configuration instead of the natural *cis* position (hence the name *trans fat*). Our bodies do not have the breakdown enzymes for this type of fat and it becomes a toxin and source of oxidative stress.

Food manufacturers love *partially hydrogenated* or trans fats. They are relatively cheap to make and have useful properties for industrial baking. Foods containing trans fat have an increased shelf life and need less refrigeration. Until recently, most margarine and vegetable shortening in the United States contained trans fat.

Major food manufacturers no longer include trans fats in their food products. The use of trans fats has been banned in restaurants in New York City. Since January 2006, all food manufacturers in America have been required to list the trans fat content of their products. From June 2018 they will be banned outright.

Nevertheless, a few smaller companies may still be holding out. Until the government ban is operative, watch out for trans fat in: margarines, household shortening, crackers, baked cookies and cakes, chips, deep-fried products such as fish sticks and chicken nuggets, non-dairy creamers and microwave popcorn.

## Drinking regular soda – a risk for heart disease, insulin resistance and diabetes

It was discussed previously that excessive amounts of sugar-containing soda promote weight gain. But extra calories are not the only problem with this type of drink. Regular soda also promotes heart disease and diabetes due to its high sugar content and in particular its high content of fructose.[9] Fructose is currently the most commonly used caloric sweetener in America.

Fructose is a natural constituent of fruits and when consumed in a modest amount is perfectly safe and healthy. The problem comes when one drinks large amounts of fructose, for example from sweetened soft drinks, power drinks, iced tea and fruit juices – since all these drinks contain substantial amounts of fructose.

Years ago, the predominant sweetener in America was table sugar. Table sugar contains equal amounts of glucose and fructose. About 40 years ago, table sugar began to be replaced by high-fructose corn syrup. High-fructose corn sweetener contains 55% fructose and 45% glucose and therefore more fructose than table sugar. In actuality, the fructose content of soda may be even higher than this, since the manufacturers add extra fructose to make the drinks sweeter. This is not illegal, since the government allows some wiggle room.

When consumed in large amounts, sugars such as table sugar and fructose can overwhelm the body's ability to metabolize them efficiently and they then become a source of oxidative stress. Many nutritional experts are concerned that much of the fatty liver disease, insulin resistance and hypertriglyceridemia, all of which are common in the obese, may be promoted by too much fructose.[8]

Many people imagine that because they are natural, fruit juices are healthy. In small amounts this is true. However, if one drinks fruit juices *plus* soft drinks *plus* sweetened iced tea, this can easily lead to fructose overloading. In addition, some fruit juices – grape juice and apple juice for example – are naturally high in fructose. Sweetened canned fruit and applesauce may also contain substantial amounts of fructose.

Many American Hispanics have gotten used to drinking lots of fruit juice, since they did this in their country of origin. It was not such a great idea then but is an even worse idea in America since our diets are already high in fructose. High-fructose corn syrup is not used in South America.

**Everyone should limit their use of regular soda – and particularly people with a weight problem, high insulin levels, high blood lipids or abnormal liver function tests.**

## WHAT ABOUT SALT?

Conventional wisdom has been that everyone should limit their salt intake in order to prevent hypertension and heart disease.

It makes sense. Salt increases blood pressure in many people and hypertension leads to heart attacks and strokes.

Recommendations in the past were for everyone to limit their sodium intake to between 1,500 to 2,300 milligram per day, since this amount of sodium has no influence on blood pressure. A teaspoon of salt contains 2,400 milligrams of sodium, so we are talking about limiting salt to just less than 1 teaspoon a day. The average salt consumption in the US and around the world is about 3,400 milligrams a day, or just less than 1½ teaspoons.

But is it really true that salt restriction prevents heart disease? When these recommendations were made no large-scale studies had been done to substantiate this claim.

It turns out that it is not true at all!

Recently, the US government asked the Institute of Medicine to review the latest evidence on salt and the latter convened a committee. Reviewing all the published scientific literature, this committee concluded that there is no reason for people to aim for a sodium intake below 2,300 milligram a day, since new studies show that the risk for heart disease actually *increases* for those who consume *less* than 2,300 milligram or *more* than 7,000 milligram of sodium a day.[10] An acceptable sodium intake therefore seems to be between 2,300 milligram to 7,000 milligram of sodium a day.

The recommendations of this committee are controversial and the safe zone for sodium intake is still a matter of debate. Nevertheless, it seems very likely that the salt consumption of many, if not most, people is in an OK range. People who need to be concerned about their salt intake are those who eat a lot of salty foods such as salty snack foods and prepared meats (neither of which are healthy) and pickles, since these foods can easily lead into the more harmful range of sodium intake.

The problem with a low-salt diet is that as one severely lowers one's salt intake unfavorable metabolic changes start to occur, such as an increase in triglyceride levels and increased insulin resistance, and these changes can increase one's risk for heart disease.

Having said all this, anyone who has been placed on a low-salt diet by a physician should check with his or her physician before making any changes, and anyone with a blood pressure problem should check with their physician before making any changes in their current salt intake.

The moral of this story? There are a lot of nutritional myths out there!

## CONCLUSIONS:

An Israeli-style Mediterranean diet is not a low-fat diet. It contains a moderate amount of fat. However, these are healthful fats, such as olive oil and canola oil that protect against heart disease, and it is far better to have them in your diet rather than out.

If you have gotten used to low-fat cooking, you may not realize how much this limits the types of foods you can serve to your family. Add back healthy fats and your meals will taste better and you will discover a wealth of delicious new dishes to try out.

The focus of this chapter is on cardiovascular disease, but it is becoming increasingly evident that the Mediterranean diet is helpful for many other medical conditions that involve oxidative stress besides heart disease – and the list keeps on growing. The Mediterranean diet has been reported to provide protection from Alzheimer disease and dementia, some forms of cancer, type 2 diabetes, asthma and depression.[11] Some of these claims are from limited studies and warrant substantiation, but their sheer number is evidence that the Mediterranean diet has widespread health benefits.

So what are you waiting for?

## CHAPTER 14

# Improve Your Blood Sugars Using Low-Glycemic Carbohydrate

Mediterranean-style meal planning helps prevent diet-induced type 2 diabetes and improves diabetes control.[1]

But are any other nutritional measures useful for improving blood sugar control?

There most certainly are.

If you are obese, weight loss works wonders. As explained in chapter 13, a weight loss of 10% of current weight markedly improves blood sugars and may even eliminate mild diabetes. Even a weight loss of less than 10% can be helpful.

In addition, eating *low-glycemic carbohydrate* lowers blood sugars in individuals with a blood sugar problem, whether this be type 2 diabetes, type 1 diabetes or impaired glucose tolerance.[2]

A quick review of the glycemic system. We met the figure below in chapter 10. It compares blood glucose responses after eating two starches – white bread and Italian pasta. Both these starches are made from wheat and both consist of long chains of glucose molecules. However, the similarities end there, since what happens to them in the gut is very different. The starch in white bread is broken down rapidly and large amounts of glucose enter quickly into the blood stream. This leads to higher peak blood glucose levels. White bread is therefore called a high-glycemic carbohydrate. Italian pasta, on the other hand, is made from semolina. Semolina is milled flour in which the grain particles are larger and coarser than in regular white flour. Pasta is also made from durum wheat, which is the hardest of all forms of wheat. The starch granules get trapped in the dough and are broken down only slowly in the gut. This leads to a smaller and more prolonged rise in blood glucose. Pasta is therefore considered to be a low-glycemic carbohydrate.

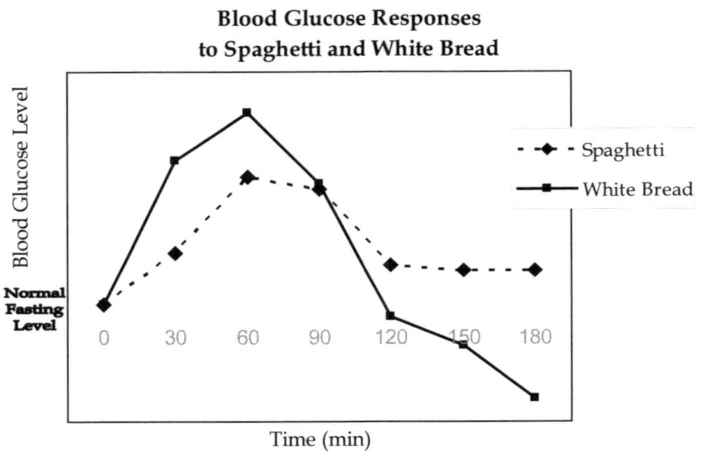


Note the high peak of glucose with white bread compared to the lower and more prolonged peak with spaghetti.

The glycemic index of a food is defined empirically as the area under its 2-hour glucose curve after eating 25 grams of digestible carbohydrate of that food, divided by the area under the curve for a similar amount of a carbohydrate "standard," which is usually table sugar.

**By convention, a food with a glycemic index of 70 or more is considered high-glycemic, 56 to 69 moderate-glycemic, and 55 or less low-glycemic.**

The rational for advising low-glycemic foods for diabetes is very simple. High-glycemic carbohydrate leads to higher blood sugars, whereas low-glycemic carbohydrate leads to lower blood sugars. If you have diabetes your blood sugars are higher than normal. Therefore, to improve your diabetes control, you should eat predominantly low-glycemic carbohydrate.

Eating low-glycemic carbohydrate should lead to a reduction of about 0.5% in hemoglobin A1c (the test used to assess diabetes control) – which is a meaningful reduction.[2] As a result of this you may need less diabetes medications, or a lower dose of medication, and in a borderline case of diabetes no medication at all. If you are taking insulin, you may be able to reduce your insulin dose, and in a situation in which it is unclear whether you need insulin or not it may just tip the balance against using insulin.

If the usefulness of low-glycemic carbohydrate is so obvious, how come your endocrinologist or diabetes educator never mentioned this to you??

One answer is that claims were made years ago about low-glycemic diets, particularly regarding weight loss, that did not fulfill expectations and this led many nutrition experts to view low-glycemic diets with suspicion. Also, a low-glycemic diet is not necessarily an ideal diet since it ignores other important aspects of carbohydrate quality such as fiber and content of anti-oxidants. Nevertheless, there is one claim about the low-glycemic diet that has never been disputed – and that is that it lowers blood sugars. In other words, it improves diabetes control.

To date, the Australian Diabetes Association is the only diabetes association that advises a low-glycemic diet for diabetics. The American Diabetes Association admits that the glycemia system can be helpful for fine-tuning blood sugar control but it is not part of their standard recommendations. Other diabetes associations think the system is too complicated and not worth the educational effort involved to teach it. To a degree, this is understandable. It is not an intuitive system.

For example, watermelon is a high-glycemic food, but because most of its content is water and not carbohydrate its glycemic effect is low and is of little concern. In the technical language of this field we say this fruit has a low *glycemic load*. In other words, it is not just the glycemic index of a food that is important, but how much carbohydrate is within the food. This means that for many foods, particularly veggies and fruits, their glycemic index figure may not be that important, and it is their glycemic load figure that is more informative.

The ripeness of a fruit may affect its glycemic index, since the glycemic index rising as the fruit ripens.

Non-carbohydrate foods within a meal can also influence the glycemia of its carbohydrate. Fat, for example, subdues the glucose response of its carbohydrate, whereas a low-fat meal permits the full impact of its glycemic response.

All this means that glycemic index figures may not be quite as meaningful as glycemic index tables seem to indicate.

Despite this, there are good reasons for diabetics to understand the glycemic index system and to use it selectively.

I will now go over how to make the glycemic system work for you.

## LIMIT HIGH-GLYCEMIC SNACK FOODS AND DRINKS!

Limiting highly refined high-glycemic snack foods is important for reducing your blood sugar levels during the day – as well as for reasons discussed in previous chapters. Therefore, be sure to restrict the following high-glycemic snack foods:

- Potato chips (baked tortilla chips are not high glycemic)
- Cakes, cookies, and donuts
- Crackers
- Pretzels made from refined carbohydrate
- High sugar-containing foods such as candies and fruit roll-ups.

Also limit the following sugar-containing drinks, whether the sugar is added or natural:

- Regular soda
- Sports drinks such as Gatorade
- Sweetened ice tea
- Fruit juices

I often see diabetics eating sugar-free cookies made out of highly refined carbohydrate, since they assume that the lack of added sugar makes them an appropriate food. This makes little sense. Even without the sugar, these cookies are a high-glycemic food. All their starch is rapidly broken down to glucose and this leads to high blood glucose levels. Although admittedly with the added sugar the blood glucose rise will be even higher. This is a good example of how knowledge of the glycemic system can help you make appropriate food choices.

## Choose low-glycemic breads!

Bread is an important constituent of many people's diets and it is worthwhile knowing which breads lead to lower blood sugars.

White bread has a high glycemic index.

Lower glycemic breads include:

- Whole-wheat bread
- Certain mixed grain breads
- Rye bread
- Pumpernickel bread
- Sourdough bread

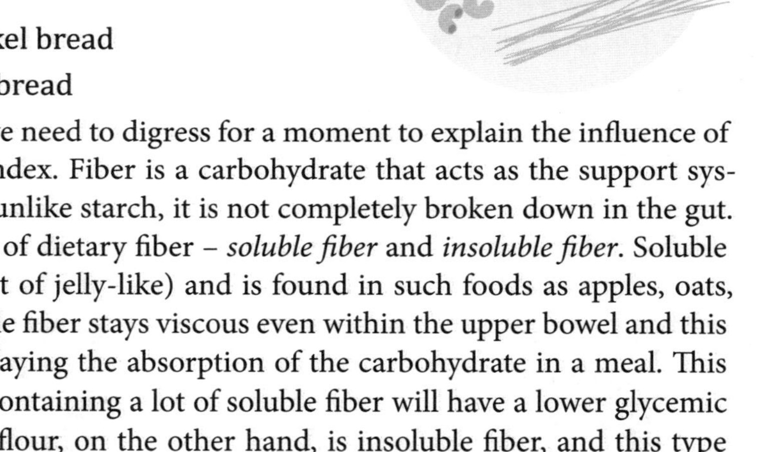

At this point, we need to digress for a moment to explain the influence of fiber on glycemic index. Fiber is a carbohydrate that acts as the support system for plants, but unlike starch, it is not completely broken down in the gut. There are two types of dietary fiber – *soluble fiber* and *insoluble fiber*. Soluble fiber is viscous (sort of jelly-like) and is found in such foods as apples, oats, and legumes. Soluble fiber stays viscous even within the upper bowel and this has the effect of delaying the absorption of the carbohydrate in a meal. This means that a food containing a lot of soluble fiber will have a lower glycemic index. The fiber in flour, on the other hand, is insoluble fiber, and this type of fiber has very little influence on carbohydrate absorption. Therefore, the glycemic index of whole-wheat bread is only slightly lower than that of white bread, even though whole-wheat bread contains a lot more fiber. Nevertheless, for reasons explained in previous chapters, whole-wheat bread is a far healthier choice than white bread.

*Stone ground whole-wheat flour* is less finely milled than machine ground whole-wheat flour and this reduces its glycemic index further.[4] With a bit of searching, you may be able to find whole-wheat bread made from this type of flour in your grocery store.

From the perspective of glycemic-index, bread containing a lot of kernels of grain is even better that whole-wheat bread. This type of bread is often sold as *mixed grain bread*, since it contains a mixture of whole-grains.[5] It is difficult to give a figure for the glycemic index of a mixed grain bread, since it depends on how many grain kernels it contains, but it can be as low as 35 and as high as 70.

Other breads with a moderately low glycemic index include rye bread (glycemic index of about 41-63), pumpernickel bread (glycemic index of about 41-62), and sourdough bread (glycemic index of about 54-66). Sourdough bread does not contain whole grains, but its acidic nature has the effect of slowing its glucose absorption from the gut. Pumpernickel bread is a type of sourdough made from a combination of rye meal and rye flour. The rye meal is more coarsely ground than the rye flour. You may be able to find a rye bread with intact grains and from the perspective of glycemic index this bread is even better than regular rye bread.

## Eat low-glycemic starches and beans

Healthy low-glycemic starches include the following:

- Spaghetti
- Pasta
- Corn
- Lentils
- Pearl barley
- Most beans

Also the following whole grains:

- Bulgur wheat
- Cracked wheat
- Whole oats
- Barley
- Quinoa
- Buckwheat
- Wheat berries

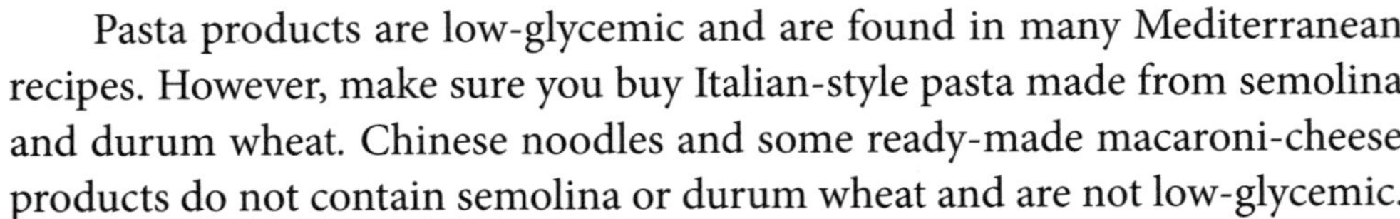

Pasta products are low-glycemic and are found in many Mediterranean recipes. However, make sure you buy Italian-style pasta made from semolina and durum wheat. Chinese noodles and some ready-made macaroni-cheese products do not contain semolina or durum wheat and are not low-glycemic.

The difference in glycemic index between white and whole grain pasta is small. However, whole grain pasta contains more fiber, minerals and antioxidants and is a healthier choice irrespective of its glycemia.

## Eat the right type of rice!

The glycemic index of boiled white rice is between 72 to 102, which means that white rice is quite a high-glycemic food.

Types of rice with a lower glycemic index include:

- Basmati rice (glycemic index of about 43-69)
- Brown rice (glycemic index of about 62-72)
- Long grain rice (glycemic index of about 50-69)
- Uncle Ben's white rice (glycemic index about 56)

Uncle Ben's rice is parboiled and this process congeals the surface starch grains, resulting in it having a lower glycemic index. Nevertheless, from a health perspective, brown rice is a better choice that parboiled white rice or regular white rice because of its fiber content. The husk, bran and germ are removed from white rice and this leaves it with a negligible content of fiber.

## Eat quality breakfast cereals!

If you are accustomed to starting the day with a breakfast cereal, then this should be a low-glycemic breakfast cereal containing whole grains.

Unfortunately, many of the popular breakfast cereals are high-glycemic.

Below are the glycemic index values of some popular breakfast cereals. Much of this data is for brands manufactured outside the United States, since this is where the measurements were made, but American brands are probably not a lot different. You will recall that a food with a glycemic index of 70 and above is considered high-glycemic, 56-69 moderate-glycemic, and 55 and less low-glycemic:

- All-Bran (Kellogg's, USA) 38
- Cheerios (General Mills, Canada) 74
- Coco Pops (Australia) 77
- Cornflakes (Kellogg's USA) 92

- Crispix (Kellogg's Canada) 87
- Froot Loops (Kellogg's Australia) 69
- Golden Grahams (General Mills, Canada) 71
- Grapenuts (Kraft, USA) 75
- Kashi Seven Whole Grains breakfast cereal (Kashi Company) 65
- Life (Quaker Oats, Canada) 66
- Muesli (Alpen) 55
- Puffed Wheat (Quaker Oats, Canada) 67
- Raisin Bran (Kellogg's, USA) 61
- Rice Chex (Nabisco, Canada) 89
- Rice Krispies (Kellogg's, Canada) 82
- Shredded Wheat (Nabisco, Canada) 83
- Total (General Mills, Canada) 76
- Weetabix (Weetabix, Canada 75

You will notice that most of the breakfast cereals in this list have either a high or moderately high glycemic index.

Low-glycemic cereals, all of which are high in fiber, include the following:

- Many Mueslis
- Oatmeal (made from Old Fashioned oats)
- The Original Shredded Wheat
- Post Bran Flakes
- General Mills Fiber One Bran
- Kellog's All-Bran Original

## Veggies forever!

Green, red and other colored vegetables, legumes and root vegetables are essential constituents of the Mediterranean diet. These vegetables are also in the main low-glycemic. Be aware though that potatoes have a high glycemic index, especially if baked or mashed. If you are trying to keep your meals low-glycemic, this is a vegetable to limit.

Also be aware that if you eat a salad dressing containing oil and vinegar with a meal this tends to lower its glycemic index. This is because both the fat and vinegar lower the glycemic index of carbohydrate.

## Wrapping up

The Mediterranean diet tends to be a low glycemic diet and will help improve diabetes control. This is because this diet contains lots of high fiber foods and many of these are low-glycemic. Nevertheless, for individuals with type 1 or type 2 diabetes, or for those who have blood glucose levels that are abnormal but not quite in the diabetic range, understanding the glycemic system and using it selectively together with Mediterranean style meal planning can be very helpful for further improving your blood sugar levels and hemoglobin A1c test results.

# CHAPTER 15

# The Carbohydrate and Fiber Content of Groups of Foods

## Beverages

| Beverage | Carbohydrate content |
|---|---|
| | |
| Apple juice, canned or bottled, unsweetened, 1 cup | 29 g |
| Beer, light, 1 can or bottle, 12 fl oz | 5 g |
| Beer, regular, 1 can or bottle, 12 fl oz | 10 g |
| Beers, non-alcoholic brews, 12 fl oz | 14 g |
| Chocolate syrup, 1 serving, 2 tablespoon | 25 g |
| Cocoa mix, Nestle, Carnation, No Sugar Added Hot Cocoa Mix, 1 envelope | 8 g |
| Cocoa mix, Nestle, Carnation Rich Chocolate Hot Cocoa Mix, 1 envelope | 24 g |
| Coffee, brewed from grounds, prepared with tap water, decaffeinated, 1 cup | 0 g |
| Coffee, brewed, espresso, restaurant-prepared, 100g | 2 g |
| Cola, contains caffeine, 1 can 12 fl oz | 39 g |
| Cola, contains caffeine, 1 bottle 16 fl oz | 51 g |
| Cranberry juice, unsweetened, 1 cup | 28 g |
| Cream soda, 1 can or bottle (12 fl oz) | 47 g |
| Cream soda, 1 can or bottle (16 fl oz) | 63 g |
| Fruit punch, frozen concentrate, prepared with water, 1 cup | 29 g |
| Gatorade Thirst Quencher, 8 fl oz | 14 g |
| Gatorade, Carbohydrate Energy, 12 fl oz | 79 g |
| Ginger ale, 1 can or bottle, 12 fl oz | 31 g |
| Grape juice, canned or bottled, unsweetened, 1 cup | 37 g |
| Grapefruit juice, pink, 1 cup | 22 g |
| Grapefruit juice, white, frozen concentrate, diluted, 1 cup | 24 g |

| Beverage | Carbohydrate content |
|---|---|
| | |
| Lemon juice, frozen, unsweetened, 1 cup | 12 g |
| Lemonade, frozen concentrate, pink, prepared with water, 1 cup | 24 g |
| Lemonade, frozen concentrate, white, prepared with water, 1 cup | 33 g |
| Limeade, frozen concentrate, prepared with water, 1 cup | 26 g |
| Orange drink, breakfast type, with juice and pulp, frozen concentrate, prepared with water, 1 cup | 28 g |
| Orange juice drink, drink box, 8.45 fl oz | 34 g |
| Orange-strawberry-banana juice, 1 cup | 26 g |
| Orange soda, 1 can or bottle, 12 fl oz | 45 g |
| Orange soda, 1 can or bottle, 16 fl oz | 60 g |
| Pineapple juice, canned, unsweetened, 1 cup | 34 g |
| Pineapple and grapefruit juice drink, canned, 1 cup | 29 g |
| Pineapple and orange juice drink, canned, 1 cup | 28 g |
| Root beer, 1 can or bottle, 12 fl oz | 38 g |
| Root beer, 1 can or bottle, 16 fl oz | 51 g |
| Snapple, Snapple Kiwi Strawberry Cocktail, ready-to-drink, 8 fl oz | 29 g |
| Starbucks, Coffee, 1 bottle, 9.5 fl oz | 37 g |
| Starbucks, Frappuccino, Caramel, 1 bottle, 9.5 fl oz | 37 g |
| Tea, instant, sweetened with sugar, lemon-flavored, without added ascorbic acid, powder, prepared, 1 cup | 22 g |
| V8 100% Vegetable Juice, 5.5 fl oz can | 7 g |
| Wine, dessert, dry, 1 glass, 3.5 fl oz | 12 g |
| Wine, dessert, sweet, 1 glass, 3.5 fl oz | 14 g |

# Breads and Bread-substitutes

| Breads and Bread-substitutes | Carbohydrate content | Fiber content |
|---|---|---|
| | | |
| 1 small bagel, plain/onion, 2 oz | 29 g | 1.5 g |
| 1 medium bagel, plain/onion, 3 oz | 45 g | 2.3 g |
| 1 large bagel, plain/onion, 4 oz | 56 g | 2.9 g |
| Bread crumbs, plain or seasoned, 1 oz | 20 g | 1.3 g |
| 6" bread roll, plain, average, 21⁄2 oz | 38 g | 0 g |
| Challah slice, 3⁄4 oz | 17 g | 1 g |
| Cornbread, prepared from recipe, made with low fat (2%) milk, 1 piece | 28 g | 1.6 g |
| Corn tortilla, 6", 1 oz each | 15 g | 1.35 g |
| Flour tortilla, 8", 1.75 oz | 26 g | 2.2 g |
| Hamburger roll, regular, 1.5 oz | 21 g | 0.9 g |
| Hamburger roll, large, | 36 g | 1 |
| Italian bread, 1 medium slice | 10 g | 0.3 g |
| Kaiser roll, small, 2 oz | 35 g | 1.3 g |
| Kaiser roll, large, 31⁄2 oz | 61 g | 2 g |
| Mixed-grain bread (includes whole-grain, 7-grain), 1 slice, 1.3 oz | 17 g | 3 g |
| Oat bran bread, 1 slice | 12 g | 1.35 g |

| BREADS AND BREAD-SUBSTITUTES | CARBOHYDRATE CONTENT | FIBER CONTENT |
|---|---|---|
| | | |
| Oatmeal bread, 1 slice | 13 g | 1.1 g |
| Onion roll, small, 2.4 oz size | 34 g | 0 g |
| Pita, white, enriched, 1 small | 16 g | 0.6 g |
| Pita, white, enriched, 1 large | 33 g | 1.3 g |
| Pita, whole-wheat, 1 small | 15 g | 2.1 g |
| Pita, whole-wheat, 1 large | 35 g | 4.7 g |
| Pumpernickel bread, snack-size slice | 3 g | 0 g |
| Pumpernickel bread, 1 thin slice | 9 g | 1 g |
| Pumpernickel bread, 1 regular slice | 12 g | 2 g |
| Rice cake, regular size, 1 cake, 9 g | 7.5 g | 0.4 g |
| Rye bread, 1 snack-size slice | 3 g | 0.4 g |
| Rye bread, 1 thin slice | 10 g | 0 g |
| Rye bread, 1 slice | 15 g | 1.9 g |
| Sourdough, 1 medium piece | 33 g | 1 g |
| Taco, mini size | 3 g | 0 g |
| Taco, regular size | 8 g | 1 g |
| Taco, large | 13 g | 1 g |
| Wheat bread (including wheat berry), 1 slice, 1 oz | 14 g | 1.2 g |

## BREAKFAST CEREALS

This list is not intended to endorse any particular brand of cereal, but only to provide illustrative examples. Details should be checked with the figures on the cereal box.

| BREAKFAST CEREALS | CARBOHYDRATE CONTENT | FIBER CONTENT |
|---|---|---|
| | | |
| Alpen, 1 cup | 86 g | 10.3 g |
| Cheerios Honey Nut, 3⁄4 cup | 22 g | 2 g |
| Corn Flakes, 1 cup | 24 g | 0.9 g |
| Cream of rice, cooked with water, 3⁄4 cup | 21 g | 0 g |
| Cream of wheat, prepared with water, 3⁄4 cup | 24 g | 1 g |
| Farina, cooked with water, 3⁄4 cup | 18 g | 1 g |
| General Mills, Apple Cinnamon Cheerios, 3⁄4 cup | 25 g | 1.2 g |
| General Mills, Coca Puffs, 3⁄4 cup | 23 g | 1.75 g |
| General Mills, Fiber 1, 1⁄2 cup | 24 g | 8.2 g |
| General Mills, Reese's Puffs, 3⁄4 cup | 22 g | 1.2 g |
| General Mills, Wheaties, 3⁄4 cup | 22 g | 3.2 g |
| Kellogg's, All Bran, original, 1⁄2 cup | 23 g | 4 g |
| Kellogg's, Corn Flakes, original, 1 cup | 24 g | 0.7 g |
| Kellogg's, Fruit Loops, original, 1 cup, 1 oz | 25 g | 3 g |
| Kellogg's Frosted Flakes, 3⁄4 cup | 26 g | <1 g |
| Kellogg's Low Fat Granola with Raisins, 0.7 cup | 43 g | 4 g |
| Kellogg's Raisin Bran, regular, 1 cup | 45 g | 7 g |
| Kellogg's Rice Krispies, 11⁄4 cup | 29 g | 0.1 g |

| Breakfast Cereals | Carbohydrate content | Fiber content |
|---|---|---|
| | | |
| Kellogg's Special K, 1 cup | 23 g | 1 g |
| Oats, instant, plain, prepared with water, 1 packet | 33 g | 5 g |
| Post Fruity pebbles, 3⁄4 cup | 24 g | 0 g |
| Post Grape-Nuts cereal, 1⁄2 cup | 47 g | 5 g |
| Post Honey Bunches of Oats with Almonds Cereal, 3⁄4 cup | 24 g | 2 g |
| Post Raisin Bran Cereal, 1 cup | 46 g | 7 g |
| Post The Original Shredded Wheat, 2 biscuits | 38 g | 6 g |
| Post The Original Shredded Wheat Spoon Size, 1 cup | 41 g | 6 g |
| Puffed wheat, 1 cup | 9.6 g | 0.5 g |
| Quaker, Captain Crunch, regular, 3⁄4 cup | 23 g | 0.7 g |
| Quaker, Instant Oatmeal, Regular, 1 packet, 1 oz | 19 g | 2.8 g |
| Quaker, Instant Oatmeal, Maple Brown Sugar, 1 packet, 1.9 oz | 33 g | 2.8 g |
| Quaker, Life, 3⁄4 cup | 26 g | 2.0 g |
| Quaker, Oatmeal Squares, Brown Sugar, 3⁄4 cup | 44 g | 5.0 g |
| Raisin Nut Bran, General Mills, 1 cup | 41 g | 6.5 g |
| Total, Honey Clusters, 3⁄4 cup | 38 g | 3 g |
| Weetabix Whole Wheat, 1 cup | 44 g | 4 g |

# Dairy

| Dairy | Carbohydrate content |
|---|---|
| | |
| Burger King, Chocolate Shake, 12 fl oz | 53 g |
| Buttermilk, fluid, cultured, lowfat, 1 cup | 12 g |
| Cheese, Cheddar, shredded, 1 cup | 1 g |
| Cheese, Parmesan, grated, 1 cup | 4 g |
| Chocolate milk, 1 cup | 26 g |
| Cottage, creamed, large and small curd, 1 cup | 6 g |
| Cow's milk, 2% and regular, 1 cup | 12 g |
| Cow's milk, skim and 1%, 1 cup | 11 g |
| Cream, fluid, half and half | 10 g |
| Cream, fluid, heavy whipping, 1 cup whipped | 3 g |
| Ensure plus, 1 cup | 50 g |
| Feta cheese, 1 cup crumbled | 6 g |
| Milk shakes, thick chocolate, 1 container (11 oz) | 55 g |
| Mozzarella cheese, 1 cup | 4 g |
| Muenster cheese, 1 cup shredded | 1 g |
| Parmesan cheese, grated, 1 cup | 4 g |
| Sour cream, cultured, 1 cup | 10 g |
| Yogurt, fruit variety, nonfat, 1 container (8-oz) | 43 g |
| Yogurt, plain, low fat, 1 container (8-oz) | 16 g |
| Yogurt, plain, whole milk, 1 container (8-oz) | 10 g |

Most cheese and cream contain only small amounts of carbohydrate and are shown here for comparison.

# Pasta and Grains

| Pasta and Grains | Carbohydrate content | Fiber content |
|---|---|---|
| | | |
| Barley, pearled, cooked, 1 cup | 44 g | 5.9 g |
| Brown rice, long-grain, cooked, 1 cup | 45 g | 3.5 g |
| Brown Rice, raw, 1 cup | 143 g | 6.5 g |
| Buckwheat groats, roasted, dry, 1 cup | 122 g | 16.8 g |
| Buckwheat groats, roasted, cooked, 1 cup | 34 g | 4.5 g |
| Bulgur, cooked, 1 cup | 34 g | 8.2 g |
| Bulgur, dry, 1 cup | 106 g | 25.6 g |
| Cornmeal, self-rising, plain, enriched, white, 1 cup | 86 g | 10.7 g |
| Cornstarch, 1 cup | 117 g | 1.1 g |
| Couscous, cooked, 1 cup | 36 g | 2.2 g |
| Couscous, dry, 1 cup | 134 g | 8.6 g |
| Noodles, egg, cooked, enriched, 1 cup | 40 g | 1.9 g |
| Noodles, egg, dry, enriched, 1 cup | 27 g | 1.25 g |
| Macaroni, small shells, cooked, 1 cup | 33 g | 2.1 g |
| Macaroni, spiral shaped, cooked, 1 cup | 38 g | 2.4 g |
| Macaroni, elbow shaped, cooked, 1 cup | 40 g | 2.5 g |
| Macaroni, whole-wheat, elbow shaped, cooked, 1 cup | 37 g | 3.9 g |
| Macaroni, whole-wheat, elbow shaped, dry, 1 cup | 79 g | 8.7 g |
| Matzo Meal, 1⁄2 cup, 2.2 oz | 48 g | 1.9 g |
| Millet, cooked, 1 cup | 41 g | 2.2 g |
| Millet, raw, 1 cup | 146 g | 17 g |
| Oat bran, cooked, 1 cup | 18 g | 6 g |
| Oat bran, raw, 1 cup | 46 g | 14.5 g |
| Oats, rolled, Old Fashioned, dry, 1 cup | 54 g | 9 g |
| Oats, cooked, 1⁄2 cup | 13 g | 8.2 g |
| Quinoa grain, 1 cup | 117 g | 11.9 g |
| Rye flour, medium, 1 cup | 79 g | 12 g |
| Semolina, 1 cup | 122 g | 6.5 g |
| Spaghetti, cooked, 1 cup | 40 g | 2.4 g |
| Spaghetti, dry, 16 oz | 308 g | 1.8 g |
| Spaghetti, whole-wheat, cooked, 1 cup | 37 g | 6 g |
| Tapioca, pearl, dry, 1 cup | 135 g | 1.4 g |
| Wheat bran, 1 cup | 37 g | 25 g |
| Wheat flour, white, all-purpose, enriched, bleached, 1 cup | 95 g | 3.4 g |
| Wheat flour, white, all-purpose, self-rising, enriched, 1 cup | 93 g | 3.4 g |
| Wheat flour, white, cake, enriched, 1 cup | 107 g | 2.3 g |
| Wheat flour, whole-grain, 1 cup | 87 g | 12.8 g |
| Wheat germ, 1 cup | 60 g | 15.1 g |
| White rice, cooked, 1 cup | 37 g | 0.6 g |
| White rice, dry, 1 cup | 151 g | 1.8 g |
| Wild rice, cooked, 1 cup | 35 g | 2.9 g |
| Wild rice, raw, 1 cup | 120 g | 11 g |

# VEGETABLES

| VEGETABLES | CARBOHYDRATE CONTENT | FIBER CONTENT |
|---|---|---|
| | | |
| Asparagus, green, cooked, from raw, 1 cup | 8 g | 3.6 g |
| Beets, cooked, drained, slices, 1 cup | 17 g | 3.4 g |
| Broccoli, raw, chopped, 1 cup | 6 g | 2 g |
| Broccoli, cooked, from raw, chopped, 1 cup | 12 g | 6 g |
| Brussels sprouts, cooked, from raw, 1 cup | 14 g | 4 g |
| Cabbage, common varieties, shredded, raw, 1 cup | 4 g | 2.2 g |
| Cabbage, red, raw, 1 cup | 4 g | 1.5 g |
| Carrot juice, canned, 1 cup | 22 g | 1.9 g |
| Carrots, cooked, sliced, 1 cup | 12 g | 4.7 g |
| Cauliflower, raw, 1 cup | 5 g | 2 g |
| Cauliflower, cooked, from raw | 5 g | 2.8 g |
| Celery, raw, 1 stalk | 1 g | 0.6 g |
| Celery, cooked, medium stalk | 2 g | 0.6 g |
| Corn, sweet, yellow, cooked, kernels on cob, 1 ear | 14 g | 2 g |
| Corn, sweet, yellow, cooked, from frozen, 1 cup | 36 g | 4 g |
| Corn, sweet, yellow, canned, cream style, 1 cup | 46 g | 3.1 g |
| Corn, sweet, yellow, canned, 1 cup | 31 g | 3 g |
| Cucumber, peeled or unpeeled, sliced, 1 cup | 3 g | 0.5 g |
| Garlic, raw, 1 clove | 1 g | 0.06 g |
| Lettuce, iceberg, raw, 1 head | 11 g | 9.4 g |
| Lettuce, romaine, shredded, 1 cup | 1 g | 1 g |
| Mushrooms, raw, slices, 1 cup | 3 g | 2 g |
| Onions, raw, chopped, 1 cup | 14 g | 2.7 g |
| Onion rings, 2"-3"diameter, breaded, from frozen, oven heated, 10 rings | 23 g | 0.8. g |
| Peas, green, boiled, from frozen, 1 cup | 23 g | 6.5 g |
| Peppers, green or red, raw, chopped, 1 cup | 10 g | 2.5 g |
| Potatoes, baked, 21/3" x 43/4", with skin, 1 potato | 51 g | 3 g |
| Potatoes, baked, 21/3" x 43/4", flesh only, 1 potato | 34 g | 2.3 g |
| Potatoes, boiled, 21/2" diameter, 1 cup | 31 g | 3.3 g |
| Potato products, french fried, from frozen, oven heated, 10 strips | 16 g | 2.9 g |
| Potato, mashed, homemade, whole milk, 1 cup | 37 g | 3.1 g |
| Potato salad, home prepared, 1 cup | 28 g | 3.2 g |
| Pumpkin, canned, 1 cup | 20 g | 7.1 g |
| Sauerkraut, canned, solids and liquid, 1 cup | 10 g | 4.1 g |
| Spinach, raw, chopped, 1 cup | 1 g | 0.7 g |
| Spinach, cooked, from frozen, 1 cup | 10 g | 4.5 g |
| Squash, summer (all varieties), cooked, 1 cup | 8 g | 2 g |
| Sweet potato, medium, baked, with skin | 24 g | 4 g |
| Sweet potato, medium, boiled, without skin<br>Tomatoes, raw, chopped or sliced, 1 cup | 27 g<br>8 g | 3.8 g<br>2.2 g |
| Tomatoes, stewed, canned, 1 cup | 17 g | 2.5 g |
| Tomato juice, canned, 1 cup | 10 g | 1.9 g |
| Tomato sauce, canned, 1 cup | 18 g | 3.7 g |

# CHAPTER 16

# References for the Scientifically Curious

## References for Chapter 10: The Israeli Mediterranean Diet: Debunking the Myths and Moving Forward


1. My website eatforhealth.com contains extensive information on the health benefits of the Mediterranean diet.
2. Slyper AH. New directions in the prevention of pediatric atherogenesis and obesity. Journal of the American College of Nutrition 2013; 32: 355-358.

   My commentary article explains why low-fat diets promote obesity and are unhelpful for heart disease prevention, and contains the main ideas on which this book is based.
3. Slyper AH. The influence of carbohydrate quality on cardiovascular disease, the metabolic syndrome, type 2 diabetes, and obesity – an overview. Journal of Pediatric Endocrinology and Metabolism 2013; 26: 617-629.

   When I first appreciated the importance of carbohydrate quality I searched for scientific articles on what constitutes "good" and "bad quality" carbohydrate and why. To my surprise, I could find no article that put everything nicely together. There was only one option and this was to write my own article! In preparing this scientific paper, I found a wealth of information on how carbohydrate quality affects obesity, cardiovascular disease, the metabolic syndrome and type 2 diabetes. The carbohydrate qualities I wrote about were dietary fiber, whole grains, glycemic index, content of bioactive compounds (such as anti-oxidants), physical form, and fructose content. Some of this material is included in this book.

4. Schwingshakl L et al. Monounsaturated fatty acids, olive oil and health status: a systematic review and meta-analysis of cohort studies. Lipids in Health and Disease 2014; 13: 154.

5. Bertelli AA et al. Grapes, wines and resveratrol, and heart health. Cardiovascular Pharmacology 2009; 54: 468-476.

   This article presents a nice summary of the health benefits of wine and its constituent resveratrol. The reference to the meta-analysis that produced the J-shaped curve for wine consumption is Di Castelnuovo A et al. Meta-analysis of wine and beer consumption in relation to vascular risk. Circulation 2002; 105: 2836-2844p.

6. Chowdhurry R et al. Association of Dietary, Circulating, and Supplement Fatty Acids With Coronary Risk: A Systematic Review and Meta-analysis. Annals of Internal Medicine 2014:160:398-406.

   A "prospective study" follows a group of volunteers over time to see how factors of interest, in this case dietary fat, influence disease, in this case cardiovascular disease. When done well, this type of study is quite sensitive in picking up harmful effects. This particular meta-analysis analyzed 32 prospective studies that looked at dietary fat intake in 512,420 participants, and 17 prospective studies that looked at blood biomarkers of fat intake in 25,721 participants. Comparing the top and bottom thirds of baseline dietary fatty acid intake, the relative risk for coronary artery disease for saturated, monounsaturated, and w-6 polyunsaturated fat were all insignificant. In other words, there was no increase in risk from consuming any of these fats.

7. Jakobsen MU et al. Intake of carbohydrates compared with intake of saturated fatty acids and risk of myocardial infarction: importance of the glycemic index. American Journal of Clinical Nutrition 2010; 91: 1764-1768.

   This prospective study followed 53,644 men and women over a period of 12 years and during this time there were 1,943 occurrences of myocardial infarction. The researchers found an inverse association between risk of myocardial infarction and substitution of saturated fat with carbohydrate that had a low-glycemic index, although the relationship was non-significant. In other words, one cannot say for sure that low-glycemic index carbohydrate protects against cardiovascular disease, since the relationship was not strong enough to be certain. However, there was a statistically significant positive association between substitution of fat with carbohydrate of high-glycemic index and risk of myocardial infarction. In other words, these results indicate that substitution of fat with high-glycemic carbohydrate likely promotes cardiovascular disease.

8. German JB. A reappraisal of the impact of dairy foods and milk fat on cardiovascular disease risk. European Journal of Nutrition 2009; 48: 191-203.

   A number of prospective studies have looked at the relationship between milk intake and subsequent heart disease and none have found that milk presents a risk. Some of these studies were done before the use of low-fat milk was widespread. These studies in whole milk drinkers also failed to show that milk constituted a health problem. After reviewing this topic the authors conclude: *"Despite the contribution of dairy products to the saturated fatty acid composition of the diet, and given the diversity of dairy foods of widely differing composition, there is no clear evidence that dairy food consumption is consistently associated with a higher risk for coronary vascular disease."*

Tholstrup T. Dairy products and cardiovascular disease. Current Opinion in Lipidology 2006; 17: 1-10.

This authors of this paper wrote the following on the basis of their review of dairy products and cardiovascular disease: "*When guiding principles such as balance, variety and moderation are stressed, there is no strong evidence that dairy products increase the risk of coronary heart disease in healthy men of all ages or young and middle-aged healthy women.*"

9. Slyper, AH et al Milk, dairy fat and body weight in Pediatrics: Time for reappraisal. Infant, Child and Adolescent Nutrition 2008; 1: 148-159.

Many studies in adults and kids have shown that milk protects against excessive weight gain. Four pediatric studies looked specifically at the fat content of milk and three of these raise the possibility that only whole and 2% milk provide this protection and not low-fat milk.

10. Scharf, RJ et al. Longitudinal evaluation of milk type consumed and weight status in preschoolers. Archives of Disease in Childhood 2013; 98: 335–340.

This study followed 10,700 preschool children and examined the children again after 2 and 4 years. Those who drank 1% or skim milk had higher BMI z-scores than those who drank 2% and whole milk and were more likely to become obese or overweight between 2 to 4 years (BMI z-score is a measure of BMI in relation to the normal BMI for that age). A highly significant inverse association was also found between the fat content of the milk and BMI z-score. As mentioned in this chapter, these findings do not prove that low-fat milk leads to excessive weight gain, but they do raise this possibility.

11 Ludwig DS et al. Three daily servings of reduced-fat milk. An evidence-based recommendation? JAMA Pediatrics 2013; 167: 788-789.

The authors of this review article suggest that whole milk is beneficial for children with poor quality diets, but they are not convinced that milk consumption confers additional health benefits for those already consuming a high quality diet. The authors are battling here with the issue that milk within the context of a Western diet seems to be good for health, whereas people living in Mediterranean countries seem to manage quite well with a much lower intake of milk. There is no answer yet to this paradox.

12. Rong Y et al. Egg consumption and risk of coronary heart disease and stroke: dose-response meta-analysis of prospective cohort studies. British Medical Journal 2013; 346e8539 (http://www.bmj.com/content/346/bmj.e8539) (published 7 January 2013).

This meta-analysis analyzed 17 prospective studies in which there were 5,847 cases of coronary artery disease and 7,579 cases of stroke, and compared groups of subjects with varying egg intakes, from nothing to more than 1 per day. Those eating one or more eggs a day were bundled together as one group. No association was found between egg consumption and risk of coronary heart disease or stroke. Nevertheless, for diabetics the risk for coronary heart disease was slightly but significantly higher. The authors discuss the result for diabetics and suggest it needs to be interpreted with caution since few diabetic subjects were followed in these studies.

13. McNamara DJ. The impact of egg limitations on coronary heart disease risk: do the numbers add up? Journal of the American College of Nutrition 2000; 19(5): 540S-548S.

This is an informative article for those interested in the topic of dietary cholesterol and heart disease.

14. Etemadi A et al. British Medical Journal 2017;357:j1957;1-11.

This important paper looked at mortality from all causes, and death due to nine specific disease states, in 536,969 US volunteers aged 50 to 71. A dietary assessment using a dietary questionnaire was performed at baseline and the volunteers were followed for up to 16 years. The specific diseases examined were heart disease, stroke or cerebrovascular disease, respiratory disease, diabetes, infections, Alzheimer disease, kidney disease, chronic liver disease, and all other causes. The investigators found a significant increase in all cause mortality and specific mortality for many of the conditions comparing the highest fifth to the lowest fifth intake of processed and unprocessed red meat. The increased mortality for unprocessed red meat was independently associated with heme iron, which accounted for 20.9 to 24.1% of the association, and nitrate/nitrite accounted for 37 to 72% of the increased mortality for processed red meat, depending on the disease analyzed. For white meat (fish, chicken and turkey) there was a 25% reduction in all cause mortality comparing the highest fifth intake with the lowest fifth. How much meat is safe? Unfortunately, there is not enough information to make recommendations. Meat is far less toxic than trans fats, which is harmful in even small amounts. Moreover, since the adverse effects of red meat are likely due to oxidative stress one can speculate that people who eat a lot of natural anti-oxidants from vegetables, fruits and whole grains will be more protected than those who do not (see reference 17). In sum, the results of this study are not a reason to completely eliminate unprocessed and processed red meat from one's diet but if you eat a lot of red meat they are a reason to limit it. The whole field of preventive nutrition is an evolving science.

15. Mozaffarian D et al. Viewpoint. The 2015 US Dietary Guidelines. Lifting the ban on total dietary fat. The Journal of the American Medical Association 2015: 313: 2421-2422.

The authors write that limiting total fat promotes the consumption of harmful low-fat foods and undermines attempts to limit refined starch and added sugar. They argue that a restructuring of national nutritional policy is needed. I could not agree more!

16. Estruch R et al. Primary prevention of cardiovascular disease with a Mediterranean diet. New England Journal of Medicine 2013; 368: 1279-1290.

7,447 Spanish men and women without cardiovascular disease at enrollment but at high risk for such were randomly assigned to one of three diets – a Mediterranean diet supplemented with extra-virgin olive oil (approximately 4 tablespoons a day), a Mediterranean diet supplemented with mixed nuts (30 g of nuts a day), or a diet in which the participants were advised to reduce their intake of dietary fat. After almost 5 years, both Mediterranean diets resulted in a substantial reduction in risk of major cardiovascular events compared to the low-fat diet.

17. Orlich MJ et al. Vegetarian dietary patterns and mortality in Adventist Health Study 2. JAMA Cardiology 2013: 173: 1230-1238.

Key TJ et al. Mortality in British vegetarians: results from the European Prospective Investigation in Cancer and Nutrition (EPIC-Oxford). American Journal of Clinical Nutrition 2008; 89(supplement): 1613S-1619S.

These are two large studies comparing mortality in vegetarians to that of non-vegetarians. The first study was done in 96,469 Seventh-day Adventists in the US over 5.79 years and it found that vegetarian diets were associated with significantly lower all-cause mortality and cause-specific mortality (cardiovascular, non-cardiovascular non-cancer, renal and endocrine), especially in males. The second study was done in the UK among 64,234 participants and found no difference between vegetarian and non-vegetarian in all-cause and cardiovascular mortality. Why the difference between these two studies, and which one was correct? A closer look at the details provides some clues. In the British study, volunteers were recruited from health stores and health magazines. Probably because of this, mortality in both groups was low compared to national rates in Britain. This could suggest that an otherwise healthy diet containing plenty of vegetables, fruits and grains may be able to counteract some of the oxidative effects of red meat.

# References for Chapter 11: Prevent Excessive Weight Gain by Controlling Your Hunger


1. Slyper AH et al. Increased hunger and speed of eating in obese children and adolescents. Journal of Pediatric Endocrinology and Metabolism DOI 10.1515/jpem-2013-0271.

   Food frequency questionnaires were given to the parents of 127 obese and 42 normal-weight patients, and perceived hunger, food intake and speed of eating were rated. 62.2% of obese patients reported "eating a lot" and being "always" or "often" hungry compared to 21.4% of normal weight patients. This difference was highly significant statistically. Patients who reporting being hungrier were 6 times more likely to be obese.

2. Ludwig DS et al. Relation between consumption of sugar-sweetened drinks and childhood obesity: a prospective, observational analysis. The Lancet 2001; 357: 505-508.

   This was one of the first studies to show a relationship between soft drink consumption and obesity in kids. The authors advance the idea, and there is general agreement that this is correct, *"that consumption of sugar-sweetened drinks leads to obesity because of imprecise and incomplete compensation for energy consumed in liquid form."* In other words, soft drinks have limited satiety value.

3. Festi D et al. Gut microbiota and metabolic syndrome. World Journal of Gastroenterology. 2014; 20: 16079-16094.

   This is one of a number of review articles published on the subject of gut bacteria. The first evidence about the role of gut microbiota came from the study of germ-free mice (i.e. mice raised in an environment such that their bowels are not colonized by bacteria). Body fat was 40% higher in conventionally raised mice compared to mice raised in a germ-free environmental, and this was independent of their food intake. Transplantation of stool from obese mice to germ-free mice led to greater weight gain in these mice than stool transplanted from lean mice to germ-free mice. There is also a specific pattern of gut microbes associated with the obese phenotype (a drop in Bacteroides bacteria and increase in Firmicutes). The data in humans is more limited but also supports the notion that fat storage is favored by the presence of certain gut bacteria.

4. Howarth NC et al. Dietary fiber and weight regulation. Nutrition Reviews 2001; 59: 129-139.

   This review article summarizes 38 studies that examined the influence of fiber on hunger or satiety in healthy subjects. Almost all these studies showed that satiety was increased with high-fiber meals and this was unrelated to whether the fiber was soluble or insoluble, whether fiber supplements or high-fiber foods were used, and whether the study was short or longer term (greater than 2 days).

   Wanders AJ et al. Effects of dietary fibre on subjective appetite, energy intake and body weight: a systemic review of randomized controlled trials. Obesity Reviews 2011; 12; 724-739.

   This paper reviews numerous studies that have examined the effect of fiber on appetite, acute and long-term energy intake and body weight. The authors conclude that fiber (they use the alternative spelling fibre) reduces appetite and acute energy intake, although this depends somewhat on the nature of the fiber. Fiber also reduces long-term energy intake and body weight. The effect was relatively small in many studies and there were large differences between studies. Nevertheless, the authors suggest that even a small effect would have clinical relevance over time.

Koh-Banerjee P et al. Changes in whole-grain, bran and cereal fiber consumption in relation to 8-y weight gain among men. American Journal of Clinical Nutrition 2004; 80: 1237-1245.

This prospective study involving 27,082 American women found that an increased intake of whole grains was strongly and inversely associated with long-term weight gain – in other words, the higher the intake of whole grains, the less the weight gain.

Liu S et al. Relation between changes in intakes of dietary fiber and grain products and changes in weight and development of obesity among middle-aged women. American Journal of Clinical Nutrition 2003; 78: 920-927.

This study, the Nurses Health Study, found that weight gain was inversely associated with intake of high-fiber whole-grain foods and positively associated with refined grain intake. Nurses with the greatest increase in dietary fiber gained an average of 1.52 Kg less over 12 years than those with the smallest increase, and women in the top fifth of dietary fiber intake had a 49% lower risk of major weight gain than those in the lowest.

5. Slyper AH. The influence of carbohydrate quality on cardiovascular disease, the metabolic syndrome, type 2 diabetes, and obesity. Journal of Pediatric Endocrinology and Metabolism 2013; 26: 617-629.

My article reviews the influence of carbohydrate "quality" on cardiovascular disease, the metabolic syndrome, type 2 diabetes and obesity. This paper notes that the effect of dietary fiber on coronary artery disease was examined in a pooled analysis of 10 prospective studies and a 27% reduction in coronary mortality and 14% reduction in coronary disease were noted for each 10 g/day increment in daily fiber. In the few prospective studies performed, dietary fiber has emerged as a significant predictor of insulin resistance and obesity.

6. Isaksson H et al. Rye kernel breakfast increases satiety in the afternoon – an effect of food structure. Nutrition Journal 2011; 10: 31.

This study showed that a breakfast of rye bread containing milled or whole kernels resulted in higher satiety rating in the morning and afternoon compared to sifted wheat bread, and that rye whole kernel porridge suppressed hunger in the afternoon more than milled kernel porridge.

7. Ludwig DS et al. High glycemic index foods, overeating, and obesity. Pediatrics 199; 103: e26.

A number of studies have shown that high-glycemic foods lead to hunger, but this particular study illustrates this effect very nicely.

8. Chaput J-P et al. The glucostatic theory of appetite control and the risk of obesity and diabetes. International Journal of Obesity 2009; 33: 46-53.

This is a very comprehensive review of the *glucostatic theory* **of appetite control. The** initial glucostatic theory was that an increase in blood glucose decreases the feeling of satiety, whereas a drop in blood glucose has the opposite effect. However, this has not been shown to be case and more recent versions of the theory focus on the dynamic pattern of blood glucose levels. However, its importance is still a matter of debate. There is little scientific evidence that consumption of carbohydrate with high glycemia is responsible for widespread obesity in the US.

Page et al. Circulating glucose levels modulate neural control of desire for high-calorie foods in humans. The Journal of Clinical Investigation 2011: 121(10); 4161-69.

Using functional MRI in human volunteers, these investigators showed that mild hypoglycemia (as might occur several hours after eating high glycemic foods) preferentially activates centers in the brain that produce a greater desire for high-calorie foods, and this may explain the influence of food glycemia on hunger.

To sum matters up, the importance of carbohydrate quality on hunger seems well established, but the mechanism whereby food glycemia influences hunger and whether it is related to changes in blood glucose is still unknown.

9. Slyper, AH et al Milk, dairy fat and body weight in Pediatrics: Time for reappraisal. Infant, Child and Adolescent Nutrition 2008; 1: 148-159.

Pfeuffer M et al. Diagnostic in obesity comorbidities: milk and the metabolic syndrome. Obesity Reviews 2006; 8: 109-118.

A number of observational studies in adults and children have shown a negative association between consumption of milk and body mass index, (i.e. body weight is lower in those who drink milk,). Many interventional studies with dairy have also shown that dairy has a beneficial effect on adiposity.

10. Gilbert J-A et al. Milk supplementation facilitates appetite control in obese women during weight loss: a randomized, single-blind, placebo-controlled trial. British Journal of Nutrition 2011; 105: 133-143.

In this study, females with low calcium consumption were given a milk supplement or a placebo during a 6-month energy-restricted program. Both groups lost weight, but there was less hunger and desire to eat in those receiving milk supplementation. This study suggests that milk has an effect on appetite. However, this is a single study and needs to be repeated before definite conclusions can be made.

11. Sanchez M et al. Childhood obesity: A role for gut microbiota? International Journal of Environmental Research and Public Health 2015: 12: 162-175.

The bowel flora of obese adults and kids is different from that of normal-weight people and it is likely that this difference in bacteria promotes their obesity. It is possible to change to a healthier flora by introducing new bacteria into the gut (and foods that do this are called probiotics) or by changing the diet in a way that positively influences bowel flora (and these foods are called prebiotics). Dietary fiber acts as a prebiotic. This paper summarizes studies showing a beneficial effect of probiotic yoghurt and fermented milk products on body fat and BMI.

12. Szajewska H et al. Systematic review demonstrating that breakfast consumption influences body weight outcomes in children and adolescents in Europe. Critical Reviews in Food Science and Nutrition 2010; 50: 113-119.

This review reports on 16 cross-sectional studies that examined the effect of breakfast consumption on body weight in 59,000 European children and adolescents. A cross-sectional study is a like a snapshot of a population. A consistent finding was that breakfast-eaters had a lower BMI than those who skipped breakfast. As this review points out, cross-sectional studies do not prove causality, but these particular studies are consistent with several small prospective studies from outside Europe.

13. Flood JE. Rolls BJ. Soup preloads in a variety of forms reduce meal intake. Appetite 2007; 49: 626-634.

    Eating a vegetable soup before a meal reduces the calories consumed at that meal by 20%. This study shows that it makes no difference whether the soup is chunky or pureed. However, at least one other study has shown that it does make a difference and that food intake is significantly less following a chunky vegetable soup than a strained one. (Himaya A et al. The effect of soup on satiation. Appetite 1998; 30: 199-210).

14. Suez J et al. Artificial sweeteners induce glucose intolerance by altering the gut microbiota. Nature doi.10.1038/nature13793.

    Commonly used non-caloric artificial sweeteners lead to glucose intolerance in mice by altering intestinal flora. This effect was seen after fecal transplantation to germ free mice from animals that had been given diet drinks. The effect was prevented by giving antibiotics to the germ-free mice after the transplantation. These investigators also found that administration of artificial sweeteners over 1 week to a small group of healthy humans led to abnormal glucose responses in most of the volunteers. The gut flora of these volunteers showed a change from baseline, and the stool of these volunteers also induced glucose intolerance when transplanted into germ-free mice. This research is pretty convincing but does need to be repeated by other groups.

15. Ford et al. Treatment of childhood obesity by retraining eating behavior: randomised controlled trial. British Medical Journal 2010; 340: b5388.

    This 12-month study used a feedback device to control eating speed in 109 obese young people aged 9-17 years. Significant long-term weight loss occurred compared to standard care, with mean meal size falling by 45 g.

# References for Chapter 12: Lose Weight by Regulating Carbs!

1. Martin W et al. Dietary protein and renal function. Nutrition Metabolism 2005; 2: 25.

The safety of high-protein diets has been the subject of debate for some time. A concern is that high-protein diets can cause deterioration in kidney function in people with kidney disease, and we already know that obesity is a risk factor for kidney dysfunction. Obesity, overweight and the metabolic syndrome increase the risk for kidney disease from between 40 to 83%. Nevertheless, there have been no reports in the medical literature of deterioration in renal function from these diets, even in populations at risk for kidney disease, such as the obese and those with hypertension. Does this mean that high-protein diets are perfectly safe? The reality is that the long-term risks of high-protein diets have never been studied and this is unlikely to be done in the future. Not too many people would be willing to stay on a diet like this for decades! One scientific article advised that those intending to go on a high-protein diet should have their kidney function checked out. This is not difficult to do and sounds like a wise precaution. Kidney function could also be checked periodically thereafter for anyone on a long-term high-protein diet.

Miller M et al. Comparative effects of 3 popular diets on lipids, endothelial function and C-reactive protein during weight maintenance. Journal of the American Dietetic Association 2009: 109 (4): 713-717.

This study looked at lipids and a measure of arterial health (flow-mediated vasodilation of the brachial artery) in patients in the weight-maintenance stage of three popular diets, Atkins (high-fat), South Beach (high-protein) and Ornish diets (vegetarian, low-fat). They found that arterial function was inversely related to saturated fat. In other words, the higher the saturated fat in the diet the worse was arterial function. The Atkins diet was also associated with higher blood lipids. Studies such as these indicate that a low-carb high-fat diet containing a lot of saturated fat is not a healthy one.

2. Shai et al. Weight loss with a low-carbohydrate, Mediterranean, or low-fat diet. New England Journal of Medicine 2008; 359: 229-241.

Obese volunteers were randomized to three low-calorie diets – a Mediterranean diet, a low-carb high-fat diet, and a low-fat diet. The low-carbohydrate diet was not restricted in calories and provided 20 g of carbohydrates per day during the induction phase, with a gradual increase to a maximum of 120 g per day. The Mediterranean diet in this study was moderate in fat (35% of total calories) and calorie restricted. The low-fat diet was also calorie restricted and aimed for 30% fat. In terms of initial weight loss, the low-carb diet was the clear winner. However, the weight loss was not maintained and by about 16 months the weight loss from the low-carb diet and the Mediterranean diet were about the same. In other words, the steep decline in body weight with the low-carb diet turned out to be a complete waste of time.

# References for Chapter 13: Go Mediterranean And Save Your Arteries – And Your Life!

1. de Lorgeril M et al. Mediterranean diet, traditional risk factors, and the rate of cardiovascular complications after myocardial infarction. Final report of the Lyon Diet Heart Study. Circulation 1999: 99; 779-785.

The results of the Lyon Diet Heart Study made quite a splash when they first appeared. The Mediterranean diet tested was similar to the diet once used by the Greeks in Crete (their diet has since become more westernized), while the control or comparison diet was approaching an American Heart Association "Step 1 diet". In a conventional step 1 diet, total fat is reduced to 30% of total calories and saturated fat to 10%. In actuality, dietary fat for the control subjects in this study was 32.7 % of total calories and saturated fat 11.7%, so that the subjects were not quite on a Step 1 Diet, but more on a what-happens-in-actual-practice low-fat diet. The reference above is the final report of their 4-year data.

2. Estruch R et al. Primary prevention of cardiovascular disease with a Mediterranean diet. New England Journal of Medicine 2013; 368: 1279-1290.

3. Blumhoff R. Dietary antioxidants and cardiovascular disease. Current Opinion in Lipidology 2005; 16: 47-54 and Kay CD, Holub BJ. The postprandial effects of dietary antioxidants in humans. Current Atherosclerosis Reports 2003; 5: 452-458.

The anti-oxidant hypothesis is still a hypothesis and not yet proven. However, it explains many of the clinical observations regarding cardiovascular disease and an increasing number of scientific papers support this theory.

4. Deuteronomy 8:7-10.

All the foods mentioned in this verse were stables of the ancient Israelite diet. According to Jewish tradition, the "honey" mentioned in this verse is from the date palm.

Berry EM et al. The Middle Eastern and biblical origins of the Mediterranean diet. Public Health Nutrition 2011; 14: 2288-2295.

This paper provides an excellent summary of the antioxidant status of the "seven species" and other Mediterranean foods mentioned in the Bible. The authors conclude "The biblical seven species, together with other indigenous foods from the Middle East, are now scientifically recognized as healthy foods, and further improve the many beneficial effects of the Mediterranean diet."

5. Schwingshackl et al. Monounsaturated fatty acids, olive oil and health status: a systematic review and meta-analysis of cohort studies. Lipids in Health and Disease 2014; 13: 154

Increasing one's intake of olive oil results in a significantly reduced risk of mortality, cardiovascular events and stroke, which is not the case for monounsaturated fat of mixed animal and plant origin. In other words, it is not the fat content of olive oil that leads to its beneficial effect but other constituents of the oil.

6. Alberto AA et al. Grapes, wines, resveratrol, and heart health. Journal of Cardiovascular Pharmacology 2009; 54: 468-476.

Wine and grapes attenuate atherosclerosis and ischemic heart disease. The vascular benefits follow a J-shaped curve with the plateau being at 150 mL of wine a day. In other words, this is the amount of daily wine providing maximum health benefit. Wine increases life span and also induces longevity genes.

7. Adom KK et al. Phytochemicals and antioxidant activity of milled fractions of different wheat varieties. Journal of Agricultural Food Chemistry 2005; 53: 2297-2306.

   Eat only white bread and you are missing out on anti-oxidants. White flour has only about 20% of the antioxidant capacity of whole grain flour.

8. Hu FB et al. Nut consumption and risk of coronary heart disease: a review of epidemiologic evidence. Current Atherosclerosis Reports 1999; 1: 204-209.

   This review article discusses five studies showing that diets containing a lot of nuts have a favorable influence on cardiovascular disease. The authors suggest that nuts warrant a more prominent position in the Food Pyramid.

9. Fung TT et al. Sweetened beverage consumption and risk of coronary heart disease in women. American Journal of Clinical Nutrition. 2009: 89(4): 1037-42.

   A *cohort study* follows a group of volunteers for a number of years and is quite sensitive in picking up disease associations, although this type of study is not able to prove disease causation. Nevertheless, if a positive effect is demonstrated, the study is getting close to the cause and may actually be picking up the causative factor. This study in nurses found after 24 years of follow-up that there was a slight but significantly higher risk for coronary heart disease for those drinking more than 2 servings a day of sweetened beverages compared to nurses drinking less than 1 serving per month.

   Slyper AH. The influence of carbohydrate quality on cardiovascular disease, the metabolic syndrome, type 2 diabetes, and obesity – an overview. Journal of Pediatric Endocrinology and Metabolism 2013; 26: 617-629.

   The evidence that high amounts of fructose cause metabolic changes is reviewed in this article. The evidence that large amounts of fructose are harmful is suggestive but not quite a closed case and more research is needed.

10. This is a link to a news report from the Institute of Medicine. The full report is many pages long:

    http://www8.nationalacademies.org/onpinews/newsitem.aspx?RecordID=18311

    For more information on this topic, see the web page "Other health benefits of the Mediterranean diet" on my website eatforhealth.org.

# References for Chapter 14: Improve Your Blood Sugars Using Low-Glycemic Carbohydrate

1. Esposito et al. Prevention and control of type 2 diabetes by Mediterranean diet. A systemic review. Diabetes Research and Clinical Practice 2010; 89: 97-102.

   This review article reports that two large prospective studies found the risk of developing type 2 diabetes much reduced on a Mediterranean diet, with a 35% to 83% lower risk. Five intervention control trials found that the Mediterranean diet reduced fasting glucose in type 2 diabetics between 7 to 40 mg/dL and hemoglobin A1c between 0.1 to 0.6%.

2. Elliott TD et al. Low glyceamic index, or low glycaemic load, diets for diabetes mellitus. Cochrane Library 2009:3.

   This Cochrane review identified eleven randomized controlled trials lasting 1 to 12 months and involving 402 participants. Metabolic control measured by glycosylated haemoglobinA1c, which is a measure of long-term diabetes control, decreased by 0.5% with the low glycemic index diet. This was statistically and clinically significant. Hypoglycemic episodes also significantly decreased with the low glycemic index diets compared to the high glycemic index diets.

3. http://www.glycemicindex.com/ This is a useful website for looking up the glycemic index and glycemic load of commonly eaten foods.

4. Heaton KW, Marcus SN, Emmett PM, Bolton CH. Particle size of wheat, maize, and oat test meals: effects on plasma glucose and insulin responses and on the rate of starch digestion in vitro. The American Journal of Clinical Nutrition 1988; 47: 675-682.

   The glycemic indices for wheat, maize and oats are lower when in the form of whole grains than cracked grains. The glycemic indices for cracked grains are lower than for coarse flours, and the glycemic indices for coarse flours lower than for fine flours.

5. Jenkins DJ, WessonV, Wolever TM et al. Wholemeal versus wholegrain breads: proportion of whole or cracked grain and the glycaemic response. The British Medical Journal 1988; 297: 958-960.

   This study found that the glycemic indices of breads were a function of the quantity of intact grains or kernels relative to flour – i.e. the more whole grains, the lower the glycemic index. By *wholemeal bread*, the authors mean bread containing wholegrain flour, whereas a *wholegrain bread* is one containing intact kernels of grain within the bread.